ISBN 0-8373-0224-2

C-224   CAREER EXAMINATION SERIES

This is your PASSBOOK® for...

Electrician

Test Preparation Study Guide

Questions & Answers

NATIONAL LEARNING CORPORATION

PASSBOOK®

NOTICE

This book is SOLELY intended for, is sold ONLY to, and its use is RESTRICTED to *individual*, bona fide applicants or candidates who qualify by virtue of having seriously filed applications for appropriate license, certificate, professional and/or promotional advancement, higher school matriculation, scholarship, or other legitimate requirements of educational and/or governmental authorities.

This book is NOT intended for use, class instruction, tutoring, training, duplication, copying, reprinting, excerption, or adaptation, etc., by:

(1) Other publishers

(2) Proprietors and/or Instructors of "Coaching" and/or Preparatory Courses

(3) Personnel and/or Training Divisions of commercial, industrial, and governmental organizations

(4) Schools, colleges, or universities and/or their departments and staffs, including teachers and other personnel

(5) Testing Agencies or Bureaus

(6) Study groups which seek by the purchase of a single volume to copy and/or duplicate and/or adapt this material for use by the group as a whole without having purchased individual volumes for each of the members of the group

(7) Et al.

Such persons would be in violation of appropriate Federal and State statutes.

PROVISION OF LICENSING AGREEMENTS. — Recognized educational commercial, industrial, and governmental institutions and organizations, and others legitimately engaged in educational pursuits, including training, testing, and measurement activities, may address a request for a licensing agreement to the copyright owners, who will determine whether, and under what conditions, including fees and charges, the materials in this book may be used by them. In other words, a licensing facility exists for the legitimate use of the material in this book on other than an individual basis. However, it is asseverated and affirmed here that the material in this book *CANNOT* be used without the receipt of the express permission of such a licensing agreement from the Publishers.

NATIONAL LEARNING CORPORATION
212 Michael Drive
Syosset, New York 11791

Inquiries re licensing agreements should be addressed to:
The President
National Learning Corporation
212 Michael Drive
Syosset, New York 11791

PASSBOOK® SERIES

THE *PASSBOOK® SERIES* has been created to prepare applicants and candidates for the ultimate academic battlefield – the examination room.

At some time in our lives, each and every one of us may be required to take an examination – for validation, matriculation, admission, qualification, registration, certification, or licensure.

Based on the assumption that every applicant or candidate has met the basic formal educational standards, has taken the required number of courses, and read the necessary texts, the *PASSBOOK® SERIES* furnishes the one special preparation which may assure passing with confidence, instead of failing with insecurity. Examination questions – together with answers – are furnished as the basic vehicle for study so that the mysteries of the examination and its compounding difficulties may be eliminated or diminished by a sure method.

This book is meant to help you pass your examination provided that you qualify and are serious in your objective.

The entire field is reviewed through the huge store of content information which is succinctly presented through a provocative and challenging approach – the question-and-answer method.

A climate of success is established by furnishing the correct answers at the end of each test.

You soon learn to recognize types of questions, forms of questions, and patterns of questioning. You may even begin to anticipate expected outcomes.

You perceive that many questions are repeated or adapted so that you can gain acute insights, which may enable you to score many sure points.

You learn how to confront new questions, or types of questions, and to attack them confidently and work out the correct answers.

You note objectives and emphases, and recognize pitfalls and dangers, so that you may make positive educational adjustments.

Moreover, you are kept fully informed in relation to new concepts, methods, practices, and directions in the field.

You discover that you are actually taking the examination all the time: you are preparing for the examination by "taking" an examination, not by reading extraneous and/or supererogatory textbooks.

In short, this PASSBOOK®, used directedly, should be an important factor in helping you to pass your test.

ELECTRICIAN

DUTIES

Electricians, under direction, perform work on the installation, repair and maintenance of high or low tension electrical systems for light, heat, power and communications in or on buildings, structures and highways; may serve as a special electrician, making applications and obtaining permits and approvals required by rule, regulation and/or statute; prepare reports and maintain records; install, repair, replace and maintain electric wiring systems and components, equipment and apparatus in or on buildings and structures in accordance with the electrical code, pertinent plans, specifications and job orders; install, repair, replace, and maintain electric wiring and equipment, traffic signals and controllers; install conduits, raceways and electrical conductors; conduct tests on existing installations to determine faults and make necessary repairs; when assigned as a special electrician, obtain permits for electrical work to be performed; conduct and/or witness tests on electrical wiring systems, equipment and/or appliances; prepare applications, reports, notices and other documents; prepare required sketches, drawings and layouts; keep job and other records; in the temporary absence of the supervisor, may perform the duties of that position; supervise assigned personnel; may drive motor vehicles; and perform related work.

SCOPE OF THE EXAMINATION

The multiple-choice test may include questions on: A.C. and D.C. circuits, machinery and applied electronics; the electrical code; electrical diagrams and specifications; electrical calculations; methods and procedures for the installation, alteration, maintenance, and repair of electrical wiring and equipment; installation of conduit; tools, fittings, materials, measuring instruments and meters used in the electrician's trade; principles of supervision; record keeping; preparation of reports; safety; and other related areas, including: principles; installations; fundamentals; services, feeders and branch circuits; grounding and bonding; conductors and cables; low-voltage circuits and communications; special occupancies; special equipment; motors; power and conditioning equipment; lighting; raceways and boxes; emergency systems; fire detection and alarm systems.

HOW TO TAKE A TEST

I. YOU MUST PASS AN EXAMINATION

A. WHAT EVERY CANDIDATE SHOULD KNOW

Examination applicants often ask us for help in preparing for the written test. What can I study in advance? What kinds of questions will be asked? How will the test be given? How will the papers be graded?

As an applicant for a civil service examination, you may be wondering about some of these things. Our purpose here is to suggest effective methods of advance study and to describe civil service examinations.

Your chances for success on this examination can be increased if you know how to prepare. Those "pre-examination jitters" can be reduced if you know what to expect. You can even experience an adventure in good citizenship if you know why civil service exams are given.

B. WHY ARE CIVIL SERVICE EXAMINATIONS GIVEN?

Civil service examinations are important to you in two ways. As a citizen, you want public jobs filled by employees who know how to do their work. As a job seeker, you want a fair chance to compete for that job on an equal footing with other candidates. The best-known means of accomplishing this two-fold goal is the competitive examination.

Exams are widely publicized throughout the nation. They may be administered for jobs in federal, state, city, municipal, town or village governments or agencies.

Any citizen may apply, with some limitations, such as the age or residence of applicants. Your experience and education may be reviewed to see whether you meet the requirements for the particular examination. When these requirements exist, they are reasonable and applied consistently to all applicants. Thus, a competitive examination may cause you some uneasiness now, but it is your privilege and safeguard.

C. HOW ARE CIVIL SERVICE EXAMS DEVELOPED?

Examinations are carefully written by trained technicians who are specialists in the field known as "psychological measurement," in consultation with recognized authorities in the field of work that the test will cover. These experts recommend the subject matter areas or skills to be tested; only those knowledges or skills important to your success on the job are included. The most reliable books and source materials available are used as references. Together, the experts and technicians judge the difficulty level of the questions.

Test technicians know how to phrase questions so that the problem is clearly stated. Their ethics do not permit "trick" or "catch" questions. Questions may have been tried out on sample groups, or subjected to statistical analysis, to determine their usefulness.

Written tests are often used in combination with performance tests, ratings of training and experience, and oral interviews. All of these measures combine to form the best-known means of finding the right person for the right job.

II. HOW TO PASS THE WRITTEN TEST

A. NATURE OF THE EXAMINATION

To prepare intelligently for civil service examinations, you should know how they differ from school examinations you have taken. In school you were assigned certain definite pages to read or subjects to cover. The examination questions were quite detailed and usually emphasized memory. Civil service exams, on the other hand, try to discover your present ability to perform the duties of a position, plus your potentiality to learn these duties. In other words, a civil service exam attempts to predict how successful you will be. Questions cover such a broad area that they cannot be as minute and detailed as school exam questions.

In the public service similar kinds of work, or positions, are grouped together in one "class." This process is known as *position-classification*. All the positions in a class are paid according to the salary range for that class. One class title covers all of these positions, and they are all tested by the same examination.

B. FOUR BASIC STEPS

1) Study the announcement

How, then, can you know what subjects to study? Our best answer is: "Learn as much as possible about the class of positions for which you've applied." The exam will test the knowledge, skills and abilities needed to do the work.

Your most valuable source of information about the position you want is the official exam announcement. This announcement lists the training and experience qualifications. Check these standards and apply only if you come reasonably close to meeting them.

The brief description of the position in the examination announcement offers some clues to the subjects which will be tested. Think about the job itself. Review the duties in your mind. Can you perform them, or are there some in which you are rusty? Fill in the blank spots in your preparation.

Many jurisdictions preview the written test in the exam announcement by including a section called "Knowledge and Abilities Required," "Scope of the Examination," or some similar heading. Here you will find out specifically what fields will be tested.

2) Review your own background

Once you learn in general what the position is all about, and what you need to know to do the work, ask yourself which subjects you already know fairly well and which need improvement. You may wonder whether to concentrate on improving your strong areas or on building some background in your fields of weakness. When the announcement has specified "some knowledge" or "considerable knowledge," or has used adjectives like "beginning principles of…" or "advanced … methods," you can get a clue as to the number and difficulty of questions to be asked in any given field. More questions, and hence broader coverage, would be included for those subjects which are more important in the work. Now weigh your strengths and weaknesses against the job requirements and prepare accordingly.

3) Determine the level of the position

Another way to tell how intensively you should prepare is to understand the level of the job for which you are applying. Is it the entering level? In other words, is this the position in which beginners in a field of work are hired? Or is it an intermediate or advanced level? Sometimes this is indicated by such words as "Junior" or "Senior" in the class title. Other jurisdictions use Roman numerals to designate the level – Clerk I, Clerk II, for example. The word "Supervisor" sometimes appears in the title. If the level is not indicated by the title,

2

check the description of duties. Will you be working under very close supervision, or will you have responsibility for independent decisions in this work?

4) Choose appropriate study materials

Now that you know the subjects to be examined and the relative amount of each subject to be covered, you can choose suitable study materials. For beginning level jobs, or even advanced ones, if you have a pronounced weakness in some aspect of your training, read a modern, standard textbook in that field. Be sure it is up to date and has general coverage. Such books are normally available at your library, and the librarian will be glad to help you locate one. For entry-level positions, questions of appropriate difficulty are chosen – neither highly advanced questions, nor those too simple. Such questions require careful thought but not advanced training.

If the position for which you are applying is technical or advanced, you will read more advanced, specialized material. If you are already familiar with the basic principles of your field, elementary textbooks would waste your time. Concentrate on advanced textbooks and technical periodicals. Think through the concepts and review difficult problems in your field.

These are all general sources. You can get more ideas on your own initiative, following these leads. For example, training manuals and publications of the government agency which employs workers in your field can be useful, particularly for technical and professional positions. A letter or visit to the government department involved may result in more specific study suggestions, and certainly will provide you with a more definite idea of the exact nature of the position you are seeking.

III. KINDS OF TESTS

Tests are used for purposes other than measuring knowledge and ability to perform specified duties. For some positions, it is equally important to test ability to make adjustments to new situations or to profit from training. In others, basic mental abilities not dependent on information are essential. Questions which test these things may not appear as pertinent to the duties of the position as those which test for knowledge and information. Yet they are often highly important parts of a fair examination. For very general questions, it is almost impossible to help you direct your study efforts. What we can do is to point out some of the more common of these general abilities needed in public service positions and describe some typical questions.

1) General information

Broad, general information has been found useful for predicting job success in some kinds of work. This is tested in a variety of ways, from vocabulary lists to questions about current events. Basic background in some field of work, such as sociology or economics, may be sampled in a group of questions. Often these are principles which have become familiar to most persons through exposure rather than through formal training. It is difficult to advise you how to study for these questions; being alert to the world around you is our best suggestion.

2) Verbal ability

An example of an ability needed in many positions is verbal or language ability. Verbal ability is, in brief, the ability to use and understand words. Vocabulary and grammar tests are typical measures of this ability. Reading comprehension or paragraph interpretation questions are common in many kinds of civil service tests. You are given a paragraph of written material and asked to find its central meaning.

3) Numerical ability

Number skills can be tested by the familiar arithmetic problem, by checking paired lists of numbers to see which are alike and which are different, or by interpreting charts and graphs. In the latter test, a graph may be printed in the test booklet which you are asked to use as the basis for answering questions.

4) Observation

A popular test for law-enforcement positions is the observation test. A picture is shown to you for several minutes, then taken away. Questions about the picture test your ability to observe both details and larger elements.

5) Following directions

In many positions in the public service, the employee must be able to carry out written instructions dependably and accurately. You may be given a chart with several columns, each column listing a variety of information. The questions require you to carry out directions involving the information given in the chart.

6) Skills and aptitudes

Performance tests effectively measure some manual skills and aptitudes. When the skill is one in which you are trained, such as typing or shorthand, you can practice. These tests are often very much like those given in business school or high school courses. For many of the other skills and aptitudes, however, no short-time preparation can be made. Skills and abilities natural to you or that you have developed throughout your lifetime are being tested.

Many of the general questions just described provide all the data needed to answer the questions and ask you to use your reasoning ability to find the answers. Your best preparation for these tests, as well as for tests of facts and ideas, is to be at your physical and mental best. You, no doubt, have your own methods of getting into an exam-taking mood and keeping "in shape." The next section lists some ideas on this subject.

IV. KINDS OF QUESTIONS

Only rarely is the "essay" question, which you answer in narrative form, used in civil service tests. Civil service tests are usually of the short-answer type. Full instructions for answering these questions will be given to you at the examination. But in case this is your first experience with short-answer questions and separate answer sheets, here is what you need to know:

1) Multiple-choice Questions

Most popular of the short-answer questions is the "multiple choice" or "best answer" question. It can be used, for example, to test for factual knowledge, ability to solve problems or judgment in meeting situations found at work.

A multiple-choice question is normally one of three types—
- It can begin with an incomplete statement followed by several possible endings. You are to find the one ending which *best* completes the statement, although some of the others may not be entirely wrong.
- It can also be a complete statement in the form of a question which is answered by choosing one of the statements listed.

- It can be in the form of a problem – again you select the best answer.

Here is an example of a multiple-choice question with a discussion which should give you some clues as to the method for choosing the right answer:

When an employee has a complaint about his assignment, the action which will *best* help him overcome his difficulty is to
  A. discuss his difficulty with his coworkers
  B. take the problem to the head of the organization
  C. take the problem to the person who gave him the assignment
  D. say nothing to anyone about his complaint

In answering this question, you should study each of the choices to find which is best. Consider choice "A" – Certainly an employee may discuss his complaint with fellow employees, but no change or improvement can result, and the complaint remains unresolved. Choice "B" is a poor choice since the head of the organization probably does not know what assignment you have been given, and taking your problem to him is known as "going over the head" of the supervisor. The supervisor, or person who made the assignment, is the person who can clarify it or correct any injustice. Choice "C" is, therefore, correct. To say nothing, as in choice "D," is unwise. Supervisors have and interest in knowing the problems employees are facing, and the employee is seeking a solution to his problem.

2) True/False Questions

The "true/false" or "right/wrong" form of question is sometimes used. Here a complete statement is given. Your job is to decide whether the statement is right or wrong.

SAMPLE: A roaming cell-phone call to a nearby city costs less than a non-roaming call to a distant city.

This statement is wrong, or false, since roaming calls are more expensive.
This is not a complete list of all possible question forms, although most of the others are variations of these common types. You will always get complete directions for answering questions. Be sure you understand *how* to mark your answers – ask questions until you do.

V. RECORDING YOUR ANSWERS

Computer terminals are used more and more today for many different kinds of exams.
For an examination with very few applicants, you may be told to record your answers in the test booklet itself. Separate answer sheets are much more common. If this separate answer sheet is to be scored by machine – and this is often the case – it is highly important that you mark your answers correctly in order to get credit.
An electronic scoring machine is often used in civil service offices because of the speed with which papers can be scored. Machine-scored answer sheets must be marked with a pencil, which will be given to you. This pencil has a high graphite content which responds to the electronic scoring machine. As a matter of fact, stray dots may register as answers, so do not let your pencil rest on the answer sheet while you are pondering the correct answer. Also, if your pencil lead breaks or is otherwise defective, ask for another.

Since the answer sheet will be dropped in a slot in the scoring machine, be careful not to bend the corners or get the paper crumpled.

The answer sheet normally has five vertical columns of numbers, with 30 numbers to a column. These numbers correspond to the question numbers in your test booklet. After each number, going across the page are four or five pairs of dotted lines. These short dotted lines have small letters or numbers above them. The first two pairs may also have a "T" or "F" above the letters. This indicates that the first two pairs only are to be used if the questions are of the true-false type. If the questions are multiple choice, disregard the "T" and "F" and pay attention only to the small letters or numbers.

Answer your questions in the manner of the sample that follows:

32. The largest city in the United States is
    A. Washington, D.C.
    B. New York City
    C. Chicago
    D. Detroit
    E. San Francisco

1) Choose the answer you think is best. (New York City is the largest, so "B" is correct.)
2) Find the row of dotted lines numbered the same as the question you are answering. (Find row number 32)
3) Find the pair of dotted lines corresponding to the answer. (Find the pair of lines under the mark "B.")
4) Make a solid black mark between the dotted lines.

VI. BEFORE THE TEST

Common sense will help you find procedures to follow to get ready for an examination. Too many of us, however, overlook these sensible measures. Indeed, nervousness and fatigue have been found to be the most serious reasons why applicants fail to do their best on civil service tests. Here is a list of reminders:

- Begin your preparation early – Don't wait until the last minute to go scurrying around for books and materials or to find out what the position is all about.
- Prepare continuously – An hour a night for a week is better than an all-night cram session. This has been definitely established. What is more, a night a week for a month will return better dividends than crowding your study into a shorter period of time.
- Locate the place of the exam – You have been sent a notice telling you when and where to report for the examination. If the location is in a different town or otherwise unfamiliar to you, it would be well to inquire the best route and learn something about the building.
- Relax the night before the test – Allow your mind to rest. Do not study at all that night. Plan some mild recreation or diversion; then go to bed early and get a good night's sleep.
- Get up early enough to make a leisurely trip to the place for the test – This way unforeseen events, traffic snarls, unfamiliar buildings, etc. will not upset you.
- Dress comfortably – A written test is not a fashion show. You will be known by number and not by name, so wear something comfortable.

- Leave excess paraphernalia at home – Shopping bags and odd bundles will get in your way. You need bring only the items mentioned in the official notice you received; usually everything you need is provided. Do not bring reference books to the exam. They will only confuse those last minutes and be taken away from you when in the test room.
- Arrive somewhat ahead of time – If because of transportation schedules you must get there very early, bring a newspaper or magazine to take your mind off yourself while waiting.
- Locate the examination room – When you have found the proper room, you will be directed to the seat or part of the room where you will sit. Sometimes you are given a sheet of instructions to read while you are waiting. Do not fill out any forms until you are told to do so; just read them and be prepared.
- Relax and prepare to listen to the instructions
- If you have any physical problem that may keep you from doing your best, be sure to tell the test administrator. If you are sick or in poor health, you really cannot do your best on the exam. You can come back and take the test some other time.

VII. AT THE TEST

The day of the test is here and you have the test booklet in your hand. The temptation to get going is very strong. Caution! There is more to success than knowing the right answers. You must know how to identify your papers and understand variations in the type of short-answer question used in this particular examination. Follow these suggestions for maximum results from your efforts:

1) Cooperate with the monitor

The test administrator has a duty to create a situation in which you can be as much at ease as possible. He will give instructions, tell you when to begin, check to see that you are marking your answer sheet correctly, and so on. He is not there to guard you, although he will see that your competitors do not take unfair advantage. He wants to help you do your best.

2) Listen to all instructions

Don't jump the gun! Wait until you understand all directions. In most civil service tests you get more time than you need to answer the questions. So don't be in a hurry. Read each word of instructions until you clearly understand the meaning. Study the examples, listen to all announcements and follow directions. Ask questions if you do not understand what to do.

3) Identify your papers

Civil service exams are usually identified by number only. You will be assigned a number; you must not put your name on your test papers. Be sure to copy your number correctly. Since more than one exam may be given, copy your exact examination title.

4) Plan your time

Unless you are told that a test is a "speed" or "rate of work" test, speed itself is usually not important. Time enough to answer all the questions will be provided, but this does not mean that you have all day. An overall time limit has been set. Divide the total time (in minutes) by the number of questions to determine the approximate time you have for each question.

5) Do not linger over difficult questions

If you come across a difficult question, mark it with a paper clip (useful to have along) and come back to it when you have been through the booklet. One caution if you do this – be sure to skip a number on your answer sheet as well. Check often to be sure that you have not lost your place and that you are marking in the row numbered the same as the question you are answering.

6) Read the questions

Be sure you know what the question asks! Many capable people are unsuccessful because they failed to *read* the questions correctly.

7) Answer all questions

Unless you have been instructed that a penalty will be deducted for incorrect answers, it is better to guess than to omit a question.

8) Speed tests

It is often better NOT to guess on speed tests. It has been found that on timed tests people are tempted to spend the last few seconds before time is called in marking answers at random – without even reading them – in the hope of picking up a few extra points. To discourage this practice, the instructions may warn you that your score will be "corrected" for guessing. That is, a penalty will be applied. The incorrect answers will be deducted from the correct ones, or some other penalty formula will be used.

9) Review your answers

If you finish before time is called, go back to the questions you guessed or omitted to give them further thought. Review other answers if you have time.

10) Return your test materials

If you are ready to leave before others have finished or time is called, take ALL your materials to the monitor and leave quietly. Never take any test material with you. The monitor can discover whose papers are not complete, and taking a test booklet may be grounds for disqualification.

VIII. EXAMINATION TECHNIQUES

1) Read the general instructions carefully. These are usually printed on the first page of the exam booklet. As a rule, these instructions refer to the timing of the examination; the fact that you should not start work until the signal and must stop work at a signal, etc. If there are any *special* instructions, such as a choice of questions to be answered, make sure that you note this instruction carefully.

2) When you are ready to start work on the examination, that is as soon as the signal has been given, read the instructions to each question booklet, underline any key words or phrases, such as *least, best, outline, describe* and the like. In this way you will tend to answer as requested rather than discover on reviewing your paper that you *listed without describing*, that you selected the *worst* choice rather than the *best* choice, etc.

3) If the examination is of the objective or multiple-choice type – that is, each question will also give a series of possible answers: A, B, C or D, and you are called upon to select the best answer and write the letter next to that answer on your answer paper – it is advisable to start answering each question in turn. There may be anywhere from 50 to 100 such questions in the three or four hours allotted and you can see how much time would be taken if you read through all the questions before beginning to answer any. Furthermore, if you come across a question or group of questions which you know would be difficult to answer, it would undoubtedly affect your handling of all the other questions.

4) If the examination is of the essay type and contains but a few questions, it is a moot point as to whether you should read all the questions before starting to answer any one. Of course, if you are given a choice – say five out of seven and the like – then it is essential to read all the questions so you can eliminate the two that are most difficult. If, however, you are asked to answer all the questions, there may be danger in trying to answer the easiest one first because you may find that you will spend too much time on it. The best technique is to answer the first question, then proceed to the second, etc.

5) Time your answers. Before the exam begins, write down the time it started, then add the time allowed for the examination and write down the time it must be completed, then divide the time available somewhat as follows:
   - If 3-1/2 hours are allowed, that would be 210 minutes. If you have 80 objective-type questions, that would be an average of 2-1/2 minutes per question. Allow yourself no more than 2 minutes per question, or a total of 160 minutes, which will permit about 50 minutes to review.
   - If for the time allotment of 210 minutes there are 7 essay questions to answer, that would average about 30 minutes a question. Give yourself only 25 minutes per question so that you have about 35 minutes to review.

6) The most important instruction is to *read each question* and make sure you know what is wanted. The second most important instruction is to *time yourself properly* so that you answer every question. The third most important instruction is to *answer every question.* Guess if you have to but include something for each question. Remember that you will receive no credit for a blank and will probably receive some credit if you write something in answer to an essay question. If you guess a letter – say "B" for a multiple-choice question – you may have guessed right. If you leave a blank as an answer to a multiple-choice question, the examiners may respect your feelings but it will not add a point to your score. Some exams may penalize you for wrong answers, so in such cases *only*, you may not want to guess unless you have some basis for your answer.

7) Suggestions
   a. Objective-type questions
      1. Examine the question booklet for proper sequence of pages and questions
      2. Read all instructions carefully
      3. Skip any question which seems too difficult; return to it after all other questions have been answered
      4. Apportion your time properly; do not spend too much time on any single question or group of questions

5. Note and underline key words – *all, most, fewest, least, best, worst, same, opposite,* etc.
6. Pay particular attention to negatives
7. Note unusual option, e.g., unduly long, short, complex, different or similar in content to the body of the question
8. Observe the use of "hedging" words – *probably, may, most likely,* etc.
9. Make sure that your answer is put next to the same number as the question
10. Do not second-guess unless you have good reason to believe the second answer is definitely more correct
11. Cross out original answer if you decide another answer is more accurate; do not erase until you are ready to hand your paper in
12. Answer all questions; guess unless instructed otherwise
13. Leave time for review

b. Essay questions
   1. Read each question carefully
   2. Determine exactly what is wanted. Underline key words or phrases.
   3. Decide on outline or paragraph answer
   4. Include many different points and elements unless asked to develop any one or two points or elements
   5. Show impartiality by giving pros and cons unless directed to select one side only
   6. Make and write down any assumptions you find necessary to answer the questions
   7. Watch your English, grammar, punctuation and choice of words
   8. Time your answers; don't crowd material

8) Answering the essay question

Most essay questions can be answered by framing the specific response around several key words or ideas. Here are a few such key words or ideas:

M's: manpower, materials, methods, money, management
P's: purpose, program, policy, plan, procedure, practice, problems, pitfalls, personnel, public relations
   a. Six basic steps in handling problems:
      1. Preliminary plan and background development
      2. Collect information, data and facts
      3. Analyze and interpret information, data and facts
      4. Analyze and develop solutions as well as make recommendations
      5. Prepare report and sell recommendations
      6. Install recommendations and follow up effectiveness

   b. Pitfalls to avoid
      1. *Taking things for granted* – A statement of the situation does not necessarily imply that each of the elements is necessarily true; for example, a complaint may be invalid and biased so that all that can be taken for granted is that a complaint has been registered

2. *Considering only one side of a situation* – Wherever possible, indicate several alternatives and then point out the reasons you selected the best one
3. *Failing to indicate follow up* – Whenever your answer indicates action on your part, make certain that you will take proper follow-up action to see how successful your recommendations, procedures or actions turn out to be
4. *Taking too long in answering any single question* – Remember to time your answers properly

IX. AFTER THE TEST

Scoring procedures differ in detail among civil service jurisdictions although the general principles are the same. Whether the papers are hand-scored or graded by machine we have described, they are nearly always graded by number. That is, the person who marks the paper knows only the number – never the name – of the applicant. Not until all the papers have been graded will they be matched with names. If other tests, such as training and experience or oral interview ratings have been given, scores will be combined. Different parts of the examination usually have different weights. For example, the written test might count 60 percent of the final grade, and a rating of training and experience 40 percent. In many jurisdictions, veterans will have a certain number of points added to their grades.

After the final grade has been determined, the names are placed in grade order and an eligible list is established. There are various methods for resolving ties between those who get the same final grade – probably the most common is to place first the name of the person whose application was received first. Job offers are made from the eligible list in the order the names appear on it. You will be notified of your grade and your rank as soon as all these computations have been made. This will be done as rapidly as possible.

People who are found to meet the requirements in the announcement are called "eligibles." Their names are put on a list of eligible candidates. An eligible's chances of getting a job depend on how high he stands on this list and how fast agencies are filling jobs from the list.

When a job is to be filled from a list of eligibles, the agency asks for the names of people on the list of eligibles for that job. When the civil service commission receives this request, it sends to the agency the names of the three people highest on this list. Or, if the job to be filled has specialized requirements, the office sends the agency the names of the top three persons who meet these requirements from the general list.

The appointing officer makes a choice from among the three people whose names were sent to him. If the selected person accepts the appointment, the names of the others are put back on the list to be considered for future openings.

That is the rule in hiring from all kinds of eligible lists, whether they are for typist, carpenter, chemist, or something else. For every vacancy, the appointing officer has his choice of any one of the top three eligibles on the list. This explains why the person whose name is on top of the list sometimes does not get an appointment when some of the persons lower on the list do. If the appointing officer chooses the second or third eligible, the No. 1 eligible does not get a job at once, but stays on the list until he is appointed or the list is terminated.

X. HOW TO PASS THE INTERVIEW TEST

The examination for which you applied requires an oral interview test. You have already taken the written test and you are now being called for the interview test – the final part of the formal examination.

You may think that it is not possible to prepare for an interview test and that there are no procedures to follow during an interview. Our purpose is to point out some things you can do in advance that will help you and some good rules to follow and pitfalls to avoid while you are being interviewed.

What is an interview supposed to test?

The written examination is designed to test the technical knowledge and competence of the candidate; the oral is designed to evaluate intangible qualities, not readily measured otherwise, and to establish a list showing the relative fitness of each candidate – as measured against his competitors – for the position sought. Scoring is not on the basis of "right" and "wrong," but on a sliding scale of values ranging from "not passable" to "outstanding." As a matter of fact, it is possible to achieve a relatively low score without a single "incorrect" answer because of evident weakness in the qualities being measured.

Occasionally, an examination may consist entirely of an oral test – either an individual or a group oral. In such cases, information is sought concerning the technical knowledges and abilities of the candidate, since there has been no written examination for this purpose. More commonly, however, an oral test is used to supplement a written examination.

Who conducts interviews?

The composition of oral boards varies among different jurisdictions. In nearly all, a representative of the personnel department serves as chairman. One of the members of the board may be a representative of the department in which the candidate would work. In some cases, "outside experts" are used, and, frequently, a businessman or some other representative of the general public is asked to serve. Labor and management or other special groups may be represented. The aim is to secure the services of experts in the appropriate field.

However the board is composed, it is a good idea (and not at all improper or unethical) to ascertain in advance of the interview who the members are and what groups they represent. When you are introduced to them, you will have some idea of their backgrounds and interests, and at least you will not stutter and stammer over their names.

What should be done before the interview?

While knowledge about the board members is useful and takes some of the surprise element out of the interview, there is other preparation which is more substantive. It *is* possible to prepare for an oral interview – in several ways:

1) Keep a copy of your application and review it carefully before the interview

This may be the only document before the oral board, and the starting point of the interview. Know what education and experience you have listed there, and the sequence and dates of all of it. Sometimes the board will ask you to review the highlights of your experience for them; you should not have to hem and haw doing it.

2) Study the class specification and the examination announcement

Usually, the oral board has one or both of these to guide them. The qualities, characteristics or knowledges required by the position sought are stated in these documents. They offer valuable clues as to the nature of the oral interview. For example, if the job involves supervisory responsibilities, the announcement will usually indicate that knowledge of modern supervisory methods and the qualifications of the candidate as a supervisor will be tested. If so, you can expect such questions, frequently in the form of a hypothetical situation which you are expected to solve. NEVER go into an oral without knowledge of the duties and responsibilities of the job you seek.

3) Think through each qualification required

Try to visualize the kind of questions you would ask if you were a board member. How well could you answer them? Try especially to appraise your own knowledge and background in each area, *measured against the job sought*, and identify any areas in which you are weak. Be critical and realistic – do not flatter yourself.

4) Do some general reading in areas in which you feel you may be weak

For example, if the job involves supervision and your past experience has NOT, some general reading in supervisory methods and practices, particularly in the field of human relations, might be useful. Do NOT study agency procedures or detailed manuals. The oral board will be testing your understanding and capacity, not your memory.

5) Get a good night's sleep and watch your general health and mental attitude

You will want a clear head at the interview. Take care of a cold or any other minor ailment, and of course, no hangovers.

What should be done on the day of the interview?

Now comes the day of the interview itself. Give yourself plenty of time to get there. Plan to arrive somewhat ahead of the scheduled time, particularly if your appointment is in the fore part of the day. If a previous candidate fails to appear, the board might be ready for you a bit early. By early afternoon an oral board is almost invariably behind schedule if there are many candidates, and you may have to wait. Take along a book or magazine to read, or your application to review, but leave any extraneous material in the waiting room when you go in for your interview. In any event, relax and compose yourself.

The matter of dress is important. The board is forming impressions about you – from your experience, your manners, your attitude, and your appearance. Give your personal appearance careful attention. Dress your best, but not your flashiest. Choose conservative, appropriate clothing, and be sure it is immaculate. This is a business interview, and your appearance should indicate that you regard it as such. Besides, being well groomed and properly dressed will help boost your confidence.

Sooner or later, someone will call your name and escort you into the interview room. *This is it.* From here on you are on your own. It is too late for any more preparation. But remember, you asked for this opportunity to prove your fitness, and you are here because your request was granted.

What happens when you go in?

The usual sequence of events will be as follows: The clerk (who is often the board stenographer) will introduce you to the chairman of the oral board, who will introduce you to the other members of the board. Acknowledge the introductions before you sit down. Do not be surprised if you find a microphone facing you or a stenotypist sitting by. Oral interviews are usually recorded in the event of an appeal or other review.

Usually the chairman of the board will open the interview by reviewing the highlights of your education and work experience from your application – primarily for the benefit of the other members of the board, as well as to get the material into the record. Do not interrupt or comment unless there is an error or significant misinterpretation; if that is the case, do not hesitate. But do not quibble about insignificant matters. Also, he will usually ask you some question about your education, experience or your present job – partly to get you to start talking and to establish the interviewing "rapport." He may start the actual questioning, or turn it over to one of the other members. Frequently, each member undertakes the questioning on a particular area, one in which he is perhaps most competent, so you can expect each member to participate in the examination. Because time is limited, you may also expect some rather abrupt switches in the direction the questioning takes, so do not be upset by it. Normally, a board member will not pursue a single line of questioning unless he discovers a particular strength or weakness.

After each member has participated, the chairman will usually ask whether any member has any further questions, then will ask you if you have anything you wish to add. Unless you are expecting this question, it may floor you. Worse, it may start you off on an extended, extemporaneous speech. The board is not usually seeking more information. The question is principally to offer you a last opportunity to present further qualifications or to indicate that you have nothing to add. So, if you feel that a significant qualification or characteristic has been overlooked, it is proper to point it out in a sentence or so. Do not compliment the board on the thoroughness of their examination – they have been sketchy, and you know it. If you wish, merely say, "No thank you, I have nothing further to add." This is a point where you can "talk yourself out" of a good impression or fail to present an important bit of information. Remember, *you close the interview yourself.*

The chairman will then say, "That is all, Mr. _____, thank you." Do not be startled; the interview is over, and quicker than you think. Thank him, gather your belongings and take your leave. Save your sigh of relief for the other side of the door.

How to put your best foot forward
Throughout this entire process, you may feel that the board individually and collectively is trying to pierce your defenses, seek out your hidden weaknesses and embarrass and confuse you. Actually, this is not true. They are obliged to make an appraisal of your qualifications for the job you are seeking, and they want to see you in your best light. Remember, they must interview all candidates and a non-cooperative candidate may become a failure in spite of their best efforts to bring out his qualifications. Here are 15 suggestions that will help you:

1) Be natural – Keep your attitude confident, not cocky
If you are not confident that you can do the job, do not expect the board to be. Do not apologize for your weaknesses, try to bring out your strong points. The board is interested in a positive, not negative, presentation. Cockiness will antagonize any board member and make him wonder if you are covering up a weakness by a false show of strength.

2) Get comfortable, but don't lounge or sprawl
Sit erectly but not stiffly. A careless posture may lead the board to conclude that you are careless in other things, or at least that you are not impressed by the importance of the occasion. Either conclusion is natural, even if incorrect. Do not fuss with your clothing, a pencil or an ashtray. Your hands may occasionally be useful to emphasize a point; do not let them become a point of distraction.

3) Do not wisecrack or make small talk
This is a serious situation, and your attitude should show that you consider it as such. Further, the time of the board is limited – they do not want to waste it, and neither should you.

4) Do not exaggerate your experience or abilities

In the first place, from information in the application or other interviews and sources, the board may know more about you than you think. Secondly, you probably will not get away with it. An experienced board is rather adept at spotting such a situation, so do not take the chance.

5) If you know a board member, do not make a point of it, yet do not hide it

Certainly you are not fooling him, and probably not the other members of the board. Do not try to take advantage of your acquaintanceship – it will probably do you little good.

6) Do not dominate the interview

Let the board do that. They will give you the clues – do not assume that you have to do all the talking. Realize that the board has a number of questions to ask you, and do not try to take up all the interview time by showing off your extensive knowledge of the answer to the first one.

7) Be attentive

You only have 20 minutes or so, and you should keep your attention at its sharpest throughout. When a member is addressing a problem or question to you, give him your undivided attention. Address your reply principally to him, but do not exclude the other board members.

8) Do not interrupt

A board member may be stating a problem for you to analyze. He will ask you a question when the time comes. Let him state the problem, and wait for the question.

9) Make sure you understand the question

Do not try to answer until you are sure what the question is. If it is not clear, restate it in your own words or ask the board member to clarify it for you. However, do not haggle about minor elements.

10) Reply promptly but not hastily

A common entry on oral board rating sheets is "candidate responded readily," or "candidate hesitated in replies." Respond as promptly and quickly as you can, but do not jump to a hasty, ill-considered answer.

11) Do not be peremptory in your answers

A brief answer is proper – but do not fire your answer back. That is a losing game from your point of view. The board member can probably ask questions much faster than you can answer them.

12) Do not try to create the answer you think the board member wants

He is interested in what kind of mind you have and how it works – not in playing games. Furthermore, he can usually spot this practice and will actually grade you down on it.

13) Do not switch sides in your reply merely to agree with a board member

Frequently, a member will take a contrary position merely to draw you out and to see if you are willing and able to defend your point of view. Do not start a debate, yet do not surrender a good position. If a position is worth taking, it is worth defending.

14) Do not be afraid to admit an error in judgment if you are shown to be wrong

The board knows that you are forced to reply without any opportunity for careful consideration. Your answer may be demonstrably wrong. If so, admit it and get on with the interview.

15) Do not dwell at length on your present job

The opening question may relate to your present assignment. Answer the question but do not go into an extended discussion. You are being examined for a *new* job, not your present one. As a matter of fact, try to phrase ALL your answers in terms of the job for which you are being examined.

Basis of Rating

Probably you will forget most of these "do's" and "don'ts" when you walk into the oral interview room. Even remembering them all will not ensure you a passing grade. Perhaps you did not have the qualifications in the first place. But remembering them will help you to put your best foot forward, without treading on the toes of the board members.

Rumor and popular opinion to the contrary notwithstanding, an oral board wants you to make the best appearance possible. They know you are under pressure – but they also want to see how you respond to it as a guide to what your reaction would be under the pressures of the job you seek. They will be influenced by the degree of poise you display, the personal traits you show and the manner in which you respond.

ABOUT THIS BOOK

This book contains tests divided into Examination Sections. Go through each test, answering every question in the margin. We have also attached a sample answer sheet at the back of the book that can be removed and used. At the end of each test look at the answer key and check your answers. On the ones you got wrong, look at the right answer choice and learn. Do not fill in the answers first. Do not memorize the questions and answers, but understand the answer and principles involved. On your test, the questions will likely be different from the samples. Questions are changed and new ones added. If you understand these past questions you should have success with any changes that arise. Tests may consist of several types of questions. We have additional books on each subject should more study be advisable or necessary for you. Finally, the more you study, the better prepared you will be. This book is intended to be the last thing you study before you walk into the examination room. Prior study of relevant texts is also recommended. NLC publishes some of these in our Fundamental Series. Knowledge and good sense are important factors in passing your exam. Good luck also helps. So now study this Passbook, absorb the material contained within and take that knowledge into the examination. Then do your best to pass that exam.

———

EXAMINATION SECTION

EXAMINATION SECTION
TEST 1

DIRECTIONS: Each question or incomplete statement is followed by several suggested answers or completions. Select the one that BEST answers the question or completes the statement. *PRINT THE LETTER OF THE CORRECT ANSWER IN THE SPACE AT THE RIGHT.*

1. For a given level of illumination, the cost of electrical energy with fluorescent lighting fixtures as compared with incandescent lighting fixtures is   1.____

    A. less   B. the same
    C. more   D. dependent on the utility rate

2. The initial current of an incandescent lamp (tungsten) as compared with its normal operating current is   2.____

    A. less
    B. the same
    C. more
    D. dependent on the system frequency

3. According to the electrical code, fixtures in which the wiring may be exposed to temperatures in excess of 140° F (60° C)   3.____

    A. are prohibited
    B. shall be wired with type AF fixture wires
    C. shall be so designed or ventilated and installed to operate at temperatures which will not cause deterioration of the wiring
    D. shall have suitable thermal insulation between the fixture and any adjacent combustible material

4. The direction of rotation of a d.c. shunt motor can be reversed by   4.____

    A. reversing the line terminals
    B. reversing the field and armature
    C. reversing the field or armature
    D. flashing the field

5. A starting device which will limit the starting current of a d.c. motor is generally required because   5.____

    A. the counter e.m.f. is maximum at standstill
    B. the inertia of the driven load causes excessive starting current
    C. the counter e.m.f. is zero at standstill
    D. decreased starting current increases the starting torque

6. According to the electrical code, motor disconnecting means shall be located   6.____

    A. within 10 feet of the motor
    B. within sight of the controller
    C. within 15 feet of the motor
    D. where convenient

7. According to the electrical code, the controller for an a.c. motor shall be capable of inter-   7.__
   rupting

   A. twice the full load current of the motor
   B. three times the full load current of the motor
   C. five times the full load current of the motor
   D. the stalled rotor current

8. According to the electrical code, motor disconnecting means shall have a continuous   8.__
   duty rating, in percent, of the name plate current rating of the motor of AT LEAST

   A. 100%   B. 115%   C. 150%   D. 200%

9. The lumens per watt taken by a lamp varies with the type and size of lamp. Given that a   9.__
   one candle power light source emits 12.57 lumens, the lumens per watt taken by a 75
   candle power lamp drawing 40 watts is *approximately*

   A. 1.9   B. 6.7   C. 23.6   D. 240

10. A 230-volt, 25-cycle magnetic brake coil is to be rewound to operate properly on 60   10.__
    cycles at the same voltage. Assuming that the coil at 25 cycles has 1800 turns, at 60
    cycles the number of turns should be

    A. *reduced* to 750   B. *increased* to 2400
    C. *reduced* to 420   D. *increased* to 3000

11. Nichrome wire having a resistance of 200 ohms per 100 feet is to be used for a heater   11.__
    requiring a total resistance of 10 ohms.
    The length, in feet, of wire required is

    A. 5   B. 15   C. 25   D. 50

12. The MAIN reason for grounding conduit is to prevent the conduit from becoming   12.__

    A. corroded by electrolysis
    B. magnetized
    C. a source of radio interference
    D. accidentally energized at a higher potential than ground

13. A feeder consisting of a positive and a negative wire supplies a motor load. The feeder is   13.__
    connected to bus-bars having a constant potential of 230 volts. The feeder is 500 feet
    long and consists of two 250,000 circular-mil conductors. The maximum load on the
    feeder is 170 amps. Assume that the resistance of 1000 feet of this cable is 0.0431 ohm.
    The voltage, at the motor terminals, is MOST NEARLY

    A. 201 V   B. 209 V   C. 213 V   D. 217 V

14. With reference to question 13 above, the efficiency of transmission, in percent, is MOST   14.__
    NEARLY

    A. 83%   B. 87%   C. 91%   D. 97%

15. With reference to a.c. motors, in addition to overload, many other things cause fuses to   15.__
    blow. The fuse will blow if, in starting an a.c. motor, the operator throws the starting
    switch of the compensator to the running position

A. too slowly
B. too quickly
C. with main switch in open position
D. with main switch in close position

16. A change in speed of a d.c. motor of 10 to 15 percent can USUALLY be made by   16.____

    A. rewinding the armature
    B. rewinding the field
    C. decreasing the number of turns in the field coils
    D. increasing or decreasing the gap between the armature and field

17. In order to check the number of poles in a 3-phase wound rotor induction motor, it is nec-   17.____
essary to check the no-load speed. The no-load speed is obtained by running the motor
with load disconnected and with the rotor resistance

    A. short-circuited   B. all in
    C. half in   D. one-third in

18. A group of industrial oil burners are equipped with several electric preheaters which can   18.____
be used singly or in combination to heat the #6 oil for the burners. Electric preheater "A"
alone can heat a certain quantity of oil from $70°$ to $160°$ in 15 minutes and preheater "B"
alone can do the same job in 30 minutes. If both preheaters are used together, they will
do the job in _____ minutes.

    A. 12   B. 11   C. 10   D. 9

19. With reference to armature windings, in a wave winding, regardless of the number of   19.____
poles, ONLY _____ brushes are necessary.

    A. two   B. four   C. six   D. eight

20. The MINIMUM number of overload devices required for a 3-phase a.c. motor connected   20.____
to a 120/208 volt, 3-phase, 4 wire system is

    A. 1   B. 2   C. 3   D. 4

21. According to the electrical code, an externally operable switch may be used as the   21.____
starter for a motor of not over 2 horsepower (and not over 300 volts) provided it has a rating of AT LEAST

    A. 2 times the stalled rotor current of the motor
    B. 2 times the full load current of the motor
    C. 115% of the full load current of the motor
    D. 150% of the stalled rotor current of the motor

22. According to the electrical code, a single disconnecting means may serve a group of   22.____
motors provided

    A. all motors are 1/2 HP or less
    B. all motors are within a short distance from each other
    C. all motors are located within a single room and within sight of the disconnecting
       means
    D. one-half of the motors are located within a single room and within sight of the dis-
       connecting means

23. In a 3-phase system with 3 identical loads connected in delta, if the line voltage is 4160 volts, the line to neutral voltage is   23.____

    A. indeterminate   B. 7200 volts
    C. 2400 volts   D. 2000 volts

24. If the current in each line is 100 amperes, the currents in each of the individual loads is (under the conditions as set forth in question 23)   24.____

    A. indeterminate   B. 57.7 amps
    C. 173 amps   D. 50.0 amps

25. In a 3-phase system with 3 identical loads connected in wye, if the line to neutral voltage is 115 volts, the line voltage is   25.____

    A. indeterminate   B. 208 volts
    C. 200 volts   D. 220 volts

26. A circuit composed of a 6-ohm resistance, a 10-ohm capacitive reactance, and an 18-ohm inductive reactance connected in series is energized by a 120 volt a.c. supply. The current, in amperes, flowing in this circuit is   26.____

    A. 0   B. 12   C. 35   D. 20

27. With reference to question 26 above, the power, in watts, used in this circuit is   27.____

    A. 0   B. 1440   C. 420   D. 864

28. With reference to question 26 above, the power factor, in percent, is   28.____

    A. 100   B. 60   C. 80   D. 90

29. With reference to question 26 above, the total impedance, in ohms, of the circuit is   29.____

    A. 10   B. 34   C. 14   D. 28

30. A triode does NOT have a   30.____

    A. cathode   B. screen grid
    C. control grid   D. plate

31. An industrial plant utilizes acetone as a solvent in one area. All wiring in this area must be   31.____

    A. vaportight   B. watertight
    C. explosionproof   D. of normal construction

32. In an area where explosionproof wiring is required, each conduit entering an enclosure containing apparatus which may produce arcs, sparks, or high temperatures shall be provided with   32.____

    A. insulating bushings
    B. a cable terminator
    C. an approved sealing compound
    D. double locknuts

33. Decreasing the bias voltage on the control grid of a triode (making it less negative with respect to the cathode) causes the plate current to   33.____

    A. not change
    C. decrease
    B. increase
    D. oscillate

Questions 34-46.

DIRECTIONS: The following questions 34 to 46 inclusive are to be answered in accordance with the provisions of the electrical code.

34. The MINIMUM size of wire for signalling systems is   34.____

    A. #14AWG   B. #16AWG   C. #18AWG   D. #19AWG

35. The MINIMUM size of service entrance conductors is   35.____

    A. #2AWG   B. #4AWG   C. #6AWG   D. #8AWG

36. The MAXIMUM number of individual sets of service equipment which can be supplied from one set of service entrance conductors is   36.____

    A. 1   B. 2   C. 4   D. 6

37. Service switches of ratings larger than 1,200 amperes   37.____

    A. are prohibited
    B. shall be of the pressure contact type
    C. shall be of the air circuit breaker type
    D. shall be remotely operable

38. The rating of service switches shall be less than   38.____

    A. the computed load current
    B. twice the computed load current
    C. one and a half times the computed load current
    D. one and a quarter times the computed load current

39. The allowable current carrying capacity of conductors in raceway or cable   39.____

    A. is independent of the number of conductors
    B. shall be reduced to 70% of table values if more than three conductors are contained within the raceway or cable
    C. shall be reduced to 50% of the table values if more than six conductors are contained in the raceway or cable
    D. shall be reduced to 80% for 4-6 conductors and to 70% for 7-9 conductors in the same raceway or cable

40. The MAXIMUM number of conductors for general light and power in a single raceway is   40.____

    A. 6   B. 9   C. 15   D. unlimited

41. The number of signal wires in a conductor raceway shall be   41.___

    A. the same as for lighting and power conductors
    B. such that their total cross-sectional area shall not exceed 50% of the cross-sectional area of the conduit or raceway
    C. the maximum number which can be easily installed
    D. such that their total cross-sectional area shall not exceed 40% of the cross-sectional area of the conduit or raceway

42. Lightning arrestors for receiving station antennas shall operate at a voltage of NOT more   42.___
than _____ volts.

    A. 100   B. 200   C. 500   D. 1000

43. The MINIMUM size of copper ground connection to lightning arrestors for receiving   43.___
antennas shall be

    A. #14AWG   B. #10AWG   C. #6AWG   D. #16AWG

44. Only motor generator sets having a generated voltage of 65 volts or less may be protected by   44.___

    A. one protective device in the generator armature circuit
    B. a protective device in each armature lead
    C. the over current protective devices in the motor circuit set to trip when the generators are delivering not more than 150% of their full load rated current
    D. the motor running protective devices of the motor

45. Single pole protective devices for direct current generators MUST be activated by   45.___

    A. the total generated current, including all field current
    B. total current except that in the shunt field
    C. separate elements in each brush lead
    D. separate elements in each line lead

46. Motor control equipment for hazardous locations MUST   46.___

    A. not produce sparks
    B. be contained in an enclosure which is vaportight
    C. be capable of withstanding an external explosion
    D. be of a type specifically approved for the installation

47. A room is 20 feet wide and is to be provided with 4 rows of lighting outlets symmetrically   47.___
spaced. The distance from the wall to the center line of the first fixture row will be

    A. 5'0"   B. 10'0"   C. 7'6"   D. 2'6"

48. A fixture mounting height of 9'6" is specified for a room with a ceiling height of 12'0", utilizing fixtures with a height of 6". The size of stem required is MOST NEARLY   48.___

    A. 3'0"   B. 2'6"   C. 2'0"   D. 1'6"

49. Specifications for a project require that 40W, T-12, RS/CW lamps be installed in a given group of fixtures. The type of lamp required is   49._____

    A. 40 watt, type 12, reflector spot, clear white, incandescent
    B. 40 watt, single pin, relay start, code white, fluorescent
    C. 40 watt, bi-pin, rapid start, cool white, fluorescent
    D. type 12, medium base, recessed spot, clear white, incandescent

50. Specifications for a project require the use of indirect type of lighting fixtures. The one of the following types that will meet this requirement is   50._____

    A. RCM dome fixture
    B. concentric ring fixture with silverbowl lamp
    C. downlight with par 38 spot
    D. opal glass bowl

KEY (CORRECT ANSWERS)

1. A	11. D	21. B	31. C	41. D
2. C	12. D	22. C	32. C	42. C
3. C	13. D	23. C	33. B	43. A
4. C	14. D	24. B	34. D	44. C
5. C	15. B	25. C	35. B	45. B
6. B	16. D	26. B	36. D	46. D
7. D	17. A	27. D	37. B	47. D
8. B	18. C	28. B	38. D	48. C
9. C	19. A	29. A	39. D	49. C
10. A	20. B	30. B	40. B	50. B

TEST 2

DIRECTIONS: Each question or incomplete statement is followed by several suggested answers or completions. Select the one that BEST answers the question or completes the statement. *PRINT THE LETTER OF THE CORRECT ANSWER IN THE SPACE AT THE RIGHT.*

1. The list of symbols for the plans for a project gives and defines the following symbol:　　1._

0_{A5C} - Incandescent lighting fixture, letters, and number indicate fixture type per specifications, circuit number and controlling switch, respectively.

The symbol for a fixture connected to circuit 8, controlled by a switch designated "e" and conforming to the requirements of a type D fixture would be

A. 0_{E8d}　　　　B. 0_{d8E}　　　　C. 0_{D8e}　　　　D. $0_{8eD}{}^0$

Questions 2-5.

DIRECTIONS: The questions numbered 2 to 5 inclusive shall be answered in accordance with the diagram which appears below.

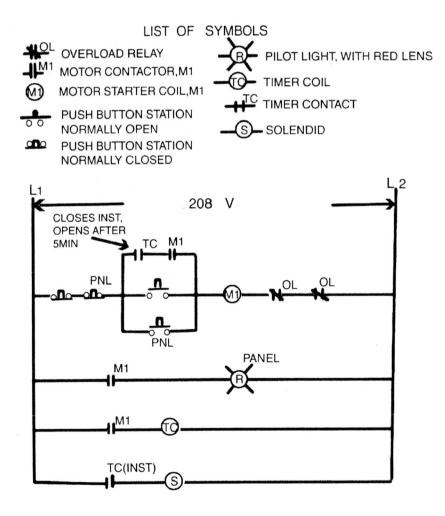

LIST OF SYMBOLS

OVERLOAD RELAY

MOTOR CONTACTOR, M1

MOTOR STARTER COIL, M1

PUSH BUTTON STATION NORMALLY OPEN

PUSH BUTTON STATION NORMALLY CLOSED

PILOT LIGHT, WITH RED LENS

TIMER COIL

TIMER CONTACT

SOLENDID

2. The above schematic diagram indicates a desired control scheme for a pump motor. The number of locations the motor can be started from is (are)   2.____

    A. 1   B. 2   C. 3   D. 4

3. Of the following, the one which contains the most complete and correct list of possible operations which will cause the already started motor to stop is   3.____

    A. pressing of stop PB after 5 minutes have elapsed since motor started, or operation of OL
    B. a lapse of 5 minutes since starting of motor, or pressing of stop PB, or operation of OL
    C. the passing of 5 minutes from the time of starting, or pressing, of stop PB, or operation of OL, or loss of voltage
    D. loss of voltage after 5 minutes have elapsed since starting motor, or operation of OL

4. The solenoid will be energized   4.____

    A. as long as the motor starter is energized
    B. only as long as the start PB is depressed
    C. for five minutes
    D. until the stop PB is depressed

5. If the timer fails to close its associated contact, the motor   5.____

    A. cannot run
    B. will run only as long as the start PB is depressed
    C. will run continuously
    D. will run for five minutes

Questions 6-8.

DIRECTIONS: The following questions 6 to 8 inclusive should be answered in accordance with the diagram below.

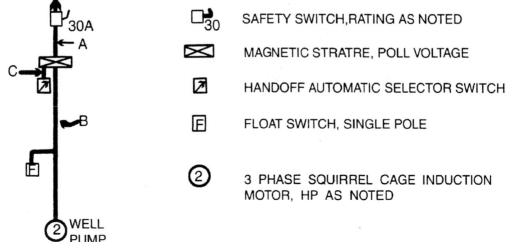

TO 208 V POWER PANEL(30)

LEGEND

SAFETY SWITCH,RATING AS NOTED

MAGNETIC STRATRE, POLL VOLTAGE

HANDOFF AUTOMATIC SELECTOR SWITCH

FLOAT SWITCH, SINGLE POLE

3 PHASE SQUIRREL CAGE INDUCTION MOTOR, HP AS NOTED

6. The required number of conductors at point "A" is   6.___

     A. 2   B. 3   C. 4   D. 5

7. The required number of conductors at point "B" is   7.___

     A. 2   B. 3   C. 4   D. 5

8. The required number of conductors at point "C" is   8.___

     A. 2   B. 3   C. 4   D. 5

9. The LEAST number of single-phase wattmeters that can be be used to measure the   9.___
power in an unbalanced 3-phase, 4-wire a.c. circuit is

     A. 1   B. 2   C. 3   D. 4

10. A note on a plan states: "All runs shall be 3/4" conduit with 2#12AWG conductors or   10.___
number of #12 conductors indicated by hatchmarks unless otherwise designated." A run
is shown as follows: —/—/—/
This run consists of

     A. 2#12, 1/2"C   B. 3#12, 1/2"C
     C. 3#12, 3/4"C   D. 2#12, 3/4"C

11. Specifications for a particular project call for a system of empty conduits and outlet boxes   11.___
for public telephones, with a galvanized steel wire installed in each conduit. The one of
the following reasons for providing this wire which is MOST acceptable is to

     A. ensure that the conduit is clear
     B. permit pulling in of wire at a later date
     C. ground the system
     D. limit corrosion of the interior surfaces of the conduit

12. An interior auxiliary fire alarm system to be installed in a building is to be of the coded   12.___
city connected shunt-trip type. The one of the following which BEST describes the operation of this system is operating any station

     A. sounds a coded signal on all bells and uses local power to trip a city box
     B. operates the city box only
     C. trips a city box using municipal system power and simultaneously sounds a coded
        signal on interior bells
     D. operates interior gongs only

13. A magnetic motor starter is to be controlled with momentary start-stop pushbuttons at   13.___
two locations. The number of control wires required, respectively, in the conduit between
the controller and the first station and in the conduit between the two stations is

     A. 3 and 3   B. 4 and 4
     C. 3 and 4   D. 2 and 4

14. If the voltage on a 3-phase squirrel cage induction motor is reduced to 90% of its rating,   14.___
the starting current

     A. increases slightly   B. is unchanged
     C. decreases 10%   D. decreases 20%

15. If the voltage on a 3-phase squirrel cage induction motor is reduced to 90% of its rating, the full load current

    A. decreases slightly   B. is unchanged
    C. increases 10%   D. increases 20%

15.____

16. A 3-conductor cable is used to provide a "hot" leg, switch leg and neutral between two outlets. The individual conductors are MOST commonly connected as follows: red is

    A. hot, white is neutral, black is switch
    B. switch, white is hot, black is neutral
    C. neutral, white is switch, black is hot
    D. switch, white is neutral, black is hot

16.____

17. To obtain a.c. current from a d.c. source of supply, it is BEST to use a(n)

    A. inverter   B. diode
    C. rectifier   D. shunt generator

17.____

18. Insulation resistance is commonly measured by means of a(n)

    A. ammeter   B. varmeter
    C. capacitance bridge   D. megger

18.____

19. A specification requires the installation of five pole, four wire, grounded 250 volt, 15 amp receptacles for 120/208 volt 3 ϕ 4 wire service, with matching plug and 15 foot #14AWG portable heavy duty cord. The number of conductors which the required cord MUST have is

    A. 3   B. 4
    C. 5   D. not clearly specified

19.____

Questions 20-21.

DIRECTIONS: The following questions 20 and 21 are to be answered in accordance with the information given below.

To get equivalent delta from wye

$$A = \frac{ab+bc+ac}{a}$$

$$B = \frac{ab+bx+ac}{b}$$

$$C = \frac{ab+bx+ac}{c}$$

To get equivalent wye from delta

$$a = \frac{BC}{A+B+C}$$

$$b = \frac{AC}{A+B+C}$$

$$c = \frac{AB}{A+B+C}$$

NOTE: The above formula indicates the relationship between equivalent wye and delta net works.

20. If, in a delta, the branches are resistors such that A=5 ohms, B=10 ohms, and C=10 ohms, the resistor of branch "a" of the equivalent wye is _____ ohms.

20.__

   A. 5   B. 10   C. 2   D. 4

21. In the problem 20 above, the resistor of branch "b" of the equivalent wye is _____ ohms.

21.__

   A. 10   B. 4   C. 2   D. 5

Questions 22-23.

DIRECTIONS: The following questions 22 and 23 should be answered in accordance with the paragraph below.

Insulation resistance tests are best made with a direct-reading Megger. These tests can also be made with a high-resistance voltmeter and a source of d.c. supply. Assume that a direct reading instrument is not available but you have on hand a 100-volt voltmeter having a sensitivity of 5000 ohms per volt and a 100-volt battery. The battery is connected in series with the voltmeter. One free battery lead is connected to the wire whose insulation resistance is to be measured, and the other free lead to the grounded circuit. With this hookup, the voltmeter reads 50 volts.

22. The insulation resistance, in ohms, of the above conductor is

22.__

   A. 500   B. 5,000   C. 250,000   D. 500,000

23. The resistance, in ohms, of the above-mentioned voltmeter is

23.__

   A. 500   B. 5,000   C. 250,000   D. 500,000

24. An ammeter and voltmeter are connected through instrument transformers to measure the KVA of a balanced three phase load connected to a 2400 volt, 3-phase, 3 wire system. The PT is rated 2400/120 volts, and the CT is rated 200/5 amperes. If the ammeter reads 4 amps and the voltmeter 100 volts, the load, in KVA, is APPROXIMATELY

24.__

   A. 0.4   B. 6.8   C. 320   D. 555

25. A note on a lighting plan states: "All fluorescent fixtures shall be symmetrically spaced and oriented so that the major axis of the fixture is parallel to the major axis of the room." For a room 20' long by 16' wide, with four-four foot fixtures, the desired arrangement is: Fixtures parallel with and centered

25.__

   A. 4' from 20' wall, 5' from 16' wall
   B. 5' from 20' wall, 4' from 16' wall
   C. 4' from 16' wall, 5' from 20' wall
   D. 5' from 16' wall, 4' from 20' wall

Questions 26-31.

DIRECTIONS: The following questions 26 to 31 inclusive are to be answered in accordance with the provisions of the electrical code.

26. Individual conductors of multi-conductor control cables shall be   26.____

    A. color coded   B. clearly tagged at each end
    C. identified by painting   D. stranded

27. Terminals of motor-starting rheostats shall be   27.____

    A. suitable for solderless external connections only
    B. clearly marked to indicate wire to which they are to be connected
    C. equipped with barriers
    D. brought out to a suitable terminal block

28. Incandescent lamps can be used for control resistors   28.____

    A. under no circumstances
    B. as protective resistances provided they do not carry the main current
    C. for loads less than 1000 watts
    D. if mounted in porcelain receptacles

29. Wiring in battery rooms shall   29.____

    A. utilize lead covered cable
    B. be installed in rigid steel conduit
    C. be installed in Greenfield
    D. be enclosed in non-corrodible conduit or be exposed

30. Control switches for emergency lights in a theater shall be located   30.____

    A. where convenient to operating personnel
    B. in the lobby where accessible to authorized persons
    C. on the stage switchboard
    D. in the projection booth

31. Signal wires of sizes #18 or #16 shall be considered as properly protected by fuses rated   31.____
    at _____ amps.

    A. 15   B. 20   C. 25   D. 30

32. If the voltage of a 3-phase squirrel cage induction motor is reduced to 90% of its rating,   32.____
    the power factor

    A. increases slightly   B. is unchanged
    C. decreases slightly   D. decreases 10 points

33. To reverse the direction of rotation of a wound rotor 3-phase induction motor, interchange   33.____

    A. all line wires   B. all rotor connections
    C. any 2 rotor connections   D. any 2-line wires

Questions 34-36.

DIRECTIONS: The following questions 34 to 36 inclusive relate to the diagram appearing on
the following page.

LEGEND

1° ALARM CONTACT, NORMALLY OPEN

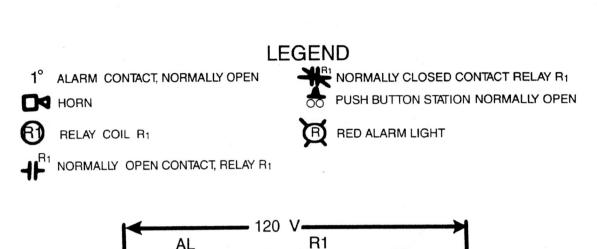

NORMALLY CLOSED CONTACT RELAY R₁

HORN

PUSH BUTTON STATION NORMALLY OPEN

RELAY COIL R₁

RED ALARM LIGHT

NORMALLY OPEN CONTACT, RELAY R₁

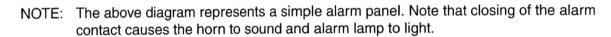

NOTE: The above diagram represents a simple alarm panel. Note that closing of the alarm contact causes the horn to sound and alarm lamp to light.

34.   Assume that the alarm contact has closed. Then, pressing the PB   34.___

    A.   causes the red alarm light to go out only as long as the button is depressed
    B.   causes the horn to be silenced until the alarm contact opens and closes again
    C.   tests the alarm light
    D.   tests the alarm horn

35.   The alarm light is illuminated   35.___

    A.   only when the pushbutton is depressed
    B.   only after the horn is silenced
    C.   as long as the alarm contact is closed
    D.   continuously

36.   The relay R₁ has the following contacts: 36.___

    A.   2 N.O.   B.   2 N.C.
    C.   1 N.O. and 1N.C.   D.   2 N.O. and 1 N.C.

37.   A blind hickey is used   37.___

    A.   to cap a spare conduit
    B.   in lieu of a fixture stud
    C.   in lieu of a fixture extension
    D.   to hang a lighting fixture on a gas outlet

Questions 38-41.

DIRECTIONS: The following questions 38 to 41 inclusive are to be answered in accordance
with the diagram below.

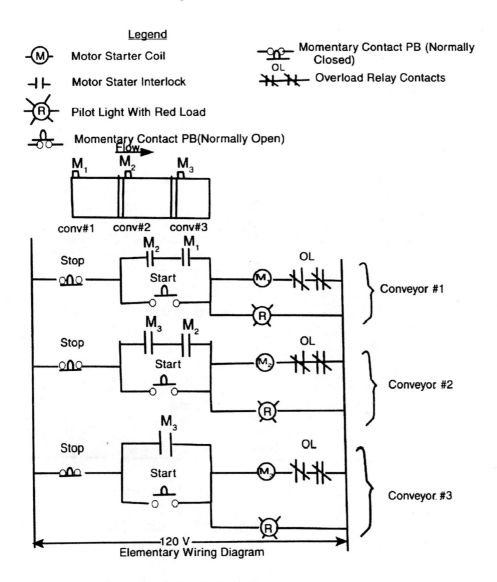

38.   For continuous operation of all conveyors,   38.____

    A.   conveyor #1 must be started first
    B.   conveyor #2 must be started first
    C.   conveyor #3 must be started first
    D.   conveyors can be started in any order

39.   Stopping of conveyor #3 will   39.____

    A.   not affect other conveyors
    B.   stop conveyor #2
    C.   stop conveyor #1
    D.   stop conveyors #1 and #2

40. Momentarily depressing the start PB of conveyor #2 before starting conveyor #3 or #1 will   40.___

    A.   start conveyors #1 and #2
    B.   start conveyor #2 and permit it to run continuously
    C.   start conveyor #2 for only the time the button is depressed
    D.   have no effect

41. When the thermal overload relays of conveyor #2 open,   41.___

    A.   motor #2 only stops
    B.   motors #1 and #2 will stop
    C.   motor #1, #2, and #3 will stop
    D.   an alarm will sound

42. An Erickson coupling is used   42.___

    A.   to join sections of EMT
    B.   to connect EMT to flexible conduit
    C.   to connect two sections of rigid conduit when one section cannot be turned
    D.   as a substitute for all thread

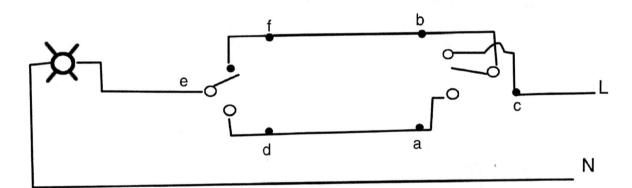

43. A light is to be controlled from two locations. It is connected with two 3-way switches as shown above and does not work properly.   43.___
To correct the wiring, the following changes should be made: Interchange connections

    A.   e and f   B.   b and c   C.   a and b   D.   a and c

44. Proper and economical control of lighting fixtures from three locations without the use of relays   44.___

    A.   cannot be done
    B.   requires a 3-way switch at each location
    C.   requires two 3-way switches and one 4-way switch
    D.   requires two 4-way switches and one 3-way switch

45. The outside diameter of a certain rigid steel conduit is measured to be approximately 2" (to the nearest 1/8 inch). The NOMINAL trade size is   45.___

    A.   2"   B.   1 1/2"   C.   1 1/4"   D.   2 1/2"

46. Electrical equipment can be secured to concrete walls by means of

    A. toggle bolts   B. wooden plugs and screws
    C. cut nails   D. lead shields

46._____

47. Continuity of an electrical circuit can conveniently be determined in the field by means of a(n)

    A. smoke test   B. bell and battery set
    C. ammeter   D. Wheatstone Bridge

47._____

48. The speed of a motor can be measured by means of a

    A. potentiometer   B. megger
    C. tachometer   D. thermocouple

48._____

49. A test for transformer polarity is made on a transformer rated 2400-240 volts by applying a voltage $V_1=120$ volts to the high voltage terminals H_1 and H_2 and measuring the voltage between terminals H_2 and X_2. (See diagram to the right.) If the transformer is of subtractive polarity, the voltmeter will read APPROXIMATELY _____ volts.

    A. 132   B. 12   C. 108   D. 0

49._____

50. An ammeter connected to the secondary of an energized metering transformer requires repairs.
Before disconnecting the instrument, the electrician should

    A. open the secondary circuit
    B. short circuit the transformer secondary terminals
    C. short circuit the transformer primary terminals
    D. remove the transformer secondary fuses

50._____

KEY (CORRECT ANSWERS)

1. C	11. B	21. C	31. A	41. B
2. B	12. C	22. D	32. A	42. C
3. C	13. C	23. D	33. D	43. B
4. A	14. C	24. D	34. B	44. C
5. B	15. C	25. A	35. C	45. B
6. B	16. D	26. A	36. C	46. D
7. D	17. A	27. B	37. D	47. B
8. B	18. D	28. B	38. C	48. C
9. C	19. C	29. D	39. D	49. C
10. C	20. D	30. B	40. C	50. B

EXAMINATION SECTION
TEST 1

DIRECTIONS: Each question or incomplete statement is followed by several suggested answers or completions. Select the one that BEST answers the question or completes the statement. *PRINT THE LETTER OF THE CORRECT ANSWER IN THE SPACE AT THE RIGHT.*

1. The PRIMARY purpose of oil in an oil circuit breaker is to

    A. quench the arc
    B. lubricate the contacts
    C. reduce the reluctance of the core
    D. lubricate between the windings and the case

1.____

2. Assume that an auto transformer has a ratio of 2 to 1. With a primary voltage of 100 volts, 60 cycles, a.c., and a secondary load of 5 ohms, the current in the load is *most nearly*

    A. 20   B. 15   C. 10   D. 5

2.____

3. Assume that an auto transformer has a ratio of 2 to 1, with a primary voltage of 100 volts, 60 cycles, a.c., and a load of 5 ohms placed across the secondary.
Under the above conditions, the current in the secondary coil of the auto transformer is *most nearly*

    A. 20   B. 15   C. 10   D. 5

3.____

4. In fire extinguishers used to fight electrical fires, the chemical used as the fire extinguishing agent is

    A. H_2O B. KH_2 C. CO_2 D. CO

4.____

5. At a frequency of 60 cycles, the reactance in ohms of a condenser having a capacitance of 10 microfarads is *most nearly*

    A. 26.6   B. 37.7   C. 266   D. 377

5.____

6. Transformation of 3-phase to 2-phase systems can be obtained by using two special transformers. The COMMON method used for connecting these transformers is called a(n)

    A. open delta   B. zig-zag
    C. differential y on z   D. Scott or T

6.____

7. The electrolyte for a lead acid storage battery is properly prepared by pouring the

    A. sulphuric acid into the water
    B. water into the sulphuric acid
    C. potassium hydroxide into the water
    D. water into the potassium hydroxide

7.____

8. The full-wave rectifier has a ripple frequency that is   8.___

    A. one-half that of the half-wave rectifier
    B. double that of the half-wave rectifier
    C. four times that of the half-wave rectifier
    D. equal to that of the half-wave rectifier

9. Of the following, the one type of resistance wire which has an extremely low temperature   9.___
co-efficient of resistance is known as

    A. Replevin   B. Ribbon   C. Maganin   D. Bifilar

10. In an a.c. dynamometer-type voltmeter, the deflections depend upon the square of the   10.___
voltage. It can CORRECTLY be said that this instrument reads _____ values.

    A. average   B. peak   C. effective   D. maximum

11. The Dobrowolsky method used for three-wire generator systems is a very efficient   11.___
means of obtaining a(n)

    A. neutral   B. V or open delta
    C. two-phase system   D. three-phase system

12. Direct current armatures, wound with coils having fractional-pitch windings, have   12.___

    A. a coil span which is less than the pole pitch
    B. a coil span which is greater than the pole pitch
    C. more than 4 poles
    D. less than 4 poles

13. To measure the current in a conductor without breaking into the conductor, you would   13.___
use a(n)

    A. ampback   B. amprobe
    C. ampule   D. ampclip

14. If two identical coils, each having an inductance of one henry, are connected in series   14.___
aiding, the combined inductance, in henries, is

    A. exactly two   B. greater than two
    C. exactly one   D. less than one

15. In a simplex lap winding, there are as many paths through the armature as there are   15.___

    A. armature slots   B. poles
    C. commutator segments   D. armature coils

16. In a wave winding, the MINIMUM number of commutator brushes required is   16.___

    A. four
    B. two
    C. dependent on the number of commutator segments
    D. dependent on the armature coils

17. Some electricians have the faculty of knowing when there is work to be done and do not have to be prompted to do it.
These electricians may be said to have   17.____

    A. initiative   B. individuality   C. virtue   D. discrimination

18. The _____ _____ ___ _____ er inch on a 1/4" diameter screw having American Standard _____ _early   18.____

    _____ 18   C. 14   D. 13

19. _____ vork, the proper tap drill size to use for a 6/32 machine screw is   19.____

    _____ 40   C. 36   D. 21

20. _____ ols used on architectural plans are those recommended by the _____ .S.A. refers to the   20.____

    _____ f Architects   B. American Standards Association
    _____ rds Association   D. Architectural Standards of America

21. _____ course of action to take if a motor bearing runs dangerously _____   21.____

    _____ old water then rapidly decrease motor speed and oil the bear-
    _____ and increase speed of motor
    _____ notor until bearing cools sufficiently then stop the water and
    _____ d any damage to bearing
    _____ ore increasing the load

22. _____ rel of a micrometer indicates an opening, in inches, of *most* _____   22.____

    _____ 0.050   C. 0.250   D. 0.270

23. _____ be designed to run on both a.c. or d.c. is the _____ motor.   23.____

    _____ repulsion   C. compound   D. series

24. _____ ertain wiring installation is broken down as follows: Materials _____ ental of equipment $400. The percentage of the total cost of _____ l to Labor is *most nearly*   24.____

    _____ 33.3   C. 40.0   D. 66.6

25. _____ rician's helpers 6 days to do a certain job. Working at the _____ nber of days it will take 3 electrician's helpers to do the same   25.____

    _____ 7   C. 8   D. 9

26. _____ cycle magnetic coil is to be rewound to operate properly on _____ ge. If the coil at 25-cycles has 1,000 turns, at 60-cycles the number of turns should be *most nearly*   26.____

    A. 2,400   B. 1,200   C. 416   D. 208

27. A coil having 50 turns of #14 wire as compared with a coil of the same diameter but hav-   27.___
ing only 25 turns of #14 wire has

    A. a smaller inductance   B. a larger inductance
    C. the same inductance   D. the same impedance

Questions 28-40.

  DIRECTIONS: The following questions 28 to 40 inclusive are to be answered in accordance
                  with the requirements of the electrical code.
                  NOTE: Questions are to be answered assuming normal procedures, as given
                  in the code. Do NOT use exceptions which are granted by special permission.

28. For elevator control wiring, conductors of 1/64 insulation may be used. The number of   28.___
such conductors that may be installed in a conduit should be such that the sum of the
cross-sectional area of all the conductors expressed as a percentage of the interior
cross-sectional area of the conduit should NOT exceed

    A. 20%   B. 30%   C. 40%   D. 60%

29. Assume that the internal diameter of a two-inch conduit is 2.067 inches. The interior   29.___
cross-sectional area, in square inches, of this conduit is *most nearly*

    A. 3.36   B. 4.79   C. 7.38   D. 9.90

30. No. 2 type R conductors in vertical raceways must be supported at intervals NOT greater   30.___
than _____ feet.

    A. 50   B. 60   C. 80   D. 100

31. A unit of an electrical system, other than a conductor, which is intended to carry but NOT   31.___
consume electrical energy is called a(n)

    A. device   B. circuit
    C. appliance   D. equipment

32. Three #4 A.W.G. rubber-covered, type R, conductors require a conduit having a diame-   32.___
ter, in inches, of NOT less than

    A. 1/2   B. 3/4   C. 1   D. 1 1/4

33. For control conductors between motors and controllers, the MAXIMUM number of #10   33.___
type R conductors that may be put into a 1 1/4" conduit or tubing is

    A. 10   B. 13   C. 15   D. 17

34. The type of wire COMMONLY used for switchboard wiring is classified by type letter or   34.___
letters

    A. TF   B. CF   C. TA   D. R

35. Wires in conduit (approved as to insulation and location) are required to have stranded   35.___
conductors if they are

    A. No. 8 or larger   B. No. 6 or larger
    C. No. 6 or smaller   D. No. 8 or smaller

36. Bends of rigid conduit should be so made that the conduit will not be injured. Where rubber conductors are used, the radius of the curve of the inner edge of any field bend should be NOT less than _____ times the internal diameter of the conduit.

    A. 15   B. 10   C. 6   D. 4

36._____

37. In Class I hazardous locations, when a conduit leads from a hazardous location to a non-hazardous location, the conduit should be sealed off with a sealing compound which is NOT affected by the surrounding atmosphere and has a melting point of NOT less than

    A. $200^{o}F$ B. $150^{o}F$ C. $100^{o}F$ D. $75^{o}F$

37._____

38. Feeders should be of such size that the voltage drop up to the final distribution point should NOT exceed

    A. 6%   B. 4 1/2%   C. 3%   D. 2 1/2%

38._____

39. For NOT more than three conductors in raceway (based on room temperature of $30^{o}C$ or $86^{o}F$), the current carrying capacity in amperes of #10 type R insulated aluminum conductor is

    A. 10   B. 15   C. 25   D. 35

39._____

40. The MAXIMUM number of No. 12 wires terminating in a 1 1/2" x 3 1/4" octagonal junction box should be

    A. 20   B. 15   C. 10   D. 5

40._____

KEY (CORRECT ANSWERS)

1.	A	11.	A	21.	C	31.	A
2.	C	12.	A	22.	C	32.	D
3.	D	13.	B	23.	D	33.	B
4.	C	14.	B	24.	B	34.	C
5.	C	15.	B	25.	C	35.	B
6.	D	16.	B	26.	C	36.	C
7.	A	17.	A	27.	B	37.	A
8.	B	18.	A	28.	C	38.	D
9.	C	19.	C	29.	A	39.	C
10.	C	20.	B	30.	D	40.	D

TEST 2

DIRECTIONS: Each question or incomplete statement is followed by several suggested answers or completions. Select the one that BEST answers the question or completes the statement. *PRINT THE LETTER OF THE CORRECT ANSWER IN THE SPACE AT THE RIGHT.*

1. Two copper conductors have the same length but the cross-section of one is twice that of the other. If the resistance of the one having a cross-section of twice the other is 10 ohms, the resistance of the other conductor, in ohms, is   1.___

   A. 5   B. 10   C. 20   D. 30

2. Assuming that copper weighs 0.32 lbs. per cubic inch, the weight, in lbs., of a bus bar 10' long and having a cross-section 2" x 1/2" is   2.___

   A. 120   B. 32   C. 3.2   D. 38.4

3. In a two-phase, three-wire system, the voltage between the common wire and either of the other two wires is 200 volts. The voltage between these other two wires is then *approximately* _____ volts.   3.___

   A. 200   B. 283   C. 141   D. 100

4. Three 30-ohm resistances are connected in delta across a 208-volt, 3-phase circuit. The line current, in amperes, is *approximately*   4.___

   A. 6.93   B. 13.86   C. 120   D. 12

5. A storage battery consists of three lead cells connected in series. On open circuit, the emf of the battery is 6.4 volts. When it delivers a current of 80 amperes, its terminal voltage drops to 4.80 volts. Its internal resistance, in ohms, is *approximately*   5.___

   A. 0.01   B. 0.02   C. 0.03   D. 0.04

6. In reference to question 5 above, the terminal voltage, in volts, when the battery delivers 50 amperes is *approximately*   6.___

   A. 5.9   B. 5.4   C. 4.9   D. 4.4

7. In order to magnetize a steel bar, a magnetomotive force of 1000 ampere turns is necessary. The voltage that MUST be applied to a coil of 100 turns and 10 ohms resistance is   7.___

   A. 1   B. 10   C. 100   D. 1000

8. Rosin is preferable to acid as a flux for soldering wire because rosin is   8.___

   A. a nonconductor   B. a dry powder
   C. a better conductor   D. noncorrosive

9. If, in tracing through an armature winding, all of the conductors are encountered before coming back to the starting point, there is but one closure and the winding is _____ reentrant.   9.___

   A. doubly   B. singly   C. triply   D. quintuply

10. A power factor meter is connected to a single-phase 2-wire circuit by means of _____ wires.

    A. 2   B. 3   C. 6   D. 5

10._____

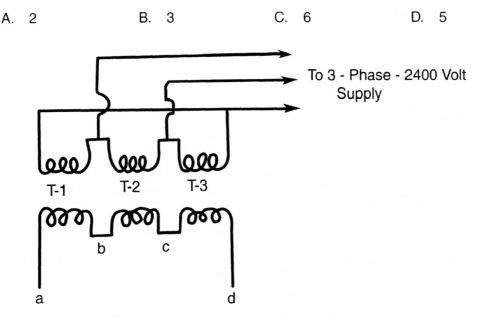

11. The above figure represents a transformer bank composed of 3 single-phase transform-   11._____
ers each having a ratio of transformation equal to 20/1. The primary is already connected
to the voltage supply, as shown in the diagram, while the secondary side is only "partly
connected".
It is desired to connect the secondary of this transformer bank in delta. Before connecting a to d, the combination of voltages should correspond to one of the following:

    A. Vab = 120, Vbc = 120, Vcd = 120 and Vad = 0
    B. Vab = 120, Vbc = 120, Vcd = 120 and Vad = 120
    C. Vab = 120, Vbc = 120, Vcd = 120 and Vad = 208
    D. Vab = 208, Vbc = 208, Vcd = 208 and Vad = 0

12. With reference to question 11 above, assuming that the combination of voltages read as   12._____
follows: Vab = 120 volts, Vbc = 120 volts, Vcd = 120 volts, Vad = 240 volts, and Vbd =
208 volts, before connecting a to d for a delta connection,

    A. do nothing as the transformer bank is already phased out
    B. secondary winding of T-1 should be reversed by interchanging its leads
    C. secondary winding of T-2 should be reversed by interchanging its leads
    D. secondary winding of T-3 should be reversed by changing its leads

13. The torque of a shunt motor varies as the   13._____

    A. armature current   B. square of the armature current
    C. cube of the armature current   D. cube of the field current

14. The armature of a synchronous converter has   14._____

    A. 3 slip rings for the ac and 2 slip rings for the dc
    B. 4 slip rings, 2 for the ac and 2 for the dc
    C. a commutator and slip rings
    D. no slip rings

15. An electrical device that transmits rotation from a driving to a driven member without mechanical contact – with stepless adjustable control and with almost instantaneous response – is the

    A. eddy current coupling   B. universal coupling
    C. planetary coupling   D. coupling transformer

16. According to the code, in order that armored cable will not be injured, the radius of the curve of the inner edge of any bend must be NOT less than _____ times the diameter of the cable.

    A. 3   B. 5   C. 7   D. 10

17. In accordance with the code, circuit breakers for motor branch circuit protection shall have continuous current ratings NOT less than _____ of the full load current of the motor.

    A. 110%   B. 115%   C. 120%   D. 125%

Meter resistance 5 Ω
Current for Full Scale deflection .01 amp

18. The above diagram represents the circuit of a multi-range ammeter. X-X is connected in series with an electric circuit for the purpose of measuring the current in that circuit. When slider S is connected to point B, the current I, in amperes, that will cause the meter to read full scale is *approximately*

    A. 30   B. 20   C. 10   D. 1

19. In reference to question 18 above, when slider S is connected to point C, the current I, in amperes, that will cause the meter to read full scale is *approximately*

    A. 30   B. 20   C. 10   D. 1

20. The code states that feeders over 40' in length supplying two branch circuits shall be NOT smaller than

    A. 2 No. 14 AWG   B. 2 No. 12 AWG
    C. 2 No. 10 AWG   D. 2 No. 8 AWG

21. Speed control by a method that requires two wound rotor induction motors with their rotors rigidly connected together is called speed control by   21._____

    A. change of poles   B. field control
    C. concatenation   D. voltage control

22. Before connecting an alternator to the bus bars and in parallel with other alternators, it is necessary that its voltage and frequency be the same as that of the bus bars but that   22._____

    A. the rotor revolve at synchronous speed
    B. the voltage be in phase opposition as well
    C. its power factor be not less than unit
    D. its power factor be greater than unit

23. A leather belt is used to drive a 3 kw dc generator by a 5 hp 3-phase induction motor. Adjustments for proper belt tension, with the generator running at full load, can be made with the aid of a   23._____

    A. 50-lb. weight as wide as the belt
    B. voltmeter and an ammeter
    C. power factor meter
    D. 3-phase wattmeter

24. The cold resistance of a 120-volt 100 watt Tungsten incandescent lamp is   24._____

    A. greater than its hot resistance
    B. smaller than the hot resistance
    C. approximately 100 ohms.
    D. equal to the hot resistance

25. The CORRECT value of the resistance of a field coil can be measured by using a(n)   25._____

    A. Schering bridge   B. ammeter and a voltmeter
    C. Kelvin double bridge   D. Maxwell bridge

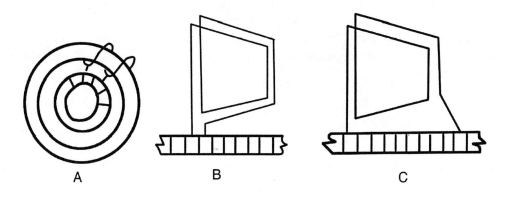

A   B   C

26. The three windings shown above belong, respectively, to the ring, lap, and wave types of _____ windings.   26._____

    A. closed-coil   B. open-coil
    C. reverse-coil   D. cumulative-coil

27. Simplex lap windings have as many armature circuits as there are   27._____

    A. commutator bars
    B. number of coils
    C. number of active conductors
    D. poles

28. The power factor of a single phase alternating current moter may be found by using one   28._____
of the following sets of ac instruments: one

    A. voltmeter and one phase-rotation meter
    B. voltmeter and one ammeter
    C. voltmeter, one ammeter, and one wattmeter
    D. voltmeter, one ammeter, and one watt-hour meter

29. When connecting wattmeters to ac motor circuits consuming large amounts of current, it   29._____
is necessary to use

    A. current transformers   B. potential transformers
    C. power shunts   D. isolation transformers

30. To control a lamp independently from five different points, you would use   30._____

    A. two 3-way and three 4-way switches
    B. four 3-way switches and one 4-way switch
    C. three 3-way and two 4-way switches
    D. three 4-way and two S.P.S.T. switches

31. The average life of a 100 watt incandescent light bulb is APPROXIMATELY _____   31._____
hours.

    A. 100   B. 400   C. 1000   D. 10,000

32. The efficiency in lumens per watt of a 40 watt fluorescent lamp   32._____

    A. is less than that of a 40 watt incandescent lamp
    B. is the same as that of a 40 watt incandescent lamp
    C. is greater than that of a 40 watt incandescent lamp
    D. may be greater or less than that of a 40 watt incandescent lamp, depending on the
       manufacturer

33. In order to use fluorescent lighting in a building which has only a 110 volt dc supply, it is   33._____
necessary to use fluorescent

    A. lamps designed for dc
    B. fixtures with an approved dc auxiliary or inductance unit and a series resistance of
       the correct value
    C. fixtures ordinarily used on ac
    D. fixtures ordinarily used on ac but equipped with a rectifier

34. Electrical contacts are opened or closed when the electrical current energizes the coils   34._____
of a device called a

    A. reactor   B. transtat
    C. relay   D. thermostat

35. Transformer cores are composed of laminated sheet steel in order to keep the _____ loss to a minimum.   35.____

    A. hysteresis
    C. eddy current
    B. windage
    D. copper

36. An auto transformer whose primary is bd is connected across a 100-volt ac supply as shown in the above diagram. The load of 5 ohms is connected across points c and d. If it is assumed that N-1 = N-2 (that is, point c is the midpoint of the winding), current I-1, in amperes, is *approximately* equal to   36.____

    A. 5   B. 10   C. 15   D. 20

37. In reference to question 36 above, current I-2, in amperes, is *approximately* equal to   37.____

    A. 5   B. 10   C. 15   D. 20

38. In reference to question 36 above, current I-3, in amperes, is *approximately* equal to   38.____

    A. 5   B. 10   C. 15   D. 20

39. The transformer is based on the principle that energy may be effectively transferred by induction from one set of coils to another by a varying magnetic flux, provided both sets of coils   39.____

    A. are not a common magnetic circuit
    B. have the same number of turns
    C. are on a common magnetic circuit
    D. do not have the same number of turns

40. In a transformer the induced emf per turn in the secondary winding is   40.____

    A. equal to the induced emf per turn in the primary winding
    B. not equal to the induced emf per turn in the primary winding
    C. equal to the induced emf per turn in the primary winding multiplied by the ratio N-1/N-2
    D. equal to the induced emf per turn in the primary winding divided by the ratio N-1/N-2

KEY (CORRECT ANSWERS)

1.	C	11.	A	21.	C	31.	C
2.	D	12.	D	22.	B	32.	C
3.	B	13.	A	23.	D	33.	B
4.	D	14.	C	24.	B	34.	C
5.	B	15.	A	25.	B	35.	C
6.	B	16.	B	26.	A	36.	A
7.	C	17.	B	27.	D	37.	B
8.	D	18.	C	28.	C	38.	A
9.	B	19.	B	29.	A	39.	C
10.	B	20.	C	30.	A	40.	A

———

TEST 3

DIRECTIONS: Each question or incomplete statement is followed by several suggested answers or completions. Select the one that BEST answers the question or completes the statement. *PRINT THE LETTER OF THE CORRECT ANSWER IN THE SPACE AT THE RIGHT.*

1. Five 100-watt, 120-volt lamps connected in series across a 600-volt circuit will draw a current, in amperes, of *most nearly*   1.____

    A. 4.2   B. .8   C. .6   D. .4

2. For a given level of illumination in a certain lighting installation, the cost of electrical energy using fluorescent lighting fixtures as compared with incandescent lighting fixtures is   2.____

    A. more   B. less
    C. the same   D. dependent on the load

3. Assume that three 20.8 ohm resistances are connected in delta across a 208-volt, 3-phase circuit. The line current, in amperes, will be *most nearly*   3.____

    A. 20.8   B. 17.3   C. 10.4   D. 8.6

4. Assume that three 10-ohm resistances are connected in wye across a 208-volt, 3-phase circuit.
The power, in watts, dissipated in this resistance load will be *most nearly*   4.____

    A. 4320   B. 1440   C. 2160   D. 720

5. A tungsten incandescent lamp has its GREATEST resistance when the lamp is   5.____

    A. cold
    B. burning at full brilliance
    C. burning at half brilliance
    D. burning at one-quarter brilliance

6. Direct current can be converted to alternating current by means of a(n)   6.____

    A. inverter   B. rectifier
    C. filter   D. selsyn

7. The direction of rotation of a d.c. shunt motor can be reversed by   7.____

    A. interchanging the line terminals
    B. reversing the field and armature current
    C. reversing the field or armature current
    D. reversing the current in any one of the commutating pole windings

8. The insulation resistance of the conductors of an electrical installation is measured or tested with a(n)   8.____

    A. strobe   B. ammeter   C. Q-meter   D. megger

9. In dealing with electrician's helpers, it is MOST important that the electrician be   9.____

    A. stern   B. fair   C. blunt   D. chummy

10. If an electrician does not understand the instructions that are given to him by his fore-   10.__
man, the BEST thing to do is to

   A. work out the solution to the problem himself
   B. do the job the way he thinks is best
   C. get one of the other electricians to do the job
   D. ask that the instructions be repeated and clarified

11. Assume that a group of dc. shunt motors is 500 ft. from a power panel and is supplied by   11.__
two 350,000 c.m. conductors with a maximum load for this circuit of 190 amps.
If the resistance of 1000 feet of 350,000 c.m. conductor is 0.036 ohm, and the voltage
at the power panel is 230 volts, the voltage at the load will be *most nearly*

   A. 217   B. 220   C. 223   D. 229

12. The power in a three-phase, three wire circuit is measured by means of the two-watt   12.__
meter method. When the reading of one wattmeter is exactly the same as the reading of
the other wattmeter, the power factor will be

   A. 1   B. .866   C. .5   D. 0

13. Assume that a fluorescent lamp blinks "on" and "off."   13.__
This may

   A. in time result in injury to the ballast
   B. cause a fuse to blow
   C. be due to a shorted switch
   D. be caused by an abnormally high voltage

14. The one of the following troubles which is NOT a cause of sparking at the commutator of   14.__
a dc. motor is

   A. a short-circuited armature coil
   B. an open-circuited armature coil
   C. vibration of the machine
   D. running below rated speed

15. The current, in amperes, of a 220-volt, 10-HP, d.c. motor having an efficiency of 90% is   15.__
approximately

   A. 37.6   B. 34   C. 28.6   D. 40.5

16. The grid-controlled gas-type electronic tube MOST often used in motor control circuits is   16.__
the

   A. ignitron   B. thyratron
   C. strobostron   D. magnetron

17. With reference to electronic control work, the vacuum tube element or electrode which is   17.__
placed in the electron stream and to which a control voltage may be applied is the

   A. plate   B. grid   C. filament   D. cathode

18. Full-wave rectifiers   18._____

    A. may be built with one tungar bulb
    B. produce a.c. current which contains some d.c.
    C. are used to change dp. current to a.c.
    D. must have at least two tungar bulbs

19. Assume that two batteries are connected in multiple. If the voltage and internal resis-   19._____
tance of one battery are 6 volts and 0.2 ohms, respectively, and the voltage and internal
resistance of the other battery are 3 volts and 0.1 ohms, respectively, the circulating current, in amperes, will be *approximately*

    A. 2   B. 5   C. 10   D. 30

20. In a single phase motor, the temporary production of a substitute for a two-phase current   20._____
so as to obtain a makeshift rotating field in starting is COMMONLY called

    A. phase splitting   B. phase spread
    C. phase transformation   D. phantom circuit

21. If a solenoid is grasped in the right hand so that the fingers point in the direction in which   21._____
the current is flowing in the wires, the thumb, extended, will point in the direction of the
_____ pole.

    A. negative   B. positive
    C. south   D. north

22. The junction of two dissimilar metals produces a flow of current when the junction is   22._____

    A. wet
    B. heated
    C. highly polished
    D. placed in a dp. magnetic field

23. The active material in the positive plates of a charged lead acid storage battery is   23._____

    A. lead carbonate   B. lead acetate
    C. lead peroxide   D. sponge lead

24. The negative plates of a charged lead acid storage battery are composed of   24._____

    A. lead carbonate   B. lead acetate
    C. lead peroxide   D. sponge lead

25. A constant horsepower two-speed squirrel cage induction motor may be made to run at   25._____
the higher speed by

    A. changing the connections to make it an eight-pole motor
    B. decreasing the rotor resistance
    C. changing the connections so that the motor has the lesser number of poles
    D. changing the connections so that the motor has the greater number of poles

26. A constant horsepower two-speed squirrel cage induction motor has its stator coils and   26._____
the line wires connected so as to form a series delta connection. Assume that the connections of the stator coils and the lines are now changed so as to form a parallel-wye
connection. Under these conditions, the motor will now have _____ poles and _____
speed.

A. fewer; higher B. fewer; lower
C. more; higher D. more; lower

27. Assume that a circuit carrying 8 amperes of d.c. current and 6 amperes of a.c. current is connected to a hot wire ammeter. The reading, in amperes, of this meter will be *most nearly*   27.___

   A. 16   B. 14   C. 12   D. 10

28. To start a 20 HP., 3-phase, 208 volt plain induction motor, it is good practice to use a   28.___

   A. compensator B. 3-point box
   C. rotor box D. 4-point box

29. A 25-ampere, 50 millivolt d.c. shunt has a resistance, in ohms, of *approximately*   29.___

   A. 0.002   B. 0.02   C. 0.5   D. 5.

30. When a relay coil is energized by applying the rated voltage across its terminals, a certain time, in seconds, must elapse from the moment the circuit is completed before the current attains approximately 2/3 of its full strength.
This elapsed time is   30.___

   A. entirely dependent on the coil resistance
   B. entirely dependent on the coil inductance
   C. proportional to the coil resistance divided by the coil inductance
   D. proportional to the coil inductance divided by the coil resistance

31. For proper operation all gas discharge lamps require   31.___

   A. a series resistor B. a parallel resistor
   C. some sort of ballast D. a starter

32. To obtain proper short-circuit protection for a service, one should use a   32.___

   A. limiting resistor B. time delay breaker
   C. time delay relay D. current limiting fuse

33. A neon test lamp can be used by an electrician to test   33.___

   A. the phase rotation of a source of supply
   B. the power factor of a source of supply
   C. a source of supply to see if it is a.c. or d.c.
   D. the field intensity of a relay magnet

34. A d.c. milliammeter may be adapted for a.c. measurements by using with it a(n)   34.___

   A. paper condenser B. instrument shunt
   C. instrument transformer D. selenium rectifier

35. A static capacitor used for power factor correction is connected to the line in   35.___

   A. parallel with a machine drawing lagging current
   B. series with a machine drawing lagging current
   C. parallel with a machine drawing leading current
   D. series with a machine drawing leading current

36. To start a squirrel cage induction motor with an across-the-line starter, without undue dis-   36.____
turbance to the line voltage, the capacity of the motor in HP should NOT exceed

    A. 100   B. 75   C. 50   D. 5

37. The type of a.c. motor MOST commonly used where considerable starting torque is   37.____
required is the

    A. squirrel cage induction motor
    B. wound rotor induction motor
    C. shunt motor
    D. synchronous motor

38. On direct current controllers where it is necessary to remove or replace blow-out coils, it   38.____
is IMPORTANT to

    A. see that the positive pole is facing down
    B. see that the negative pole is facing up
    C. insert the blow-out coils to give the proper polarity
    D. cross the coil leads before connecting them

39. The size of the fuse to be used in a circuit depends upon the   39.____

    A. connected load
    B. size of wire
    C. voltage of the line
    D. size and rating of the switch

40. Assume that a d.c. contactor coil has two turns short-circuited. In operation, it will   40.____

    A. burn out
    B. hum excessively
    C. continue to operate at reduced efficiency
    D. vibrate due to the high induced current

KEY (CORRECT ANSWERS)

1. B	11. C	21. D	31. C
2. B	12. A	22. B	32. D
3. B	13. A	23. C	33. C
4. A	14. D	24. D	34. D
5. B	15. A	25. C	35. A
6. A	16. B	26. D	36. D
7. C	17. B	27. D	37. B
8. D	18. D	28. A	38. C
9. B	19. C	29. A	39. B
10. D	20. A	30. D	40. C

EXAMINATION SECTION
TEST 1

DIRECTIONS: Each question or incomplete statement is followed by several suggested answers or completions. Select the one that *BEST* answers the question or completes the statement. *PRINT THE LETTER OF THE CORRECT ANSWER IN THE SPACE AT THE RIGHT.*

1. A spool of wire consisting of 400 turns has an average diameter of 3 inches. The APPROXIMATE total length of wire, in feet, is

    A. 1200   B. 3140   C. 314   D. 120

1._____

2. A single phase synchronous converter is connected on its d.c. side to 141.4 volt d.c. source of supply.
The a.c. single phase voltage delivered by this machine is APPROXIMATELY

    A. 300   B. 200   C. 150   D. 100

2._____

3. If the speed of a synchronous motor connected to a 60-cylce power line is 1200 rpm, the number of poles it MUST have is

    A. 2   B. 4   C. 6   D. 8

3._____

4. Under load, the current in the armature conductors of a d.c. dynamo give rise to an independent excitation which alters both the magnitude and distribution of the flux produced by the field alone.
This magnetizing action of the armature is called

    A. armature reaction   B. dynamic breaking
    C. field reaction   D. radial excitation

4._____

5. The voltage induced in a loop of wire rotating in a magnetic field is

    A. d.c.   B. pulsating d.c.   C. rectified a.c.   D. a.c.

5._____

6. The relative polarity of the windings of a transformer is determined by

    A. open circuit test   B. phasing out
    C. short ciruit test   D. polarimeter test

6._____

7. If the field of a shunt motor while running under no load opens, the motor will

    A. stop running immediately
    B. continue to run at a very slow speed
    C. run away
    D. gradually slow down until it stops

7._____

8. If, after the installation of a self-excited d.c. generator, it fails to build up on first trial run, the FIRST thing to do is

    A. increase the field resistance
    B. reverse the connections to the shunt field
    C. check the armature insulation resistance
    D. decrease the speed of the prime mover

8._____

9. In reference to question 8 above, if the generator still fails to build up, you should make sure that the

    9.__

    A. resistance of the field rheostat is all in
    B. diverter is in series with the armature
    C. resistance of the field circuit is sufficiently small
    D. diverter is in parallel with the armature

10. In reference to questions 8 and 9, if the generator still fails to build up now, you MOST probably would have to separately excite the

    10.__

    A. field for a few minutes with a battery
    B. armature for a few minutes with a battery
    C. armature with a.c. current
    D. field with a.c. current

11. Toggle bolts are MOST commonly used to fasten an outlet box to a _____ wall.

    11.__

    A. solid concrete   B. plaster or tile
    C. solid brick   D. wooden partition

Questions 12-15.

DIRECTIONS: Questions 12 through 15 refer to the diagram below

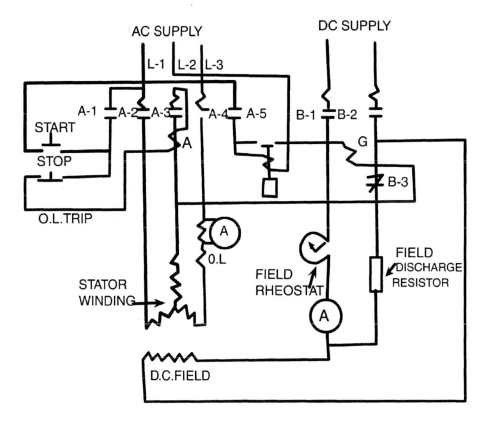

12. The above sketch represents a starter diagram of a _____ motor.

    12.__

    A. synchronous   B. d.c. series
    C. wound rotor induction   D. squirrel cage induction

13. When start P.B. is pressed, Contractor 13.____

    A. A-1, A-2, A-3, A-4, A-5, B-1 and B-2 will close at once
    B. A-1, A-2, A-3, A-4 and A-5 will close at once
    C. A-2, A-3, A-4 and B-3 will close at once
    D. A-2, A-3 and A-4 only will close at once

14. After the start button is pressed, the 14.____

    A. motor will run but will stop unless field is energized
    B. d.c. field is energized at once
    C. d.c. field is energized after a definite time
    D. motor will not run until the d.c. field is energized

15. The field discharge resistor acts to 15.____

    A. steady the d.c. field during start period
    B. improve the power factor
    C. dissipate the energy stored in the field after the d.c. field supply is cut off
    D. quench the arc

16. In accordance with the code,all wiring is to be installed so that when completed, the sys- 16.____
tem will be free from shorts or grounds.
A circuit installation of #12 wire with all safety devices in place, but lampholders, receptacles, fixtures and/or appliances not connected, shall have a resistance between conductors and between all conductors and ground NOT less than _____ ohms.

    A. 10,000   B. 100,000   C. 250,000   D. 1,000,000

17. The code states that wires, cables and cords of all kinds EXCEPT weatherproof wire 17.____
shall have a

    A. distinctive marking so that the maker may be readily identified
    B. tag showing the minimum working voltage for which the wire was tested or
       approved
    C. tag showing the maximum current passed through the conductor under test
    D. tag showing the ultimate tensile strength

18. The code states that conductors supplying an individual motor shall have a MINIMUM 18.____
carrying capacity of _____ of the motor full load current.

    A. 110%   B. 120%   C. 125%   D. 135%

19. For NOT more than three conductors in raceway, *based on a room temperature of 86° F,* 19.____
the allowable current carrying capacity, in amperes, of a No. 12, AWG type R conductor
is

    A. 15   B. 20   C. 30   D. 40

20. A 41740 CM Class A stranded copper conductor is composed of 7 wires. 20.____
The diameter, in mils, of one wire is APPROXIMATELY

    A. 109.3   B. 97.4   C. 86.7   D. 77.2

21. In accordance with the code, the number of No. 14 AWG type R conductors running through or terminating in a 1 1/2" X 3 1/4" octagonal outlet or junction box, should NOT be greater than

    A. 5   B. 6   C. 7   D. 8

  21.___

22. The part of a circuit which melts when the current abnormally exceeds the allowable carrying capacity of the conductor is called

    A. circuit breaker   B. thermo cutout
    C. overload trip   D. fuse

  22.___

23. Defects in wiring which permit current to jump from one wire to another before the intended path has been completed are called

    A. grounds   B. shorts   C. opens   D. breaks

  23.___

24. In accordance with the code, a grounding conductor for a direct current system shall have a current carrying capacity not less than that of the LARGEST conductor supplied by the system and in no case LESS than that of No. _____ copper wire.

    A. 12   B. 10   C. 8   D. 6

  24.___

25. In accordance with the code, the grounding connection for interior metal raceways and armored cable shall be made at a point

    A. not greater than 5 feet from the source of supply
    B. not greater than 10 feet from the source of supply
    C. as far as possible from the source of supply
    D. as near as practicable to the source of supply

  25.___

26. In accordance with the code, motors

    A. may be operated in series multiple
    B. may be operated in multiple series
    C. shall not be operated in series multiple
    D. shall not be operated in multiple

  26.___

27. Boxes and fittings intended for outdoor use should be of

    A. weatherproof type
    B. stamped steel of not less than No. 16 standard guage
    C. stamped steel plated with cadmium
    D. ample strength and rigidity

  27.___

28. Two 1/4 h.p. motors, under the protection of a single set of over-current devices and with or without other current consuming devices in the current, are considered as being sufficiently protected if the rating or setting of the over-current devices does NOT exceed _____ amperes at _____ volts.

    A. 15; 250   B. 15; 125   C. 30; 125   D. 30; 250

  28.___

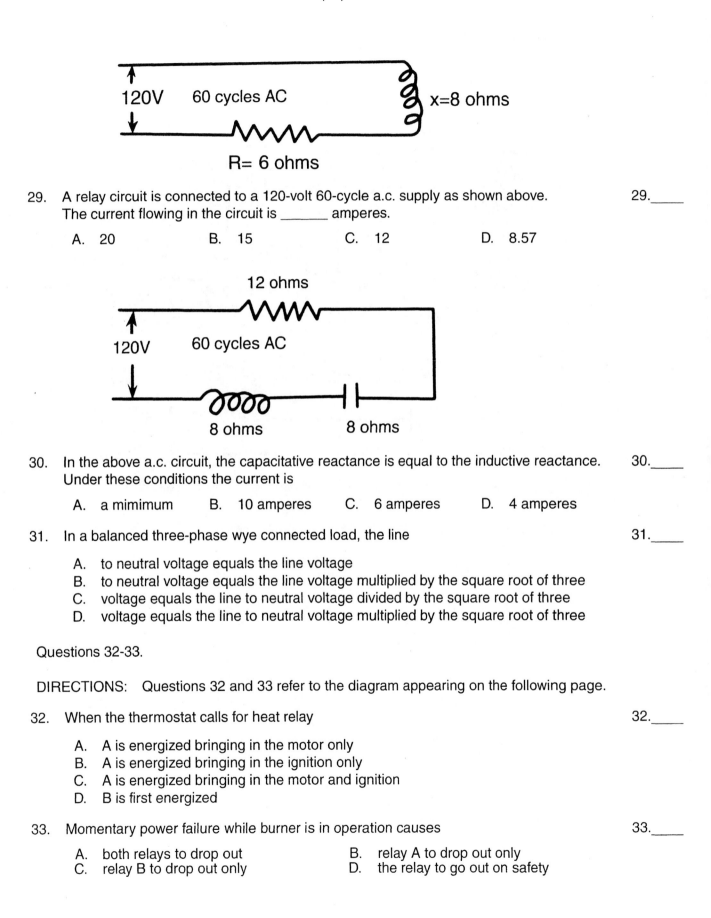

29. A relay circuit is connected to a 120-volt 60-cycle a.c. supply as shown above. The current flowing in the circuit is _____ amperes.

   A. 20   B. 15   C. 12   D. 8.57

   29._____

30. In the above a.c. circuit, the capacitative reactance is equal to the inductive reactance. Under these conditions the current is

   A. a mimimum   B. 10 amperes   C. 6 amperes   D. 4 amperes

   30._____

31. In a balanced three-phase wye connected load, the line

   A. to neutral voltage equals the line voltage
   B. to neutral voltage equals the line voltage multiplied by the square root of three
   C. voltage equals the line to neutral voltage divided by the square root of three
   D. voltage equals the line to neutral voltage multiplied by the square root of three

   31._____

Questions 32-33.

DIRECTIONS: Questions 32 and 33 refer to the diagram appearing on the following page.

32. When the thermostat calls for heat relay

   A. A is energized bringing in the motor only
   B. A is energized bringing in the ignition only
   C. A is energized bringing in the motor and ignition
   D. B is first energized

   32._____

33. Momentary power failure while burner is in operation causes

   A. both relays to drop out   B. relay A to drop out only
   C. relay B to drop out only   D. the relay to go out on safety

   33._____

Questions 34-37.

Questions 34 through 37 are based on the diagram below.

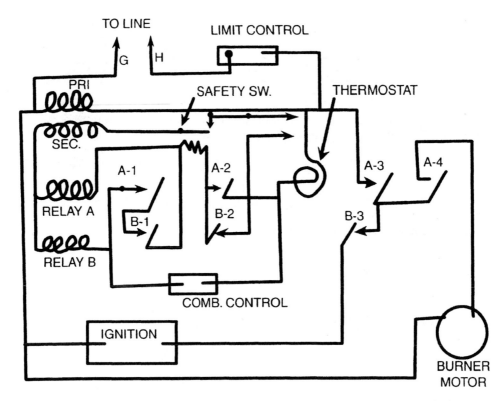

DIAGRAM OF PROTECTOR RELAY FOR OIL BURNER

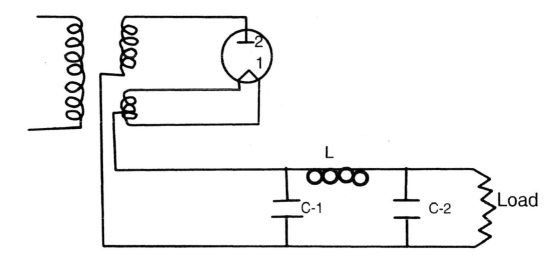

34. In order to furnish d.c. for the operation of relays and control circuits, where only a source   34.__
    of a.c. is available and the use of batteries is not convenient, gas and vacuum tubes are
    used extensively as rectifiers.
    The schematic diagram shown above represents a typical _____ rectifier.

    A. full wave   B. push pull   C. bridge   D. half wave

35. In reference to the sketch above, tube element 1 represents the   35.____

    A. filament   B. plate   C. suppressor   D. grid

36. In reference to the sketch above, tube element 2 represents the   36.____

    A. suppressor   B. filament   C. grid   D. plate

37. In reference to the sketch above, the circuit element marked L together with C-1 and C-2   37.____
act to

    A. smooth the voltage across the load
    B. change the frequency across the load
    C. rectify the incoming a.c.
    D. maintain the factor K cos ϕ intact

38. The output of a 6-pole d.c. generator is 360 amperes at 240 volts.   38.____
If its armature is simplex lap-wound, the current per path, in amperes, through the
armature is

    A. 52. 5   B. 60   C. 105   D. 210

39. In reference to question 38, the voltage per path, in volts is   39.____

    A. 120   B. 420   C. 60   D. 240

40. In reference to question 38, the kilowatt rating of the machine is APPROXIMATELY   40.____

    A. 86   B. 50   C. 14   D. 7

KEY (CORRECT ANSWERS)

1.	C	11.	B	21.	A	31.	D
2.	D	12.	A	22.	D	32.	C
3.	C	13.	B	23.	B	33.	A
4.	A	14.	C	24.	C	34.	D
5.	D	15.	C	25.	D	35.	A
6.	B	16.	D	26.	C	36.	D
7.	C	17.	A	27.	A	37.	A
8.	B	18.	C	28.	B	38.	B
9.	C	19.	B	29.	C	39.	D
10.	A	20.	D	30.	B	40.	A

TEST 2

DIRECTIONS: Each question or incomplete statement is followed by several suggested answers or completions. Select the one that *BEST* answers the question or completes the statement. *PRINT THE LETTER OF THE CORRECT ANSWER IN THE SPACE AT THE RIGHT.*

1. When five 60-watt, 120-volt lamps are connected in series across a 600-volt circuit the current, in amperes, drawn by the lamps is   1.___

   A. 2   B. 1   C. 3/4   D. 1/2

2. The resistance of a conductor, expressed in ohms, multiplied by the square of the current flowing in the conductor, expressed in amperes, is equal to the   2.___

   A. final temperature
   B. voltage across the conductor
   C. current loss in the conductor
   D. watts lost in the conductor

3. Three 20-ohm resistances are connected in wye across a 208-volt, 3 phase circuit. The line current in amperes is APPROXIMATELY   3.___

   A. 18   B. 10.4   C. 5.2   D. 6

4. Referring to question 3, the power dissipated in the load is _____ watts.   4.___

   A. 2160   B. 6480   C. 1620   D. 19,440

5. A direct-current supply may be obtained from an alternating current source by means of   5.___

   A. a frequency changer set
   B. an inductance-capacitance filter
   C. a tungar bulb rectifier
   D. none of the devices mentioned above

6. A megger is an instrument used to   6.___

   A. determine the capacity of a condenser
   B. measure the insulation resistance of wires and cables
   C. measure the voltage of a system
   D. insert a desired number of megohms in a circuit

7. To measure the value of armature circuit resistance corresponding to rated current for a 100-H.P., direct-current, 240-volt compound motor you would use a   7.___

   A. 0-50 millivoltmeter and 0-500 ammeter
   B. 0-50 millivoltmeter and a 0-500 milliammeter
   C. 0-15 voltmeter and a 0-500 ammeter
   D. megger

8. The power is measured in a three-phase, three wire circuit by means of the well-known two-wattmeter method.
   When the power factor is unity,   8.___

A. one wattmeter reads zero
B. the ratio of the readings of the two wattmeters is less than one
C. the ratio of the readings of the two wattmeters is unit
D. the ratio of the readings of the two wattmeters is greater than one

9. The internal diameter of 1/2 inch electrical conduit is APPROXIMATELY _____ inch.   9._____

    A. 0.422   B. 0.5   C. 0.552   D. 0.622

10. The resistance, in ohms, of a 25-ampere, 50 millivolt shunt is APPROXIMATELY   10._____

    A. 2   B. 0.2   C. 0.02   D. 0.002

11. A circular mil is the area of a circle whose diameter is _____ inch.   11._____

    A. 0.01   B. 0.001   C. 0.0001   D. 1

12. The current in amperes of a 220-volt, 5-H.P., d.c. motor having an efficiency of 90% is   12._____
    APPROXIMATELY

    A. 18.8   B. 17   C. 14.3   D. 20.5

13. If you attempted to start a d.c. compound motor in which the series field was open-cir-   13._____
    cuited, the motor would

    A. not start   B. blow the fuse
    C. run away   D. start in the reverse direction

14. You have a 100-ampere, 13-K.V. oil switch which has a trip coil rated up to 5 amperes.   14._____
    You wish the switch to open when the line current is 80 amperes.
    To accomplish this the trip coil should be set at _____ amperes.

    A. 4   B. 5   C. 3   D. 1

15. To control a lamp independently from three different points you would use two   15._____

    A. 3-way and one S.P.S.T. switch   B. 3-way and one 4-way switch
    C. S.P.S.T. and one 3-way switch   D. 4-way and one S.P.S.T. switch

16. The current in amperes of a one horsepower, 120-volt single-phase induction motor hav-   16._____
    ing an efficiency of 90% and operating at 0.8 power factor is APPROXIMATELY

    A. 6.9   B. 7.8   C. 8.6   D. 6.2

17. In a 5-H.P., 220-volt, shunt motor rated at 19.2 amperes and 1500 R.P.M., the armature   17._____
    resistance is _____ that of the shunt field.

    A. smaller than   B. larger than
    C. the same as   D. always one-half

18. The MOST common type of motor that can be used with both a.c. and d.c. sources is   18._____

    A. the repulsion motor   B. the series motor
    C. the rotary converter   D. the shunt motor

19. The speed of a synchronous motor having two poles and connected to a 60-cycle power supply is _____ R.P.M.   19.__

    A. 7200   B. 3600   C. 1800   D. 1200

20. To start a synchronous motor it must be brought up to synchronous speed.   20.__
If a small induction motor, on the same shaft as the synchronous motor, is used for bringing it up to speed, the induction motor MUST have

    A. more poles than the synchronous motor
    B. fewer poles than the synchronous motor
    C. the same number of poles as the synchronous motor
    D. the same number of poles and the same excitation as the synchronous motor

21. The speed of a three-phase, slip-ring, induction motor is increased with a(n)   21.__

    A. *decrease* in the secondary circuit resistance
    B. *increase* in the secondary circuit resistance
    C. *decrease* in the voltage impressed on the stator
    D. *increase* in the stator current

Questions 22-26.

DIRECTIONS: Questions 22 to 26 inclusive refer to the schematic diagram of a series motor controller illustrated below.

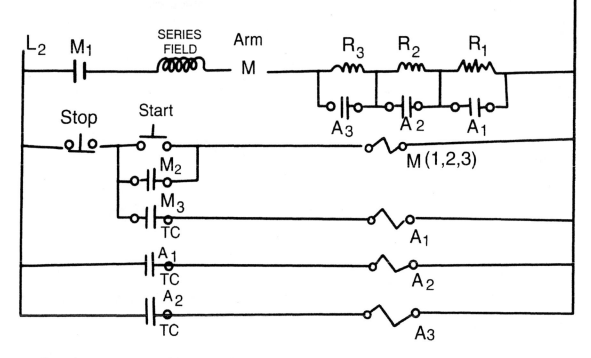

22. Certain contacts on this controller are equipped with dash pots to give time delay on closing, these contacts are marked TC.   22.__
When the start button is closed,

A. all the M-contacts will close at once
B. the motor starts first and then contact M1 closes
C. contacts M1 and M2 will close at once and contact M3 will close after a definite predetermined time
D. contacts M1 and A1 will close at once

23. With reference to the diagram which appears on the previous page, closing the start button will cause the motor to start   23._____

    A. at twice the rated speed   B. within an instant
    C. about one minute later   D. about two minutes later

24. With reference to the diagram which appears on the previous page, contact M1 is a   24._____

    A. normally closed contact
    B. normally open contact
    C. contact with time delay on opening
    D. contact with time delay on closing

25. With reference to the diagram which appears on the previous page, current flowing through the coil M causes the   25._____

    A. immediate operation of contactor A1
    B. immediate acceleration of the motor
    C. operation of contactor A1 after a definite time delay
    D. operation of contactor A2 before the operation of A1

26. With reference to the diagram which appears on the previous page, operation of the stop button causes   26._____

    A. the motor to stop immediately
    B. the ultimate opening of all contacts
    C. contact A1 to close after a definite time delay
    D. contact M1 to open after contact A1

27. The type of relay that is used to prevent the starting of a three-phase induction motor in the event that two of the line leads are accidentally interchanged is known as a(n) _____ relay.   27._____

    A. overload   B. phase-sequence
    C. polarity direction   D. reverse-current

28. The current-carrying capacity of a No. 2 rubber-insulated aluminum wire as compared to that of a No. 2 rubber-insulated copper wire is _____ percent.   28._____

    A. 80   B. 84   C. 74   D. 88

29. The secondary of a current transformer in whose primary winding current is flowing should   29._____

    A. always be short-circuited
    B. not be connected to the current coil of a wattmeter
    C. not be open-circuited
    D. not be short-circuited

30. To fasten an outlet box to a solid concrete wall you should use   30.___

    A. expansion bolts   B. toggle bolts
    C. wooden plugs and nails   D. wooden plugs and screws

31. Three single-phase transformers having ratios of 10 to one are connected with their pri-   31.___
    maries in wye and their secondaries in delta.
    If the low-voltage windings are used as the primaries and the line voltage on the pri-
    mary side is 208 volts then the line voltage on the secondary side is _____ volts.

    A. 3600   B. 2080   C. 1200   D. 692

32. Electrical metallic tubing shall   32.___

    A. be threaded for a length equal to half that of the coupling
    B. use National Fine standard pipe thread
    C. never be threaded
    D. use running threads for coupling

33. A piece of No. 1/0 emery cloth should be used to grind the commutator of a d.c. motor   33.___

    A. whenever there is sparking at the brushes
    B. under no condition
    C. when the cummutator is rough or worn
    D. when the brushes do not make good contact

34. An intercommunicating telephone system in which each station can ring any other sta-   34.___
    tion without disturbing the rest of the stations in the system and as many separate con-
    versations can be carried on simultaneously as there are pairs of stations is called a

    A. selective ringing, selective talking system
    B. selective ringing, common talking system
    C. code ringing, private talking system
    D. master station, private talking system

35. A storage battery is charged from a 120-volt d.c. line through a series resistance.   35.___
    If the charging rate is 10 amperes, the electromotive force of the battery is 20 volts and
    its internal resistance is 0.1 ohm, the value of the series resistance is _____ ohms.

    A. 2   B. 9.9   C. 10   D. 12

36. To change the direction of rotation of a cumulative compound-wound d.c. motor and   36.___
    maintain its characteristics you must reverse the connections to the _____.

    A. armature   B. shunt field
    C. series field   D. armature and the series

37. To change the direction of rotation of a 3-phase, 3-wire, wound-rotor a.c. induction motor,   37.___
    you should

    A. reverse any two leads connected to the rotor
    B. reverse any two leads connected to the stator
    C. reverse the field connections
    D. do nothing since it cannot be done

38. To change the direction of rotation of a single-phase, split-phase induction motor, you should

38.____

    A.   do nothing since it cannot be done
    B.   reverse the connections to the shunt field
    C.   reverse the connections to both windings
    D.   reverse the connections to the starting or auxiliary winding

39. To temporarily change the direction of rotation of a single-phase, shaded-pole, induction motor, you would

39.____

    A.   do nothing since it cannot be done
    B.   reverse the connections to the starting winding
    C.   shift the brushes to the opposite neutral
    D.   reverse the line leads

40. A one-microfarad condenser is connected in series with a one-half microfarad condenser.
The resulting capacity of the combination is _____ microfarad.

40.____

    A.   one-half   B.   one-third
    C.   one and one-half   D.   one

KEY (CORRECT ANSWERS)

1.	D	11.	B	21.	A	31.	C
2.	D	12.	A	22.	C	32.	C
3.	D	13.	A	23.	B	33.	B
4.	A	14.	A	24.	B	34.	A
5.	C	15.	B	25.	C	35.	B
6.	B	16.	C	26.	B	36.	A
7.	C	17.	A	27.	B	37.	B
8.	C	18.	B	28.	B	38.	D
9.	D	19.	B	29.	C	39.	A
10.	D	20.	B	30.	A	40.	B

EXAMINATION SECTION
TEST 1

DIRECTIONS: Each question or incomplete statement is followed by several suggested
answers or completions. Select the one that *BEST* answers the question or
completes the statement. *PRINT THE LETTER OF THE CORRECT ANSWER
IN THE SPACE AT THE RIGHT.*

1.   That system of electric braking in which the traction motors are used as generators and   1.____
the kinetic energy of the load is used as the actuating means for exerting a retarding
force is known as _____ braking.

   A.   track   B.   magnetic   C.   dynamic   D.   generator

2.   Thermal overload protective devices used for motor running protection protect the motor   2.____
against

   A.   a short-circuit   B.   overcurrent at starting
   C.   transient overloads   D.   normal operating overloads

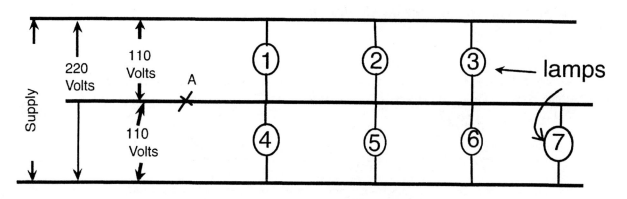

3.   In the above diagram, the center conductor breaks at point A.   3.____

   A.   Lamps 1, 2, and 3 will burn with greater brilliancy than lamps 4, 5, 6 and 7.
   B.   Lamps 1, 2, and 3 will burn dimmer than lamps 4, 5, 6, and 7.
   C.   All lamps will be extinguished.
   D.   All lamps will burn with the same brilliancy that they had before the center lead
opened.

4.   In ordering standard cartridge fuses it is necessary to specify ONLY the   4.____

   A.   current capacity
   B.   voltage of the circuit
   C.   current capacity and the voltage of the circuit
   D.   power to be dissipated

5.   The current input per phase under rated-load conditions for a 200-H.P., 3 phase, 2300-   5.____
volt, 0.8 P. F., induction motor which is 90% efficient is _____ amperes.

   A.   52   B.   90   C.   41.6   D.   46.8

6.   Referring to problem 5 above, the power input under rated-load conditions is APPROXI-   6.____
MATELY

   A.   149 K.W.   B.   96 K.W.   C.   166 K.W.   D.   332 K.W.

7. Three single-phase transformers are connected in delta on both the primary and second-   7.__
   ary sides.
   If one of the transformers burns out the system can continue to operate but its capacity, in terms of the capacity of the original arrangement, is reduced to

      A. 66 2/3%   B. 57.8%   C. 115%   D. 100%

8. In order to successfully operate two compound-wound d.c. generators in parallel it is   8.__
   necessary to use

      A. a compensating winding   B. an equalizer connection
      C. a series field diverter   D. commutating poles

9. If a given machine requires a full-load torque of 30 pound-feet and runs at a speed of   9.__
   1800 R.P.M., the size of direct-coupled motor required to drive this machine is APPROX-
   IMATELY _____ H.P.

      A. 10.3   B. 20.6   C. 15.3   D. 5.2

10. Oil is used in many large transformers to   10.__

      A. lubricate the core   B. lubricate the coils
      C. insulate the coils   D. insulate the core

11. A certain machine is driven by a 1750-R.P.M. d.c. shunt motor. If the power supply is to   11.__
   be changed to three-phase, 60 cycles, a.c., the MOST suitable replacement motor would
   be a _____ motor.

      A. series   B. repulsion
      C. squirrel-cage induction   D. capacitor

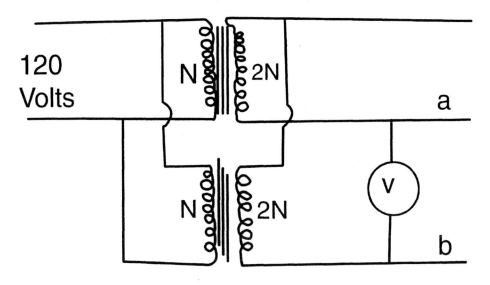

12. Two transformers with ratios of 1.2 are to be connected in parallel. To test for proper con-   12.__
    nections the circuit of the above diagram is used.
    The transformers may be connected in parallel by connecting lead a to lead b if the
    voltmeter shown reads _____ volts.

      A. 120   B. 240   C. zero   D. 480

13. You were asked to calculate the electric bill for the last month. The kilowatt-hour meter reads 99,010 K.W.-hrs. at the end of the previous month and now reads 00,110 K.W.-hrs. The demand meter reads 75 K.W.

13.____

The energy rate is:

For the first 500 K.W.-hrs.	$0.04 per K.W.-hr.
For the next 300 K.W.-hrs.	$0.03 per K.W.-hr.
For the next 200 K.W.-hrs.	$0.02 per K.W.-hr.
For all in excess of 100 K.W.-hrs.	$0.01 per K.W.-hr.

The demand rate is $0.50 per K.W.

The total electric bill is

A. $71.50   B. $67.50   C. $83.50   D. $74.50

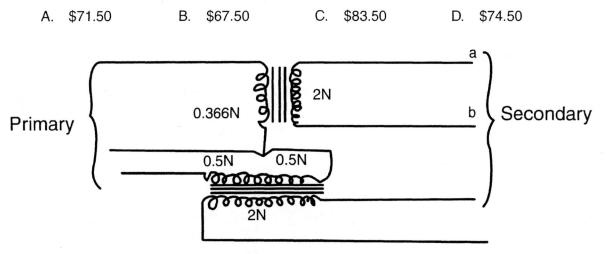

14. If the primary leads in the above diagram are connected to a three-phase, three-wire, 208 volt system and the transformation ratios are as indicated on the diagram, the secondary leads will form a _____ -phase, _____ -wire system.

14.____

A.	three	four
B.	two	four
C.	four	five
D.	three	three

15. In the circuit of the above diagram, the voltage between the secondary leads a and b is _____ volts.

15.____

A. 208   B. 120   C. 416   D. 240

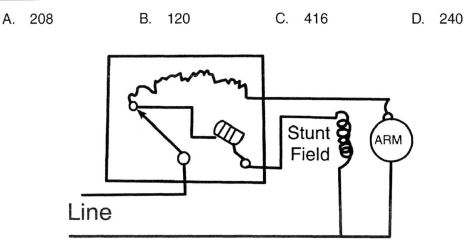

16. The circuit of the above diagram shows a d.c. motor starter.   16.___
    One of the features of this starting box is a(n) _____ release.

   A. overload   B. no-field   C. reverse-current D. underload

17. For starting a three-phase induction motor a three-phase transformer is used with its pri-   17.___
    maries connected in delta and its secondaries connected in delta for starting and in wye
    for running.
    The ratio of the running to the starting voltage is

   A. 3 : 1   B. 2 : 1   C. 1.73 : 1   D. 1.41 : 1

18. A booster transformer is a transformer connected   18.___

   A. in such a manner as to increase the load on the line by a fixed percentage
   B. as a delta-connected bank
   C. as an auto-transformer to raise the line voltage by a fixed percentage
   D. in such a manner as to raise the frequency by a fixed percentage

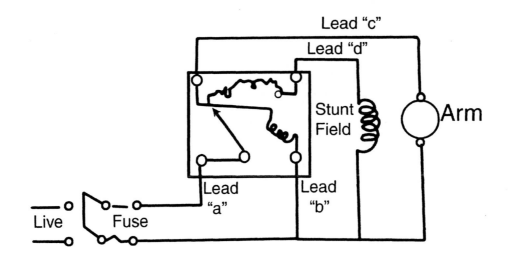

19. The motor shown in the above figure does not operate correctly. When the line switch is   19.___
    closed the fuses blow.
    To correct this fault leads _____ and _____ should be interchanged.

   A. leads *a* and *b*
   B. leads *a* and *c*
   C. leads *b* and *d*
   D. leads *c* and *d*

20. A standard stranded cable contains 19 strands. When measured with a micrometer the   20.___
    diameter of each strand is found to be 105.5 mils.
    If, under certain conditions, the allowable current density is 600 C.M. per ampere the
    allowable current-carrying capacity of this conductor is _____ amperes.

   A. 236   B. 176.3   C. 352.5   D. 705

21. For MAXIMUM safety the magnetic contactors used for reversing the direction of rotation of a motor should be   21.____

    A. electrically interlocked
    B. electrically and mechanically interlocked
    C. mechanically interlocked
    D. operated from independent sources

22. When the starter for a 250-volt, direct-current shunt motor whose full-load armature current is 20 amperes, is in the first contact postion, the total resistance in the armature circuit, to permit the motor to start with 150% of rated torque, should be APPROXIMATELY _____ ohms.   22.____

    A. 5   B. 8   C. 12   D. 20

23. If the allowable current density for copper bus bars is 1000 amperes per square inch, the current-carrying capacity of a circular copper bar having a diameter of two inches is APPROXIMATELY _____ amperes.   23.____

    A. 1050   B. 2320   C. 3140   D. 4260

24. A rotary converter, operating at unity power factor, may be made to take a leading power factor by   24.____

    A. *increasing* the d.c. field strength of the machine
    B. *decreasing* the d.c. field strength of the machine
    C. *decreasing* the speed at which it operates
    D. *increasing* the speed at which it operates

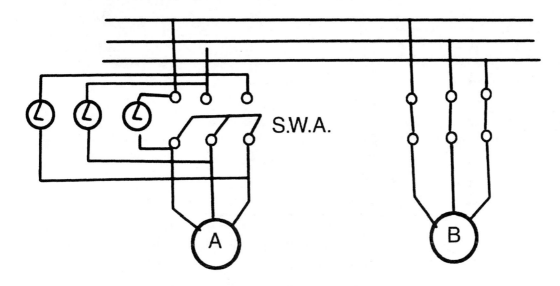

S.W.A.

25. Two alternators are to be synchronized for parallel operation, the correct synchronization being indicated by three lamps, as shown in the above diagram.   25.____
The CORRECT time to close switch *A* is

    A. when the lamps are at maximum brilliancy
    B. when the lamps are dark
    C. just before the lamps reach maximum brilliancy
    D. just after the lamps reach maximum brilliancy

26. The maximum voltage-drop between a d.c. motor and switchboard is not to exceed one percent of the supply voltage.
If the supply voltage is 200 volts, the full-load current of the motor 100 amperes, the distance from the switchboard to the motor 100 feet, and the resistivity of copper 10 ohms per C.M.-foot, the size wire required in C.M. is

   A. 25,000   B. 50,000   C. 100,000   D. 200,000

26.__

27. One foot of a certain size of nichrome wire has a resistance of 1.63 ohms.
To make a heating element for a toaster that will use 5 amperes at 110 volts, the number of feet of wire needed is APPROXIMATELY

   A. 17.9   B. 8.2   C. 5.5   D. 13.5

27.__

28. A tri-free circuit breaker is one that

   A. is tripped from a shunt-circuit through a relay
   B. can be tripped only by an operator
   C. cannot be tripped when the operating lever is held in the closed position
   D. can be tripped by the overload mechanism even though the operating lever is held in the closed position

28.__

29. The following equipment is required for a 2-*line return-call* electric bell circuit: 2 bells, 2 metallic lines,

   A. 2 ordinary push-buttons, and one set of batteries
   B. 2 return-call push-buttons and 2 sets of batteries
   C. 2 return-call push-buttons and one set of batteries
   D. one ordinary push-button, one return-call push button and one set of batteries

29.__

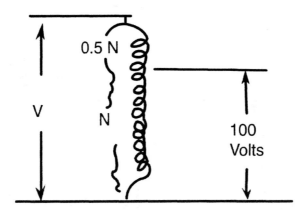

30. An auto-transformer with turns ratio as indicated in the above sketch is connected to a 100-volt, 60-cycle supply on the low-tension side.
The voltage, V, on the high tension side is _____ volts.

   A. 50   B. 100   C. 150   D. 200

30.__

31. The MINIMUM size of grounding conductor for a direct or alternating-current system is

   A. No. 14   B. No. 10   C. No. 8   D. No. 6

31.__

32. The thickness of insulation for a No. 8 rubber-covered conductor for use at NOT more than 2000 volts shall be _____ of an inch.

32.____

   A. 2/64ths   B. 3/64ths   C. 4/64ths   D. 5/64ths

33. A gutter whose width is 36 inches shall be constructed of sheet metal of thickness NOT less than No. _____ U.S. standard sheet metal gauge.

33.____

   A. 10   B. 12   C. 14   D. 16

34. The MAXIMUM voltage permitted on the push buttons of elevator signalling circuits shall be _____ volts to ground.

34.____

   A. 300   B. 125   C. 250   D. 600

35. Electric motors installed in hospital operating rooms shall be of the _____ proof type.

35.____

   A. water   B. explosion   C. dust   D. light

36. Connecting batteries in parallel instead of in series _____ of the batteries.

36.____

   A. *increases* the current output
   B. *decreases* the life
   C. *increases* the voltage
   D. *decreases* the current output

37. To charge a storage battery, one would use

37.____

   A. either a.c. or d.c.   B. a.c. only
   C. d.c. only   D. only low frequency a.c.

38. A transformer is USUALLY used to

38.____

   A. change a.c. to d.c.
   B. raise or lower a.c. voltage
   C. change d.c. to a.c.
   D. change the frequency of the a.c. supply

39. The commutator of a d.c. generator

39.____

   A. keeps the current flowing in one direction in the load circuit
   B. reverses the current direction in the armature
   C. acts only as a sliding electrical contact
   D. changes a.c. to d.c. within the armature

40. The number of fresh dry cells that should be connected in series to obtain 12 volts is

40.____

   A. 2   B. 6   C. 8   D. 12

KEY (CORRECT ANSWERS)

1.	C	11.	C	21.	B	31.	C
2.	D	12.	C	22.	B	32.	D
3.	A	13.	A	23.	C	33.	A
4.	C	14.	B	24.	A	34.	A
5.	A	15.	C	25.	B	35.	B
6.	C	16.	B	26.	C	36.	A
7.	B	17.	C	27.	D	37.	C
8.	B	18.	C	28.	D	38.	B
9.	A	19.	D	29.	B	39.	A
10.	C	20.	C	30.	C	40.	C

TEST 2

DIRECTIONS: Each question or incomplete statement is followed by several suggested answers or completions. Select the one that *BEST* answers the question or completes the statement. *PRINT THE LETTER OF THE CORRECT ANSWER IN THE SPACE AT THE RIGHT.*

1. Of the following, the BEST conductor of electricity is   1.____

    A. tungsten   B. iron   C. aluminum   D. carbon

2. A 600-volt cartridge fuse is MOST readily distinguished from a 250-volt cartridge fuse of   2.____
    the same ampere rating by comparing the

    A. insulating materials used   B. shape of the ends
    C. diameters   D. lengths

3. Many power-transformer cases are filled with oil.   3.____
    The purpose of the oil is to

    A. prevent rusting of the core
    B. reduce a.c. hum
    C. insulate the coils from the case
    D. transmit heat from the coils and core

4. In order to make certain that a 600-volt circuit is dead before working on it, the BEST pro-   4.____
    cedure is to

    A. test with a voltmeter
    B. *short* the circuit quickly with a piece of insulated wire
    C. see if any of the insulated conductors are warm
    D. disconnect one of the wires of the circuit near the feed

5. When closing an exposed knife switch on a panel, the action should be positive and rapid   5.____
    because there is less likelihood of

    A. the operator receiving a shock
    B. the operator being burned
    C. the fuse blowing
    D. injury to equipment connected to the circuit

6. Lubrication is never used on   6.____

    A. a knife switch
    B. a die when threading conduit
    C. wires being pulled into a conduit
    D. a commutator

7. If one plug fuse in a 110-volt circuit blows because of a short-circuit, a 110-volt lamp   7.____
    screwed into the fuse socket will

    A. burn dimly   B. remain dark   C. burn out   D. burn normally

8. Of the following, the LEAST undesirable practice if a specified wire size is not available   8.____
    for part of a circuit is to

A. use two wires of 1/2 capacity in parallel as a substitute
B. use the next larger size wire
C. use a smaller size wire if the length is short
D. reduce the size of the fuse and use smaller wire

9. If it is necessary to increase slightly the tension of an ordinary coiled spring in a relay, the PROPER procedure is to   9.___

A. cut off one or two turns
B. compress it slightly
C. stretch it slightly
D. unhook one end, twist and replace

10. As compared with solid wire, stranded wire of the same gage size is   10.___

A. given a higher current rating
C. larger in total diameter
B. easier to skin
D. better for high voltage

11. Motor frames are USUALLY positively grounded by a special connection in order to   11.___

A. remove static
C. provide a neutral
B. protect against lightening
D. protect against shock

12. If a live conductor is contacted accidentally, the severity of the electrical shock is determined PRIMARILY by   12.___

A. the size of the conductor
B. whether the current is a.c. or d.c.
C. the contact resistance
D. the current in the conductor

13. If a snap switch rated at 5 amperes is used for an electric heater which draws 10 amperes, the MOST likely result is that the   13.___

A. circuit fuse will be blown
B. circuit wiring will become hot
C. heater output will be halved
D. switch contacts will become hot

14. To straighten a long length of wire which has been tightly coiled, before pulling it into a conduit run, a good method is to   14.___

A. roll the wire into a coil in the opposite direction
B. fasten one end to the floor and whip it against the floor from the other end
C. draw it over a convenient edge
D. hold the wire at one end and twist it with the pliers from the other end

15. The wire size MOST commonly used for branch circuits in residences is   15.___

A. #14   B. #16   C. #12   D. #18

16. If the applied voltage on an incandescent lamp is increased 10%, the lamp will   16.___

A. have a longer life
B. burn more brightly
C. consume less power
D. fail by insulation breakdown

17. You would expect that the overload trip coil on an ordinary air circuit breaker would have   17.____

    A. heavy wire   B. fine wire
    C. many turns   D. heavily insulated wire

18. A cycle counter is an electrical timer which, when energized by alternating current,   18.____
counts the number of cycles until it is de-energized.
If a cycle counter is energized from a 60-cycle power supply for ten seconds, the reading of the instrument should be

    A. 6   B. 10   C. 60   D. 600

19. The MOST practical way to determine in the field if a large coil of #14 wire has the   19.____
required length for a given job is to

    A. weigh the coil
    B. measure one turn and count the turns
    C. unroll it into another coil
    D. make a visual comparison with a full coil

20. A frequency meter is constructed as a potential device, that is, to be connected across   20.____
the line.
A logical reason for this is that

    A. only the line voltage has frequency
    B. a transformer may then be used with it
    C. the reading will be independent of the varying current
    D. it is safer than a series device

21. It is usually not safe to connect 110 volts d.c. to a magnet coil designed for 110 volts a.c.   21.____
because the

    A. insulation is insufficient   B. iron may overheat
    C. wire may overheat   D. inductance may be too high

22. The MOST satisfactory temporary replacement for a 40-watt, 120-volt incandescent   22.____
lamp, if an identical replacement is not available, is a lamp rated at _____ watts,
_____ volts.

    A. 100; 240   B. 60; 130   C. 40; 32   D. 15; 120

23. If the following bare copper wire sizes were arranged in the order of increasing weight   23.____
per 1000 feet, the CORRECT arrangement would be

    A. #00, #40, #8   B. #40, #00, #8
    C. #00, #8, #40   D. #40, #8, #00

24. The purpose of having a rheostat in the field circuit of a d.c. shunt motor is to   24.____

    A. control the speed of the motor
    B. minimize the starting current
    C. limit the field current to a safe value
    D. reduce sparking at the brushes

25. The resistance of a 1000-ft. length of a certain size copper wire is required to be 10.0   25.__
    ohms $\pm$ 2%.
    This wire would NOT be acceptable if the resistance was _____ ohms.

    A. 10.12   B. 10.02   C. 10.22   D. 9.82

26. The LEAST important action in making a good soldered connection between two wires is   26.__
    to

    A. use the proper flux   B. clean the wires well
    C. use plenty of solder   D. use sufficient heat

27. Of the following, the BEST conductor of electricity is   27.__

    A. aluminum   B. carbon   C. copper   D. water

28. Good practice requires that the end of a piece of conduit be reamed after it has been cut   28.__
    to length.
    The purpose of the reaming is to

    A. prevent insulation damage when pulling in the wires
    B. finish the conduit accurately to length
    C. make the threading easier
    D. remove loose rust

29. According to the national electrical code, a run of conduit between two outlet boxes   29.__
    should not contain more than four quarter bends.
    The MOST likely reason for this limitation is that more bends will

    A. result in cracking the conduit
    B. make the pulling of the wire too difficult
    C. increase the wire length unnecessarily
    D. not be possible in one standard length of conduit

30. Asbestos is commonly used as the covering of electric wires in locations where there is   30.__
    likely to be high

    A. voltage   B. temperature   C. humidity   D. current

31. Portable lamp cord is LIKELY to have   31.__

    A. steel armor   B. stranded wires
    C. paper insulation   D. number 8 wire

32. The one of the following terms which could NOT correctly be used in describing a knife   32.__
    switch is

    A. quick-break   B. single throw   C. four-pole   D. toggle

33. With respect to common electric light bulbs, it is CORRECT to state that the   33.__

    A. circuit voltage has no effect on the life of the bulb
    B. filament is made of carbon
    C. base has a left hand thread
    D. lower wattage bulb has the higher resistance

34. The resistance of a 1000-foot coil of a certain size copper wire is 10 ohms.   34._____
    If 300 feet are cut off, the resistance of the remainder of the coil is _____ ohms.

    A. 7   B. 3   C. 0.7   D. 0.3

35. The term *l5 ampere* is COMMONLY used in identifying a(n)   35._____

    A. insulator   B. fuse   C. conduit   D. outlet box

36. When connecting the two lead wires of a test instrument to a live d.c. circuit, the BEST   36._____
    procedure is to first make the negative or ground connection and then the positive con-
    nection.
    The reason for this procedure is that

    A. electricity flows from positive to negative
    B. there is less danger of accidental shock
    C. the reverse procedure may blow the fuse
    D. less arcing will occur when the connection is made

37. To make a good soldered connection between two stranded wires, it is LEAST important   37._____
    to

    A. twist the wires together before soldering
    B. use enough heat to make the solder flow freely
    C. clean the wires carefully
    D. apply solder to each strand before twisting the two wires together

38. When a step-up transformer is used, it increases the   38._____

    A. voltage   B. current   C. power   D. frequency

39. Lock nuts are frequently used in making electrical connections on terminal boards.   39._____
    The purpose of such lock nuts is to

    A. make tighter connections with less effort
    B. make it difficult to tamper with the connections
    C. avoid stripping the threads
    D. keep the connections from loosening through vibration

40. The core of an electro-magnet is USUALLY   40._____

    A. aluminum   B. lead   C. brass   D. iron

41. A stranded wire is given the same size designation as a solid wire if it has the same   41._____

    A. cross-sectional area   B. weight per foot
    C. overall diameter   D. strength

42. One advantage of cutting 1" rigid conduit with a hacksaw rather than a 3-wheel pipe   42._____
    cutter is that

    A. the cut can be made with less exertion
    B. the pipe is not squeezed out of round
    C. less reaming is required after the cut
    D. no vise is needed

43. Assume that the field leads of a large, completely disconnected d.c. motor are not tagged   43.___
or otherwise marked. You could readily tell the shunt field leads from the series field
leads by the

    A. length of the leads   B. size of wire
    C. thickness of insulation   D. type of insulation

44. Standard electrician's pliers should NOT be used to   44.___

    A. bend thin sheet metal
    B. crush insulation on wires to be skinned
    C. cut off nail points sticking through a board
    D. hold a wire in position for soldering

45. The device used to change a.c. to d.c. is a   45.___

    A. frequency   B. regulator   C. transformer   D. rectifier

46. The CHIEF advantage of using stranded rather than solid conductors for electrical wiring   46.___
is that stranded conductors are

    A. more flexible   B. easier to skin
    C. smaller   D. stronger

47. One identifying feature of a squirrel-cage induction motor is that it has no   47.___

    A. windings on the stationary part
    B. commutator or slip rings
    C. air gap
    D. iron core in the rotating part

48. If a cartridge fuse is hot to the touch when you remove it to do some maintenance on the   48.___
circuit, this MOST probably indicates that the

    A. voltage of the circuit is too high
    B. fuse clips do not make good contact
    C. equipment on the circuit starts and stops frequently
    D. fuse is oversize for the circuit

49. The instrument MOST commonly used to determine the state of charge of a lead-acid   49.___
storage battery is the

    A. thermometer   B. hydrometer
    C. voltmeter   D. ammeter

50. Rigid conduit must be installed as to prevent the collection of water in it between outlets.   50.___
In order to meet this requirement, the conduit should NOT have a

    A. low point between successive outlets
    B. high point between successive outlets
    C. low point at an outlet
    D. high point at an outlet

KEY (CORRECT ANSWERS)

1. C	11. D	21. C	31. B	41. A
2. D	12. C	22. B	32. D	42. C
3. D	13. D	23. D	33. D	43. B
4. A	14. B	24. A	34. A	44. C
5. B	15. A	25. C	35. B	45. D
6. D	16. C	26. C	36. B	46. A
7. D	17. A	27. C	37. D	47. B
8. B	18. D	28. A	38. A	48. B
9. A	19. B	29. B	39. D	49. B
10. C	20. C	30. B	40. D	50. A

———

TEST 3

DIRECTIONS: Each question or incomplete statement is followed by several suggested answers or completions. Select the one that *BEST* answers the question or completes the statement. *PRINT THE LETTER OF THE CORRECT ANSWER IN THE SPACE AT THE RIGHT.*

1. When a test lamp is connected to the two ends of a cartridge fuse on an operating switchboard, the indication in ALL cases will be that this fuse is

    A. blown if the test lamp remains dark
    B. good if the test lamp lights
    C. blown if the test lamp lights
    D. good if the test lamp remains dark

1.____

2. If one copper wire has a diameter of 0.128 inch, and another copper wire has a diameter of 0.064 inch, the resistance of 1,000 feet of the first wire compared to the same length of the second wire is

    A. one half   B. one quarter   C. double   D. four times

2.____

3. If the allowable current in a copper bus bar is 1,000 amperes per square inch of cross-section, the width of a standard 1/4" bus bar designed to carry 1500 amperes would be

    A. 2"   B. 4"   C. 6"   D. 8"

3.____

4. It is not possible to obtain a 200-watt light-bulb that is as small in all dimensions as the standard 150-watt light-bulb.
The PRINCIPAL advantage to users resulting from this reduction in size is that

    A. maintenance electricians can carry many more light-bulbs
    B. two sizes of light-bulbs can be kept in the same storage space
    C. the higher wattage bulb can now fit into certain lighting fixtures
    D. less breakage is apt to occur in handling

4.____

5. A carbon brush in a d.c. motor should exert a pressure of about 1 1/2 lbs. per square inch on the commutator.
A much lighter pressure would be MOST likely to result in

    A. sparking at the commutator
    B. vibration of the armature
    C. the brush getting out of line
    D. excessive wear of the brush holder

5.____

6. The number of watts of heat given off by a resistor is expressed by the formula I^2R.
If 10 volts is applied to a 5-ohm resistor, the heat given off will be _____ watts.

    A. 500   B. 250   C. 50   D. 20

6.____

7. When a number of rubber insulated wires are being pulled into a run of conduit having several sharp bends between the two pull boxes, the pulling is likely to be hard and the wires are subjected to considerable strain.
For these reasons it is ADVISABLE in such a case to

7.____

    A.   push the wires into the feed end of the conduit at the same time that pulling is being done
    B.   pull in only one wire at a time
    C.   use extra heavy grease
    D.   pull the wires back a few inches after each forward pull to gain momentum

8. The plug of a portable tool should be removed from the convenience outlet by grasping the plug and not by pulling on the cord because   8.____

    A.   the plug is easier to grip than the cord
    B.   pulling on the cord may allow the plug to fall on the floor and break
    C.   pulling on the cord may break the wires off the plug terminals
    D.   the plug is generally better insulated than the cord

9. When using a pipe wrench, the hand should be placed so as to pull instead of push on the wrench.   9.____
The basis for this recommendation is that there is less likelihood of

    A.   the wrench slipping
    B.   injury to the hand if the wrench slips
    C.   injury to the pipe if the wrench slips
    D.   stripped pipe threads

10. High voltage switches in power plants are commonly so constructed that their contacts are submerged in oil.   10.____
The purpose of the oil is to

    A.   help quench arcing
    B.   lubricate the contacts
    C.   cool the switch mechanism
    D.   insulate the contacts from the switch framework

11. In a storage battery installation consisting of twenty 2-volt cells connected in series, a leak develops in one of the cells and all the electrolyte runs out of it.   11.____
The terminal voltage across the twenty cells will now be

    A. 40   B. 38   C. 2   D. 0

12. When removing the insulation from a wire before making a splice, care should be taken to avoid nicking the wire MAINLY because then the   12.____

    A.   current carrying capacity will be reduced
    B.   resistance will be increased
    C.   insulation will be harder to remove
    D.   wire is more likely to break

13. Good practice dictates that an adjustable open-end wrench should be used PRIMARILY when the   13.____

    A.   nut to be turned is soft and must not be scored
    B.   proper size of fixed wrench is not available
    C.   extra leverage is needed
    D.   location is cramped permitting only a small turning angle

14. It would generally be poor practice to use ordinary slip-joint pliers to   14.__

    A. pull a small nail   B. bend a wire
    C. remove a cotter pin   D. tighten a machine bolt

15. The a.c. motor which has exactly the same speed at full-load as at no load is the _____   15.__
motor.

    A. synchronous   B. repulsion   C. induction   D. condenser

16. A metal bushing is usually screwed on to the end of rigid conduit inside of a junction box.   16.__
The bushing serves to

    A. center the wires in the conduit
    B. separate the wires where they leave the conduit
    C. protect the wires against abrasion
    D. prevent sagging of the conduit

17. The PROPER abrasive for cleaning the commutator of a d.c. generator is   17.__

    A. steel wool   B. emery cloth   C. sand paper   D. soapstone

18. If a *live* 120-volt d.c. lighting circuit is connected to the 120-volt winding of an otherwise   18.__
disconnected power transformer, the result will be

    A. blowing of the d.c. circuit fuse
    B. magnetization of the transformer fuse
    C. sparking at the transformer secondary terminals
    D. burning out of lights on the d.c. circuit

19. Threaded joints in rigid conduit runs are made watertight through the use   19.__

    A. petroleum jelly   B. solder   C. red lead   D. paraffin wax

20. The letters S.P.S.T. frequently found on wiring plans refer to a type of   20.__

    A. cable   B. switch   C. fuse   D. motor

21. Renewable fuses differ from ordinary fuses in that   21.__

    A. they can carry higher overloads
    B. burned out fuses can be located more easily
    C. burned out fuse elements can be readily replaced
    D. they can be used on higher voltages

22. After No. 10 A.W.G., the next SMALLER copper wire size in common use is No.   22.__

    A. 8   B. 9   C. 11   D. 12

23. The BEST of the following tools to use for cutting off a piece of single-conductor #6 rub-   23.__
ber insulated lead covered cable is

    A. pair of electrician's pliers   B. hacksaw
    C. hammer and cold chisel   D. lead knife

24. Toggle bolts are MOST appropriate for use to fasten conduit clamps to a   24._____

    A.   steel column   B.   concrete wall
    C.   hollow tile wall   D.   brick wall

25. If a 10-24 by 3/4" machine screw is not available, the screw which could be MOST easily   25._____
modified to use in an emergency is a

    A.   10-24 by 1/2"   B.   12-24 by 3/4"
    C.   10-24 by 1 1/2"   D.   8-24 by 3/4"

26. A standard pipe thread differs from a standard screw thread in that the pipe thread   26._____

    A.   is tapered
    B.   is deeper
    C.   requires no lubrication when cutting
    D.   has the same pitch for any diameter of pipe

27. The material which is LEAST likely to be found in use as the outer covering of rubber   27._____
insulated wires or cables is

    A.   cotton   B.   varnished cambric
    C.   lead   D.   neoprene

28. In measuring to determine the size of a stranded insulated conductor, the proper place to   28._____
use the wire gauge is on

    A.   the insulation   B.   the outer covering
    C.   the stranded conductor   D.   one strand of the conductor

29. Rubber insulation on an electrical conductor would MOST quickly be damaged by contin-   29._____
uous contact with

    A.   acid   B.   water   C.   oil   D.   alkali

30. If a fuse clip becomes hot under normal circuit load, the MOST probable cause is that the   30._____

    A.   clip makes poor contact with the fuse ferrule
    B.   circuit wires are too small
    C.   current rating of the fuse is too high
    D.   voltage rating of the fuse is too low

31. If the input ot a 10 to 1 step-down transformer is 15 amperes at 2400 volts, the second-   31._____
ary output would be NEAREST to _____ amperes at _____ volts.

    A.   1.5; 24,000   B.   150; 240   C.   1.5; 240   D.   150; 24,000

32. The resistance of a copper wire to the flow of electricity   32._____

    A.   *increases* as the diameter of the wire increases
    B.   *decreases* as the diameter of the wire decreases
    C.   *decreases* as the length of the wire increases
    D.   *increases* as the length of the wire increases

33. Where galvanized steel conduit is used, the PRIMARY purpose of the galvanizing is to   33.__

    A. increase mechanical strength
    B. retard rusting
    C. provide a good surface for painting
    D. provide good electrical contact for grounding

34. The CORRECT method of measuring the power taken by an a.c electric motor is to use a   34.__

    A. wattmeter
    C. power factor meter
    B. voltmeter and an ammeter
    D. tachometer

35. Checking a piece of rigid electrical conduit with a steel scale, you measure the inside   35.__
diameter as 1 1/16" and the outside diameter as 1 5/16".
The NOMINAL size of this conduit is

    A. 3/4"   B. 1"   C. 1 1/4"   D. 1 1/2"

36. Of the following, it would be MOST difficult to solder a copper wire to a metal plate made   36.__
of

    A. copper   B. brass   C. iron   D. tin

37. After a piece of rigid conduit has been cut to length, it is MOST important to   37.__

    A. ream the inside edge to prevent injury to wires
    B. file the end flat to make an accurate fit
    C. coat the cut surface with red lead to prevent rust
    D. rile the outside edge to a taper for ease in threading

38. Rigid conduit is generally secured to sheet metal outlet boxes by means of   38.__

    A. threadless couplings
    C. locknuts and bushings
    B. box connectors
    D. conduit clamps

39. While a certain d.c. shunt motor is driving a light load, part of the field winding becomes   39.__
short circuited,
The motor will MOST likely

    A. increase its speed
    C. remain at the same speed
    B. decrease its speed
    D. come to a stop

40. Each time a certain electric heater is turned on, the incandescent lights connected to the   40.__
same branch circuit become dimmer and when the heater is turned off the lamps
become brighter.
The factor which probably contributes MOST to this effect is the

    A. voltage of the circuit
    C. current taken by the lamps
    B. size of the circuit fuse
    D. size of the circuit conductors

41. Comparing the shunt field winding with the series field winding of a compound d.c. motor,   41.__
it would be CORRECT to say that the shunt field winding has _____ resistance,

    A. *more* turns but the *lower*
    C. *fewer* turns and the *lower*
    B. *more* turns and the *higher*
    D. *fewer* turns but the *higher*

42. The most important reason for using a fuse-puller when removing a cartridge fuse from the fuse clips is to

    A. prevent blowing of the fuse
    B. prevent injury to the fuse element
    C. reduce the chances of personal injury
    D. reduce arcing at the fuse clips

42.____

43. A coil of wire wound on an iron core draws exactly 5 amperes when connected across the terminals of a ten-volt storage battery.
If this coil is now connected across the ten-volt secondary terminals of an ordinary power transformer, the current drawn will be

    A. *less* than 5 amperes
    B. *more* than 5 amperes
    C. *exactly* 5 amperes
    D. more or less than 5 amperes depending on the frequency

43.____

44. A revolution counter applied to the end of a rotating shaft reads 100 when a stop-watch is started. It reads 850 when the stop-watch indicates 90 seconds.
The average RPM of the shaft is

    A. 8.4   B. 9.4   C. 500   D. 567

44.____

45. Motor speeds are generally measured directly in RPM by the use of a

    A. potentiometer   B. manometer   C. dynamometer   D. tachometer

45.____

46. To reverse the direction of rotation of a 3-phase motor, it is necessary to

    A. increase the resistance of the rotor circuit
    B. interchange any two of the three line connections
    C. interchange all three line connections
    D. reverse the polarity of the rotor circuit

46.____

47. Mica is commonly used in electrical construction for

    A. commutator bar separators   B. switchboard panels
    C. strain insulators   D. heater cord insulation

47.____

48. The rating term *1000 ohms, 10 watts* would generally be applied to a

    A. heater   B. relay   C. resistor   D. transformer

48.____

49. According to the National Electrical Code, the identified (or grounded) conductor of the branch circuit supplying an incandescent lamp socket must be connected to the screw shell.
The MOST likely reason for this requirement is that

    A. longer lamp life results
    B. the wiring will be kept more nearly uniform
    C. persons are more likely to come in contact with the shell
    D. the shell can carry heavier currents

49.____

50. In an installation used to charge a storage battery from a motor-generator you would   50.___
LEAST expect to find a(n)

   A. rectifier   B. rheostat   C. voltmeter   D. ammeter

KEY (CORRECT ANSWERS)

1. C	11. D	21. C	31. B	41. B
2. B	12. D	22. D	32. D	42. C
3. C	13. B	23. B	33. B	43. A
4. C	14. D	24. C	34. A	44. C
5. A	15. A	25. C	35. B	45. D
6. D	16. C	26. A	36. C	46. B
7. A	17. C	27. B	37. A	47. A
8. C	18. A	28. D	38. C	48. C
9. B	19. C	29. C	39. A	49. C
10. A	20. B	30. A	40. D	50. A

ELECTRICITY
EXAMINATION SECTION
TEST 1

DIRECTIONS: Each question or incomplete statement is followed by several suggested answers or completions. Select the one that *BEST* answers the question or completes the statement. *PRINT THE LETTER OF THE CORRECT ANSWER IN THE SPACE AT THE RIGHT.*

1. The one of the following items in which the metal alloy "Alnico" is *most likely* to be found is

   A. thermocouples
   C. wire-wound resistors
   B. heating elements
   D. permanent magnets

   1.____

2. Of the following devices, the one which, when inserted between a rectifier and its load, reduces the ripple current is the

   A. wave trap
   C. inverter
   B. coupling transformer
   D. filter

   2.____

3. The Q-factor (quality factor) of an inductor equals the

   A. product of its reactance and its resistance
   B. product of its inductance and its resistance
   C. ratio of its inductance to its resistance
   D. ratio of its reactance to its resistance

   3.____

4. Of the following types of screw heads, the one which requires a cross-slot screwdriver having 45-degree flukes and a sharp pointed head, is the

   A. Phillips
   C. Torque-set
   B. Recessed
   D. Reed and Prince

   4.____

5. Of the following, the *most likely* reason why loudspeakers in a public address system might produce a loud, howling noise when the input is a normal speaking voice, is

   A. feedback
   C. squelching
   B. attenuation
   D. transient current

   5.____

6. A megohmmeter of suitable voltage is used to test the condition of an A.C. electrolytic capacitor. Two readings are taken and the test leads are reversed between readings. The capacitor is discharged before and after the readings. The meter indications will stabilize at readings which are

   A. zero for one connection and high for the other, if the capacitor is defective
   B. high for one connection and zero for the other, if the capacitor is good
   C. zero for both connections, if the capacitor is good
   D. high for both connections, if the capacitor is good

   6.____

7. Of the following terms, the one which is most frequently used to describe circuits formed by etching metal foil deposited on a base of insulating material is the   7.____

    A. printed circuit   B. wired circuit
    C. bread-board circuit   D. prototype circuit

8. The PRIMARY function of a "zero sequence" current transformer, when installed in a four-wire A.G. power distribution system, is to detect   8.____

    A. ground faults   B. metering errors
    C. phase sequences   D. power factors

9. In three-phase rectifier systems, it is common practice to connect the power transformer with its primaries in _____ and its secondaries in _____.   9.____

    A. delta; delta   B. delta; wye
    C. wye; delta   D. wye; wye

10. The tap changer in a distribution transformer is normally used to change the   10.____

    A. voltage ratio   B. insulating oil
    C. winding polarity   D. impedance matching

11. The eddy currents in a distribution transformer can BEST be reduced by   11.____

    A. laminating the iron core
    B. polarizing both windings
    C. installing a secondary capacitor
    D. increasing the primary voltage

12. Of the following procedures, the one which is a precaution that should be taken when working with an instrument current transformer is: 12.____

    A. Short the primary before disconnecting it
    B. Short the secondary before disconnecting it
    C. Ground the primary after disconnecting it
    D. Ground the secondary after disconnecting it

13. If the line voltages across the load equal the phase voltages across the load in a balanced three-phase A.C. circuit, the load is connected in   13.____

    A. delta   B. Scott   C. star   D. wye

14. Of the following motors, the one MOST commonly used to correct a lagging power factor is the   14.____

    A. induction motor   B. synchronous motor
    C. series motor   D. compound motor

15. The one of the following motors which *frequently* requires a D.C. supply for excitation is the   15.____

    A. capacitor motor   B. shaded-pole motor
    C. wound-rotor motor   D. synchronous motor

16. Of the following, the *most likely* reason why a compound D.C. motor is running more slowly at full load than it normally does is that its

    A. line voltage is too high
    B. series field bucks the shunt field
    C. shunt field is open
    D. armature has a short

16.____

17. Suppose a newly installed D.C. shunt motor rotates in the wrong direction. This condition can be corrected by reversing the connections to

    A. the armature and the field only
    B. either the armature or the field
    C. the armature, the field, and the line
    D. the line only

17.____

18. Switches used to disconnect generator or synchronous motor fields are frequently designed to connect which of the following? A discharge

    A. *resistor* across the commutator before opening the circuit
    B. *capacitor* across the commutator after opening the circuit
    C. *capacitor* across the field after opening the circuit
    D. *resistor* across the field before opening the circuit

18.____

19 After grinding a new surface on a commutator having mica-insulated copper bars, it is good practice to

    A. side-cut the bars and under-cut the mica
    B. feather-edge the bars and create mica fins
    C. under-cut the bars and side-cut the mica
    D. dress both the bars and the mica until they are flush with each other

19.____

20. In a lap-wound D.C. motor armature, the two ends of each armature coil are *usually* connected to commutator segments that are

    A. adjacent to each other
    B. opposite from each other
    C. separated by 90 electrical degrees
    D. separated by 360 electrical degrees

20.____

KEY (CORRECT ANSWERS)

1.	B	11.	A
2.	D	12.	B
3.	D	13.	A
4.	D	14.	B
5.	A	15.	D
6.	D	16.	D
7.	A	17.	B
8.	A	18.	D
9.	B	19.	A
10.	A	20.	A

———

TEST 2

DIRECTIONS: Each question or incomplete statement is followed by several suggested answers or completions. Select the one that *BEST* answers the question or completes the statement. *PRINT THE LETTER OF THE CORRECT ANSWER IN THE SPACE AT THE RIGHT.*

1. The direction of rotation of an A.C. repulsion motor can be reversed by   1._____
   A. reversing the line connections
   B. reversing the field connections
   C. shifting the shading coil past the main stator winding
   D. shifting the brushes to the reverse side of the neutral

2. The number of threads per inch usually found on the threaded section of a 1-inch   2._____
   micrometer caliper's spindle, is
   A. 25   B. 40   C. 75   D. 100

3. Three-phase A.G. motors with six leads, when connected to star-delta starters,   3._____
   are usually run _____ and started _____.
   A. delta; star   B. delta; delta
   C. star; delta   D. star; star

4. In a typical three-phase A.C. electrically-operated magnetic motor starter,   4._____
   the auxiliary contact, the start button, and the stop button are usually connected
   so that the auxiliary contact is in
   A. *series* with both buttons   B. *series* with the start button
   C. *parallel* with both buttons   D. *parallel* with the start button

5. Of the following classifications of insulating materials used in electrical machinery,   5._____
   the one with the HIGHEST maximum safe-operating temperature is class
   A. A   B. B   C. H   D. 0

6. Of the following features, the one which makes it possible to operate certain   6._____
   circuit breakers remotely, regardless of load, is the
   A. shunt trip   B. gutter tap
   C. limiter lug   D. thermal element

7. Thermal magnetic circuit breakers usually provide _____ overload protection   7._____
   and _____ short circuit protection.
   A. instantaneous; instantaneous
   B. inverse time delay; instantaneous
   C. inverse time delay; inverse time delay
   D. instantaneous; inverse time delay

8. Following are sets of branch circuit numbers for an 18-circuit, sequence-phased, lighting panelboard equipped with single-phase circuit breakers in each circuit and connected to a three-phase, four-wire feeder.
   The set which consists of circuit numbers which are usually all connected to the same phase is

   A. 1, 2, 3, 4, 5, 6   B. 1, 3, 5, 7, 9, 11
   C. 2, 4, 6, 8, 10, 12   D. 1, 2, 7, 8, 13, 14

8.____

9. Unless otherwise specified, lighting panelboard boxes are usually manufactured with knockouts *only* on the

   A. top, bottom, and back   B. top, and both sides
   C. bottom, and both sides   D. top and bottom

9.____

10. When using a 12-point box wrench to turn a nut, the MINIMUM angle through which the wrench must be swung before the next set of points can be fitted to the corners of the nut, is

    A. 15°   B. 30°   C. 45°   D. 60°

10.____

11. Suppose that the floor plans for a certain building are drawn to a scale of 1/8" = 1'0". On these plans the distance between two symbols representing receptacle outlets measures 2 7/8" on an ordinary ruler.
    The actual distance between the two receptacle outlets installed at these locations should be

    A. 2 7/8 inches   B. 2 feet 7 inches
    C. 16 feet   D. 23 feet

11.____

12. Of the following combinations of switches, the one usually used when it is necessary to control a lighting fixture from five different locations, is

    A. two three-way switches and three four-way switches
    B. two four-way switches and three three-way switches
    C. five three-way switches
    D. five four-way switches

12.____

13. Of the following, the MOST common use for a Wheatstone bridge is to

    A. shunt leakage currents   B. measure resistances
    C. bypass faulty components D. support scaffolds

13.____

14. Suppose that, when both test-tips of a neon-glow lamp tester are properly placed across a live circuit, only one of its electrodes glows. Of the following, the *most likely* reason for this is that the circuit is

    A. D.C., and the glowing electrode is connected to the negative side
    B. D.C., and the glowing electrode is connected to the positive side
    C. A.C., and the voltage is too low to permit both electrodes to glow
    D. A.C., and the glowing electrode is connected to the grounded neutral

14.____

15. The specific gravity of a fully charged lead acid storage battery is, *most nearly,*

    A. 1.000   B. 1.150   C. 1.280   D. 1,830

15.____

16. The three regions in a junction transistor cross-section are *commonly* known as the

    16.____

    A. cathode, grid, and emitter regions
    B. collector, emitter, and base regions
    C. base, grid, and plate regions
    D. emitter, cathode, and screen regions

17. An axially color-coded fixed resistor, having neither a gold nor a silver marking, is only accurate to within _____ percent of its marked value.

    17.____

    A. 5　　　　　B. 10　　　　　C. 15　　　　　D. 20

18. Of the following sizes of machine screws, the one indicating the GREATEST number of threads per inch, is the

    18.____

    A. No. 6 - 32
    C. No. 14 - 18
    B. No. 10 - 24
    D. No. 30 - 14

19. The number of threads per inch MOST commonly used on 3/4 inch rigid conduit is

    19.____

    A. 27　　　　　B. 18　　　　　C. 14　　　　　D. 8

20. Of the following three-phase, 4-wire, secondary voltage combinations, the one MOST frequently used in industrial plants and commercial buildings, is _____ volts.

    20.____

    A. 138/240　　　B. 208/260　　　C. 277/480　　　D. 347/600

KEY (CORRECT ANSWERS)

1. D		11. D	
2. B		12. A	
3. A		13. B	
4. D		14. A	
5. C		15. C	
6. A		16. B	
7. B		17. D	
8. D		18. A	
9. D		19. C	
10. B		20. C	

TEST 3

DIRECTIONS: Each question or incomplete statement is followed by several suggested answers or completions. Select the one that *BEST* answers the question or completes the statement. *PRINT THE LETTER OF THE CORRECT ANSWER IN THE SPACE AT THE RIGHT.*

1. The total resistance of ten 5-ohm resistors connected in parallel is   1.____

    A. 50 ohms   B. 10 ohms   C. 2 ohms   D. 0.5 ohm

2. The power consumed by a 100-ohm resistor carrying a D.C. current of 5 amperes is   2.____

    A. 4 watts   B. 20 watts   C. 500 watts   D. 2500 watts

3. The impedance of a series circuit consisting of a 6-ohm resistor, a 12-ohm capacitive reactance, and a 4-ohm inductive reactance, is   3.____

    A. 22 ohms   B. 18 ohms   C. 16 ohms   D. 10 ohms

4. The capacitive reactance of a 60-Hertz A.C. circuit consisting of a 50 microfarad capacitor is, *most nearly,*   4.____

    A. .0188 ohm   B. .0200 ohm   C. 53 ohms   D. 3,000 ohms

5. A coil having an inductive reactance of 100 ohms is designed to operate satisfactorily at 120 volts and 60 Hertz. This coil has negligible resistance and is energized from a 120-volt, 25-Hertz source. In order not to exceed rated current, it will be necessary to add a resistance in series with the coil. The *value* of this resistance is, *most nearly,*   5.____

    A. 40 ohms   B. 60 ohms   C. 80 ohms   D. 100 ohms

6. The power factor of a single-phase A.G. circuit consuming 1,800 watts at 120 volts while drawing 20 amperes, is   6.____

    A. .50   B. .75   C. .86   D. 1.33

7. The MAXIMUM instantaneous voltage that occurs across a circuit which is connected to a common 120-volt, 60-Hertz, single-phase supply, is, *most nearly,*   7.____

    A. 120 volts   B. 141 volts   C. 170 volts   D. 208 volts

8. The line current in a three-phase, four-wire 120/208 volt feeder circuit, supplying a balanced 120-volt lighting load totaling 36 kilowatts, *is, most nearly,*   8.____

    A. 300 amps   B. 173 amps   C. 100 amps   D. 57 amps

9. Three equal resistors connected in delta across a three-phase, 120/208 volt supply, drawing line currents of 30 amperes, will each have a resistance of, *most nearly,*   9.____

    A. 4 ohms   B. 12 ohms   C. 33 ohms   D. 70 ohms

10. The full load-line current of a squirrel cage induction motor rated at 2 H.P., having an efficiency of 70%, a power factor of 70%, and connected to a 3-phase, 208-volt, 60-Hertz supply, is *most nearly*

    A. 1.5 amperes   B. 5.0 amperes
    C. 8.5 amperes   D. 14.5 amperes

10._____

11. A D.C. circuit consists of an unknown resistance in series with a five-ohm resistor. It is found that when a voltmeter is placed across the five-ohm resistor, it reads 40 volts.
If the voltmeter reads 54 volts when placed across the unknown resistance, the value of the unknown resistance is, *most nearly,*

    A. 3.7 ohms   B. 6.8 ohms   C. 7.0 ohms   D. 14.0 ohms

11._____

12. If the diameter of a copper wire is twice the diameter of another copper wire of the same length, the resistance of the first wire will be _____ the resistance of the second wire.

    A. 1/4 of   B. 1/2 of
    C. 2 times   D. 4 times

12._____

13. A defective 120-volt, 1-kilowatt electric heater needs a new heating element. If this element is to consist of a continuous length of nichrome wire having a resistance of 1.5 ohms per foot, the length of this wire should be, *most nearly,*

    A. 3.5 feet   B. 8.5 feet   C. 9.5 feet   D. 14.5 feet

13._____

14. The diameter of a round copper bus-bar having a circular cross-section with an area of 250,000 circular mils, is, *most nearly,*

    A. 1/4 inch   B. 1/2 inch   C. 2 1/2 inches   D. 5 inches

14._____

15. The number of circular mils in a copper wire whose diameter is 1/8" is, *most nearly,*

    A. 125,000   B. 15,625   C. 3,140   D. 387

15._____

16. A 2"-wide rectangular copper bus-bar is to carry 500 amperes D.C. without exceeding a maximum allowable current density of 1,000 amperes. The MINIMUM thickness of this bus-bar must be

    A. 1/8 inch   B. 3/16 inch   C. 1/4 inch   D. 1/2 inch

16._____

17. A three-phase, 60-Hertz A.C. squirrel cage induction motor will have a synchronous speed of 1200 rpm if it has

    A. 4 poles   B. 6 poles   C. 8 poles   D. 10 poles

17._____

18. The speed of a four-pole, three-phase, 60-Hertz, squirrel cage induction motor running with a slip of 5.6% will be, *most nearly,*

    A. 850 rpm   B. 1700 rpm   C. 2550 rpm   D. 3400 rpm

18._____

19. The full load-line current of a 1-horsepower, single-phase, 60-Hertz, A.C. motor, having an efficiency of 70 percent, is, *most nearly,* _____ amperes

    A. 4   B. 6   C. 8   D. 10

19._____

20. The percent regulation of a single-phase transformer whose secondary terminal voltage varies from 126 volts at no load, to 120 volts at full load, is, *most nearly,* _____ percent.

    A. 3.6   B. 4.8   C. 5.0   D. 6.0

20.____

KEY (CORRECT ANSWERS)

1.	D	11.	B
2.	D	12.	A
3.	D	13.	C
4.	C	14.	B
5.	B	15.	B
6.	B	16.	C
7.	C	17.	B
8.	C	18.	B
9.	B	19.	C
10.	C	20.	C

TEST 4

DIRECTIONS: Each question or incomplete statement is followed by several suggested answers or completions. Select the one that *BEST* answers the question or completes the statement. *PRINT THE LETTER OF THE CORRECT ANSWER IN THE SPACE AT THE RIGHT.*

1. When preparing fresh electrolyte for a lead-acid storage battery, it is considered best to pour the concentrated acid into the water rather than adding water to the concentrated acid. The MAIN reason for following this sequence is to prevent

   A. corrosion
   C. loss of concentrated acid
   B. sedimentation
   D. production of excessive heat

   1.____

2. Fire extinguishers suitable for use on an electrical fire should be identified by a

   A. five-pointed star containing the letter "D"
   B. triangle containing the letter "A"
   C. square containing the letter "B"
   D. circle containing the letter "C"

   2.____

3. The SMALLEST size of rigid conduit that may be installed when wiring for new branch circuit receptacle outlets is

   A. 1 inch   B. 3/4 inch   C.   1/2 inch   D. 3/8 inch

   3.____

4. Of the following, the *color* of a fixed equipment ground wire should be

   A. white   B. black   C. red   D. green

   4.____

5. Of the following, the HEAVIEST fixture that may be supported directly from its outlet box is one weighing

   A. 25 pounds   B. 35 pounds   C. 45 pounds   D. 55 pounds

   5.____

6. The SMALLEST size of copper wire that may be used as a system ground on an A.C. service is

   A. No. 6   B. No. 8   C. No. 10   D. No. 12

   6.____

7. The SMALLEST size of feeder conductor that must be stranded if installed in raceways is

   A. No. 6   B. No. 2   C. No. 1/0   D. 250 MCM

   7.____

8. Of the following locations, the *ones* usually classified as Class I hazardous locations are

   A. rooms used for spray painting
   C. cotton-waste storage rooms
   B. woodworking plants
   D. janitor's sink closets

   8.____

9. In relation to the allowable current carrying capacity of wiring it is protecting, the MAXIMUM value that an instantaneous magnetic trip circuit breaker may be set for is _____ of the allowable current-carrying capacity.

   A. 75%   B. 100%   C. 125%   D. 150%

   9.____

10. When installed in vertical raceways, 500 MCM feeders must be supported at intervals NOT greater than

    A. 100 feet   B. 75 feet   C. 50 feet   D. 25 feet

10.____

11. Sections of existing conduit exceeding 3 feet in length are being used to rewire for increased load, using more than four non-lead covered conductors. The MAXIMUM percentage of the conduit's cross-sectional area which may be occupied by these conductors is

    A. 60%   B. 50%   C. 40%   D. 30%

11.____

12. The MAXIMUM length of armored cable that may be exposed at the terminal connections of a ventilating fan located in a fan room is

    A. 8 feet   B. 6 feet   C. 4 feet   D. 2 feet

12.____

13. The MAXIMUM allowable current rating for a 250-volt ferrule contact, cartridge fuse is _____ amperes.

    A. 200   B. 100   C. 60   D. 30

13.____

14. An approved attachment plug and receptacle may be used as the controller for a portable motor whose horsepower rating is NOT larger than

    A. 1/4 HP   B. ½ HP   C. 1/2 HP   D. 1 HP

14.____

15. A printed or typed directory must be mounted in an approved manner on the door of a panelboard having more than _____ circuits.

    A. 4   B. 6   C. 8   D. 10

15.____

16. Surface metal raceways should NOT be used for wires larger than

    A. No. 6   B. No. 8   C. No. 10   D. No. 12

16.____

17. The MINIMUM length of a pull box with knockouts, installed in a run of 1 1/2-inch conduit containing a set of No 4 RH lighting panel feeders, is

    A. 24 inches   B. 18 inches   C. 12 inches   D. 6 inches

17.____

18. Suppose you find some of the conductors in a cutout box identified by means of a half-inch wide band of yellow tape. Of the following, it is *most likely* that these identified conductors are in circuits that are

    A. direct current   B. alternating current
    C. grounded   D. spares

18.____

19. The MINIMUM size of wire that may be used as fixture wire is

    A. No. 14   B. No. 16   C. No. 18   D. No. 20

19.____

20. The SMALLEST size of copper wire that may be used as an equipment ground if the branch circuit over-current device is rated at 20 amperes, is a

    A. No. 10   B. No. 12   C. No. 16   D. No. 18

20.____

KEY (CORRECT ANSWERS)

1.	D	11.	C
2.	D	12.	B
3.	C	13.	C
4.	D	14.	A
5.	C	15.	A
6.	B	16.	A
7.	A	17.	C
8.	A	18.	A
9.	C	19.	C
10.	C	20.	C

REPORT WRITING

EXAMINATION SECTION
TEST 1

DIRECTIONS: Each question or incomplete statement is followed by several suggested answers or completions. Select the one that *BEST* answers the question or completes the statement. *PRINT THE LETTER OF THE CORRECT ANSWER IN THE SPACE AT THE RIGHT.*

1. Following are six steps that should be taken in the course of report preparation: 1._____
     I.   Outlining the material for presentation in the report
     II.   Analyzing and interpreting the facts
     III. Analyzing the problem
     IV.   Reaching conclusions
     V.   Writing, revising, and rewriting the final copy
     VI.   Collecting data
   According to the principles of good report writing, the CORRECT order in which these steps should be taken is:

     A. VI, III, II, I, IV, V   B. III, VI, II, IV, I, V
     C. III, VI, II, I, IV, V   D. VI, II, III, IV, I, V

2. Following are three statements concerning written reports: 2._____
     I.   Clarity is generally more essential in oral reports than in written reports.
     II.   Short sentences composed of simple words are generally preferred to complex sentences and difficult words.
     III. Abbreviations may be used whenever they are customary and will not distract the attention of the reader
   Which of the following choices correctly classifies the above statements in to whose which are valid and those which are not valid?

     A. I and II are valid, but III is not valid.
     B. I is valid, but II and III are not valid.
     C. II and III are valid, but I is not valid.
     D. III is valid, but I and II are not valid.

3. In order to produce a report written in a style that is both understandable and effective,   3._____
   an investigator should apply the principles of unit, coherence, and emphasis. The one of the following which is the BEST example of the principle of coherence is

     A. interlinking sentences so that thoughts flow smoothly
     B. having each sentence express a single idea to facilitate comprehension
     C. arranging important points in prominent positions so they are not overlooked
     D. developing the main idea fully to insure complete consideration

4. Assume that a supervisor is preparing a report recommending that a standard work pro-   4._____
   cedure be changed. Of the following, the MOST important information that he should include in this report is

     A. a complete description of the present procedure
     B. the details and advantages of the recommended procedure

A. the type and amount of retraining needed
B. the percentage of men who favor the change

5. When you include in your report on an inspection some information which you have   5.____
obtained from other individuals, it is *MOST* important that

    A. this information have no bearing on the work these other people are performing
    B. you do not report as fact the opinions of other individuals
    C. you keep the source of the information confidential
    D. you do not tell the other individuals that their statements will be included in your report.

6. Before turning in a report of an investigation of an accident, you discover some additional   6.____
information you did not know about when you wrote the report.
Whether or not you re-write your report to include this additional information should
depend *MAINLY* on the

    A. source of this additional information
    B. established policy covering the subject matter of the report
    C. length of the report and the time it would take you to re-write it
    D. bearing this additional information will have on the conclusions in the report

7. The *most desirable FIRST* step in the planning of a written report is to   7.____

    A. ascertain what necessary information is readily available in the files
    B. outline the methods you will employ to get the necessary information
    C. determine the objectives and uses of the report
    D. estimate the time and cost required to complete the report

8. In writing a report, the practice of taking up the *least* important points *first* and the *most*   8.____
important points *last* is a

    A. *good* technique since the final points made in a report will make the greatest
impression on the reader
    B. *good* technique since the material is presented in a more logical manner and will
lead directly to the conclusions
    C. *poor* technique since the reader's time is wasted by having to review irrelevant
information before finishing the report
    D. *poor* technique since it may cause the reader to lose interest in the report and
arrive at incorrect conclusions about the report

9. Which one of the following serves as the *BEST* guideline for you to follow for effective   9.____
written reports? Keep sentences

    A. *short* and limit sentences to *one* thought
    B. *short* and use *as many* thoughts as possible
    C. *long* and limit sentences to *one* thought
    D. *long* and use *as many* thoughts as possible

10. One method by which a supervisor might prepare written reports to management is to   10.____
begin with the conclusions, results, or summary, and to follow this with the supporting
data.
The *BEST* reason why management may *prefer* this form of report is that

A. management lacks the specific training to understand the data
B. the data completely supports the conclusions
C. time is saved by getting to the conclusions of the report first
D. the data contains all the information that is required for making the conclusions

11. When making written reports, it is MOST important that they be   11._____

    A. well-worded   B. accurate as to the facts
    B. brief   D. submitted immediately

12. Of the following, the *MOST* important reason for a supervisor to prepare good written   12._____
reports is that

    A. a supervisor is rated on the quality of his reports
    B. decisions are often made on the basis of the reports
    C. such reports take less time for superiors to review
    D. such reports demonstrate efficiency of department operations

13. Of the following, the *BEST* test of a good report is whether it   13._____

    A. provides the information needed
    B. shows the good sense of the writer
    C. is prepared according to a proper format
    D. is grammatical and neat

14. When a supervisor writes a report, he can *BEST* show that he has an understanding of   14_____
the subject of the report by

    A. including necessary facts and omitting nonessential details
    B. using statistical data
    C. giving his conclusions but not the data on which they are based
    D. using a technical vocabulary

15. Suppose you and another supervisor on the same level are assigned to work together on   15._____
a report. You disagree strongly with one of the recommendations the other supervisor
wants to   include in the report but you cannot change his views.
Of the following, it would be BEST that

    A. you refuse to accept responsibility for the report
    B. you ask that someone else be assigned to this project to replace you
    C. each of you state his own ideas about this recommendation in the report
    D. you give in to the other supervisor's opinion for the sake of harmony

16. Standardized forms are often provided for submitting reports.   16._____
Of the following, the *MOST* important advantage of using standardized forms for
reports is that

    A. they take less time to prepare than individually written reports
    B. the person making the report can omit information he considers unimportant
    C. the responsibility for preparing these reports can be turned over to subordinates
    D. necessary information is less likely to be omitted

17. A report which may *BEST* be classed as a *periodic* report is one which   17. __

    A. requires the same type of information at regular intervals
    B. contains detailed information which is to be retained in permanent records
    C. is prepared whenever a special situation occurs
    D. lists information in graphic form

18. In the writing of reports or letters, the ideas presented in a paragraph are usually of   18. __
unequal importance and require varying degrees of emphasis.
All of the following are methods of placing extra stress on an idea *EXCEPT*

    A. repeating it in a number of forms
    B. placing it in the middle of the paragraph
    C. placing it either at the beginning or at the end of the paragraph
    D. underlining it

Questions 19-25.

DIRECTIONS: Questions 19 to 25 concern the subject of report writing and are based on the information and incidents described in the paragraph below. (In answering these questions, assume that the facts and incidents in the paragraph are true.)

On December 15, at 8 a.m., seven Laborers reported to Foreman Joseph Meehan in the Greenbranch Yard in Queens. Meehan instructed the men to load some 50-pound boxes of books on a truck for delivery to an agency building in Brooklyn. Meehan told the men that, because the boxes were rather heavy, two men should work together, helping each other lift and load each box. Since Michael Harper, one of the Laborers, was without a partner, Meehan helped him with the boxes for a while. When Meehan was called to the telephone in a nearby building, however, Harper decided to lift a box himself. He appeared able to lift the box, but, as he got the box halfway up, he cried out that he had a sharp pain in his back. Another Laborer, Jorge Ortiz, who was passing by, ran over to help Harper put the box down. Harper suddenly dropped the box, which fell on Ortiz' right foot. By this time Meehan had come out of the building. He immediately helped get the box off Ortiz' foot and had both men lie down. Meehan covered the men with blankets and called an ambulance, which arrived a half hour later. At the hospital, the doctor said that the X-ray results showed that Ortiz' right foot was broken in three places.

19. What would be the *BEST* term to use in a report describing the injury of Jorge Ortiz?   19. ___

    A. Strain   B. Fracture   C. Hernia   D. Hemorrhage

20. Which of the following would be the MOST accurate summary for the Foreman to put in   20. ___
his report of the incident?

    A. Ortiz attempted to help Harper carry a box which was too heavy for one person, but Harper dropped it before Ortiz got there.
    B. Ortiz tried to help Harper carry a box but Harper got a pain in his back and accidentally dropped the box on Ortiz' foot.
    C. Harper refused to follow Meehan's orders and lifted a box too heavy for him; he deliberately dropped it when Ortiz tried to help him carry it.
    D. Harper lifted a box and felt a pain in his back; Ortiz tried to help Harper put the box down but Harper accidentally dropped it on Ortiz' foot.

21. One of the Laborers at the scene of the accident was asked his version of the incident. 21.___
Which information obtained from this witness would be *LEAST* important for
including in the accident report?

  A. His opinion as to the cause of the accident
  B. How much of the accident he saw
  C. His personal opinion of the victims
  D. His name and address

22. What should be the *MAIN* objective of writing a report about the incident described in the 22.___
above paragraph? To

  A. describe the important elements in the accident situation
  B. recommend that such Laborers as Ortiz be advised not to interfere in
  another's work unless given specific instructions
  C. analyze the problems occurring when there are not enough workers to perform
  a certain task
  D. illustrate the hazards involved in performing routine everyday tasks

23. Which of the following is information *missing* from the passage above but which *should* 23.___
be included in a report of the incident? The

  A. name of the Laborer's immediate supervisor
  B. contents of the boxes
  C. time at which the accident occurred
  D. object or action that caused the injury to Ortiz' foot

24. According to the description of the incident, the accident occurred *because* 24.___

  A. Ortiz attempted to help Harper who resisted his help
  B. Harper failed to follow instructions given him by Meehan
  C. Meehan was not supervising his men as closely as he should have
  D. Harper was not strong enough to carry the box once he lifted it

25. Which of the following is *MOST* important for a foreman to *avoid* when writing up an offi- 25.___
cial accident report?

  A. Using technical language to describe equipment involved in the accident
  B. Putting in details which might later be judged unnecessary
  C. Giving an opinion as to conditions that contributed to the accident
  D. Recommending discipline for employees who, in his opinion, caused the accident

KEY (CORRECT ANSWERS)

1.	B		11.	B
2.	C		12.	B
3.	A		13.	A
4.	B		14.	A
5.	B		15.	C
6.	D		16.	D
7.	C		17.	A
8.	D		18.	B
9.	A		19.	B
10.	C		20.	D

21.	C
22.	A
23.	C
24.	B
25.	D

TEST 2

1. Lieutenant X is preparing a report to submit to his commanding officer in order to get approval of a plan of operation he has developed.
The report starts off with the statement of the problem and continues with the details of the problem. It contains factual information gathered with the help of field and operational personnel. It contains a final conclusion and recommendation for action. The recommendation is supplemented by comments from other precinct staff members on how the recommendations will affect their areas of responsibility. The report also includes directives and general orders ready for the commanding officer's signature. In addition, it has two statements of objections presented by two precinct staff members.
Which one of the following, if any, is *either* an item that Lieutenant X should have included in his report and which is not mentioned above, *or* is an item which Lieutenant X improperly did include in his report?   1. ___

   A. Considerations of alternative courses of action and their consequences should have been covered in the report.
   B. The additions containing documented objections to the recommended course of action should not have been included as part of the report.
   C. A statement on the qualifications of Lieutenant X, which would support his expertness in the field under consideration, should have been included in the report.
   D. The directives and general orders should not have been prepared and included in the report until the commanding officer had approved the recommendations.
   E. None of the above, since Lieutenant X's report was both proper and complete.

2. During a visit to a section, the district supervisor criticizes the method being used by the assistant foreman to prepare a certain report and orders him to modify the method. This change ordered by the district supervisor is in direct conflict with the specific orders of the foreman. In this situation, it would be *BEST* for the assistant foreman to   2. ___

   A. change the method and tell the foreman about the change at the first opportunity
   B. change the method and rely on the district supervisor to notify the foreman
   C. report the matter to the foreman and delay the preparation of the report
   D. ask the district supervisor to discuss the matter with the foreman but use the old method for the time being

3. A department officer should realize that the *most usual* reason for writing a report is to   3. ___

   A. give orders and follow up their execution
   B. establish a permanent record
   C. raise questions
   D. supply information

4. A very important report which is being prepared by a department officer will soon be due   4. ___
on the desk of the district supervisor. No typing help is available at this time for the officer. For the officer to write out this report in longhand in such a situation would be

A. *bad;* such a report would not make the impression a typed report would
B. *good;* it is important to get the report in on time
C. *bad;* the district supervisor should not be required to read longhand reports
D. *good;* it would call attention to the difficult conditions under which this section must work

5. In a well-written report, the length of each paragraph in the report should be   5.___

    A. varied according to the content
    B. not over 300 words
    C. pretty nearly the same
    D. gradually longer as the report is developed and written

6. A clerk in the headquarters office complains to you about the way in which you are filling   6.___
out a certain report. It would be *BEST* for you to

    A. tell the clerk that you are following official procedures in filling out the report
    B. ask to be referred to the clerk's superior
    C. ask the clerk exactly what is wrong with the way in which you are filling out the report
    D. tell the clerk that you are following the directions of the district supervisor

7. The use of an outline to help in writing a report is   7___

    A. *desirable* in order to insure good organization and coverage
    B. *necessary* so it can be used as an introduction to the report itself
    C. *undesirable* since it acts as a straight jacket and may result in an unbalanced report
    D. *desirable* if you know your immediate supervisor reads reports with extreme care and attention

8. It is advisable that a department officer do his paper work and report writing as soon as   8.___
he has completed an inspection *MAINLY* because

    A. there are usually deadlines to be met
    B. it insures a steady work-flow
    C. he may not have time for this later
    D. the facts are then freshest in his mind

9. Before you turn in a report you have written of an investigation that you have made, you   9.___
discover some additional information you didn't know about before. Whether or not you
re-write your report to include this additional information should depend *MAINLY* on the

    A. amount of time remaining before the report is due
    B. established policy of the department covering the subject matter of the report
    C. bearing this information will have on the conclusions of the report
    D. number of people who will eventually review the report

10. When a supervisory officer submits a periodic report to the district supervisor, he should   10.___
realize that the *CHIEF* importance of such a report is that it

    A. is the principal method of checking on the efficiency of the supervisor and his subordinates
    B. is something to which frequent reference will be made

C. eliminates the need for any personal follow-up or inspection by higher echelons
D. permits the district supervisor to exercise his functions of direction, supervision, and control better

11. Conclusions and recommendations are usually better placed at the *end* rather than at the *beginning* of a report because   11.____

    A. the person preparing the report may decide to change some of the conclusions and recommendations before he reaches the end of the report
    B. they are the most important part of the report
    C. they can be judged better by the person to whom the report is sent after he reads the facts and investigations which come earlier in the report
    D. they can be referred to quickly when needed without reading the rest of the report

12. The use of the same method of record-keeping and reporting by *all* agency sections is   12.____

    A. *desirable, MAINLY* because it saves time in section operations
    B. *undesirable, MAINLY* because it kills the initiative of the individual section foreman
    C. *desirable, MAINLY* because it will be easier for the administrator to evaluate and compare section operations
    D. *undesirable, MAINLY* because operations vary from section to section and uniform record-keeping and reporting is not appropriate

13. The *GREATEST* benefit the section officer will have from keeping complete and accurate records and reports of section operations is that   ____

    A. he will find it easier to run his section efficiently
    B. he will need less equipment
    C. he will need less manpower
    D. the section will run smoothly when he is out

14. You have prepared a report to your superior and are ready to send it forward. But on re-reading it, you think some parts are not clearly expressed and your superior may have difficulty getting your point.
Of the following, it would be *BEST* for you to   14.____

    A. give the report to one of your men to read, and if he has no trouble understanding it send it through
    B. forward the report and call your superior the next day to ask whether it was all right
    C. forward the report as is; higher echelons should be able to understand any report prepared by a section officer
    D. do the report over, re-writing the sections you are in doubt about

15. The *BEST* of the following statements concerning reports is that   15.____

    A. a carelessly written report may give the reader an impression of inaccuracy
    B. correct grammar and English are unimportant if the main facts are given
    C. every man should be required to submit a daily work report
    D. the longer and more wordy a report is, the better it will read

16. In writing a report, the question of whether or not to include certain material could be   16.
determined *BEST* by considering the

    A. amount of space the material will occupy in the report
    B. amount of time to be spent in gathering the material
    C. date of the material
    D. value of the material to the superior who will read the report

17. Suppose you are submitting a fairly long report to your superior. The *one* of the following   17.
sections that should come *FIRST* in this report is a

    A. description of how you gathered material
    B. discussion of possible objections to your recommendations
    C. plan of how your recommendations can be put into practice
    D. statement of the problem dealt with

Questions 18-20.

DIRECTIONS: A foreman is asked to write a report on the incident described in the following
              passage. Answer Questions 18 through 20 based on the following information.

On March 10, Henry Moore, a laborer, was in the process of transferring some equipment from the machine shop to the third floor. He was using a dolly to perform this task and,
as he was wheeling the material through the machine shop, laborer Bob Greene called to him.
As Henry turned to respond to Bob, he jammed the dolly into Larry Mantell's leg, knocking
Larry down in the process and causing the heavy drill that Larry was holding to fall on Larry's
foot. Larry started rubbing his foot and then, infuriated, jumped up and punched Henry in the
jaw. The force of the blow drove Henry's head back against the wall. Henry did not fight back;
he appeared to be dazed. An ambulance was called to take Henry to the hospital, and the
ambulance attendant told the foreman that it appeared likely that Henry had suffered a
concussion. Larry's injuries consisted of some bruises, but he refused medical attention.

18. An adequate report of the above incident should give as minimum information the names   18.
of the persons involved, the names of the witnesses, the date and the time that each event
took place, *and* the

    A. names of the ambulance attendants
    B. names of all the employees working in the machine shop
    C. location where the accident occurred
    D. nature of the previous safety training each employee had been given

19. The *only* one of the following which is *NOT* a fact is   19.

    A. Bob called to Henry
    B. Larry suffered a concussion
    C. Larry rubbed his foot
    D. the incident took place in the machine shop

20. Which of the following would be, the MOST accurate summary of the incident for the foreman to put in his report of the accident?   20. ___

    A. Larry Mantell punched Henry Moore because a drill fell on his foot and he was angry. Then Henry fell and suffered a concussion.
    B. Henry Moore accidentally jammed a dolly into Larry Mantell's foot, knocking Larry down. Larry punched Henry, pushing him into the wall and causing him to bang his head against the wall.
    C. Bob Greene called Henry Moore. A dolly then jammed into Larry Mantell and knocked him down. Larry punched Henry who tripped and suffered some bruises. An ambulance was called.
    D. A drill fell on Larry Mantell's foot. Larry jumped up suddenly and punched Henry Moore and pushed him into the wall. Henry may have suffered a concussion as a result of falling.

Questions 21-25.

DIRECTIONS: Answer Questions 21 through 25 *only* on the basis of the information provided in the following passage.

A written report is a communication of information from one person to another. It is an account of some matter especially investigated, however routine that matter may be. The ultimate basis of any good written report is facts, which become known through observation and verification. Good written reports may seem to be no more than general ideas and opinions. However, in such cases, the facts leading to these opinions were gathered, verified, and reported earlier, and the opinions are dependent upon these facts. Good style, proper form and emphasis cannot make a good written report out of unreliable information and bad judgment; but, on the other hand, solid investigation and brilliant thinking are not likely to become very useful until they are effectively communicated to others. If a person's work calls for written reports, then his work is often no better than his written reports.

21. Based on the information in the passage, it can be concluded that opinions expressed in a report should be   21. ___

    A. based on facts which are gathered and reported
    B. emphasized repeatedly when they result from a special investigation
    C. kept to a minimum
    D. separated from the body of the report

22. In the above passage, the one of the following which is mentioned as a way of establishing facts is   22. ___

    A. authority
    C. reporting
    B. communication
    D. verification

23. According to the passage, the characteristic shared by *all* written reports is that they are   23. ___

    A. accounts of routine matters
    B. transmissions of information
    C. reliable and logical
    D. written in proper form

24. Which of the following conclusions can *logically* be drawn from the information given in the passage?   24.

        A. Brilliant thinking can make up for unreliable information in a report.
        B. One method of judging an individual's work is the quality of the written reports he is required to submit.
        C. Proper form and emphasis can make a good report out of unreliable information.
        D. Good written reports that seem to be no more than general ideas should be rewritten.

25. Which of the following suggested titles would be *MOST* appropriate for this passage?   25.

        A. Gathering and Organizing Facts
        B. Techniques of Observation
        C. Nature and Purpose of Reports
        D. Reports and Opinions: Differences and Similarities

---

KEY (CORRECT ANSWERS)

1. A	11. C		
2. A	12. C		
3. D	13. A		
4. B	14. D		
5. A	15. A		
6. C	16. D		
7. A	17. D		
8. D	18. C		
9. C	19. B		
10. D	20. B		

21. A
22. D
23. B
24. B
25. C

TEST 3

Questions 1-5.

DIRECTIONS: The following is an accident report similar to those used in departments for reporting accidents. Answer Questions 1 to 5 using *only* the information given in this report.

ACCIDENT REPORT

FROM *John Doe*	**DATE OF REPORT** *June 23*
TITLE *Sanitation Man*	
DATE OF ACCIDENT *June 22* time *3* ~~AM~~ PM	**CITY** *Metropolitan*
PLACE *1489 Third Avenue*	
VEHICLE NO. *1*	**VEHICLE NO.** *2*
OPERATOR John Doe, *Sanitation Man* TITLE	**OPERATOR** *Richard Roe*
VEHICLE CODE NO. *14-238*	**ADDRESS** *498 High Street*
LICENSE NO. *0123456*	**OWNER** *Henry Roe* **LIC NUMBER** *5N1492* **ADDRESS** *786 E. 83 St*

DESCRIPTION OF ACCIDENT *Light green Chevrolet sedan while trying to pass drove in to rear side of Sanitation truck which had stopped to collect garbage. No one was injured but there was property damage.*

NATURE OF DAMAGE TO PRIVATE VEHICLE *Right front fender crushed, bumper bent.*

DAMAGE TO CITY VEHICLE *Front of left rear fender pushed in. Paint scraped.*

NAME OF WITNESS *Frank Brown*	**ADRESS** *48 Kingsway*
John Doe **Signature of person making this report**	**BADGE NO.** *428*

1. Of the following, the one which has been omitted from this accident report is the

    A.   location of the accident
    B.   drivers of the vehicles involved
    C.   traffic situation at the time of the accident
    D.   owners of the vehicles involved

1. ____

2. The address of the driver of Vehicle No. 1 is not required because he

    A.   is employed by the department
    B.   is not the owner of the vehicle
    C.   reported the accident
    D.   was injured in the accident

2. ____

3. The report indicates that the driver of Vehicle No. 2 was *probably* 3._

    A. passing on the wrong side of the truck
    B. not wearing his glasses
    C. not injured in the accident
    D. driving while intoxicated

4. The number of people *specifically* referred to in this report is 4._

    A. 3   B. 4   C. 5   D. 6

5. The license number of Vehicle No. 1 is 5._

    A. 428   B. 5N1492   C. 14-238   D. 0123456

6. In a report of unlawful entry into department premises, it is *LEAST* important to include the 6._

    A. estimated value of the property missing
    B. general description of the premises
    C. means used to get into the premises
    D. time and date of entry

7. In a report of an accident, it is *LEAST* important to include the 7._

    A. name of the insurance company of the person injured in the accident
    B. probable cause of the accident
    C. time and place of the accident
    D. names and addresses of all witnesses of the accident

8. Of the following, the one which is_____ *NOT* required in the preparation of a weekly functional expense report is the

    A. hourly distribution of the time by proper heading in accordance with the actual work performed
    B. signatures of officers not involved in the preparation of the report
    C. time records of the men who appear on the payroll of the respective locations
    D. time records of men working in other districts assigned to this location

KEY (CORRECT ANSWERS)

1. C	5. D
2. A	6. B
3. C	7. A
4. B	8. B

EXAMINATION SECTION
TEST 1

DIRECTIONS: Each question or incomplete statement is followed by several suggested answers or completions. Select the one that BEST answers the question or completes the statement. *PRINT THE LETTER OF THE CORRECT ANSWER IN THE SPACE AT THE RIGHT.*

1. A supervisor was given a booklet that showed a new work method that could save time. He didn't tell his men because he thought that they would get the booklet anyway. For the supervisor to have acted like this is a

    A. *good* idea because he saves the time and bother of talking to the men
    B. *bad* idea because he should make sure his men know about better work methods
    C. *good* idea because the men would rather read about it themselves
    D. *bad* idea because a supervisor should always show his men every memo he gets from higher authority

1.____

2. A supervisor found it necessary to discipline two subordinates. One man had been oper-ating his equipment in a wrong way, while the other man came to work late for three days in a row. The supervisor decided to talk to both men together. For the supervisor to deal with the problems in this way is a

    A. *good* idea because each man will learn about the difficulties of the other person and how to solve such difficulties
    B. *bad* idea because the supervisor should wait until he can bring a larger group together and save time in discussing such questions
    C. *good* idea because he will be able to get the men to see that their problems are related
    D. *bad* idea because he should meet with each man separately and give him his full attention

2.____

3. A supervisor should try to make his men feel their jobs are important in order to

    A. get the men to say good things about their supervisor to his own superior
    B. get the men to think in terms of advancing to better jobs
    C. let higher management in the agency know that the supervisor is efficient
    D. help the men to be able to work more efficiently and enthusiastically

3.____

4. A supervisor should know approximately how long it takes to do a particular kind of job CHIEFLY because he

    A. will know how much time to take if he has to do it himself
    B. will be able to tell his men to do it even faster
    C. can judge the performance of the person doing the job
    D. can retrain experienced employees in better work habits

4.____

5. Supervisors often get their employees' opinions about better work methods because

    A. the men will know that they are respected
    B. the men would otherwise lose all their confidence in the supervisor
    C. the supervisor might find in this way a good suggestion he could use
    D. this is the best method for improvement of work methods

5.____

6. Right after you have trained your subordinates in doing a new job, you find that they   6.___
seem to be doing all right, but that it will take them several days to finish. You also have
several groups of men working at other locations. The MOST efficient way for you to
make sure that the men continue doing the new job properly is to

    A.   stay on that job with the men until it is finished just in case trouble develops
    B.   visit the men every half hour until the job is done
    C.   stay away from their job that day and visit the men the next day to ask them if they
        had any problems
    D.   visit the men a few times each day until they finish the new job

7. Assume that one of your new employees is older than you are. You also think that he   7.___
may be hard to get along with because he is older than you. The BEST way for you to
avoid any problems with the older worker is for you to

    A.   lay down the law immediately and tell the man he better not cause you any trouble
    B.   treat the man just the way you would any other worker
    C.   always ask the older worker for advice in the presence of all the men
    D.   ignore the man entirely until he realizes that you are the boss

8. Assume that you have tried a new method suggested by one of your employees and find   8.___
that it is easier and cheaper than the method you had been using.
The proper thing for you to do NEXT is to

    A.   say nothing to anyone but train your men to use the new method
    B.   train your men to use the new method and tell your crew that you got the idea from
        one of the men
    C.   continue using the old method because a supervisor should not use suggestions of
        his men
    D.   have your crew learn the new method and take credit for the idea since you are the
        boss

9. Suppose you are a supervisor and your superior tells you that the way your men are   9.___
doing a certain procedure is wrong and that you should re-train your men as soon as
possible.
When you begin to re-train the men, the FIRST thing you should do is

    A.   tell your men that a wrong procedure had been used and that a new method must
        be learned as a result
    B.   train your employees in the new method with no explanation since you are the boss
    C.   tell the crew that your superior has just decided that everyone should learn a new
        method
    D.   tell the crew that your superior says your method is wrong but that you don't agree
        with this

10. It is BAD practice to criticize a man in front of the other men because   10.___

    A.   people will think you are too strict
    B.   it is annoying to anyone who walks by
    C.   it is embarrassing to the man concerned
    D.   it will antagonize the other men

11. A supervisor decides not to put his two best men on a work detail because he knows that 11.____
they won't like it.
For the supervisor to make the work assignment this way is a

    A. *good* idea because it is only fair to give your best men a break once in a while
    B. *bad* idea because you should treat all of your men fairly and not show favoritism
    C. *good* idea because you save the strength of these men for another job
    D. *bad* idea because more of the men should be exempted from the assignment

12. Suppose you are a supervisor and you find it inconvenient to obey an established proce- 12.____
dure set by your agency. You think another procedure would be better.
The BEST thing to do first about this procedure that you don't like is for you to

    A. obey the procedure even if you don't want to and suggest your idea to your own
       supervisor
    B. disregard the procedure because a supervisor is supposed to have some privi-
       leges
    C. follow the procedure some of the time but ignore it when the men are not watching
    D. organize a group of other supervisors to get the procedure changed

13. A supervisor estimated that it would take his crew one workday per week to do a certain 13.____
job each week. However, after a month he noticed that the job averaged two and a half
days a week and this delayed other jobs that had to be done.
The FIRST thing that the supervisor should do in this case is to

    A. call his men together and warn them that they will get a poor work evaluation if they
       do not work harder
    B. talk to each man personally, asking him to work harder on the job
    C. go back and study the maintenance job by himself to see if more men should be
       assigned to the job
    D. write his boss a report describing in detail how much time it is taking the men to do
       the job

14. An employee complains to you that some of his work assignments are too difficult to do 14.____
alone.
Which of the following is the BEST way for you to handle this complaint?

    A. Go with him to see exactly what he does and why he finds it so difficult.
    B. Politely tell the man that he has to do the job or be brought up on charges.
    C. Tell the man to send his complaint to the head of your agency.
    D. Sympathize with the man and give him easier jobs.

15. The BEST way for a supervisor to keep control of his work assignments is to 15.____

    A. ask the men to report to him immediately when their jobs are finished
    B. walk around the buildings once a week and get a firsthand view of what is being
       done
    C. keep his ears open for problems and complaints, but leave the men alone to do the
       work
    D. write up a work schedule and check it periodically against the actual work done

16. A supervisor made a work schedule for his men. At the bottom of it, he wrote, *No changes or exceptions will be made in this schedule for any reason.*
For the supervisor to have made this statement is

16.___

   A. *good* because the men will respect the supervisor for his attitude
   B. *bad because* there are emergencies and special situations that occur
   C. *good* because each man will know exactly what is expected of him
   D. *bad* because the men should expect that no changes will ever be made in the work schedule without written permission

17. Which one of the following would NOT be a result of a well-planned work schedule?
The schedule

17.___

   A. makes efficient use of the time of the staff
   B. acts as a check list for an important job that might be left out
   C. will give an idea of the work to a substitute supervisor
   D. shows at a glance who the best men are

18. A new piece of equipment you have ordered is delivered. You are familiar with it, but the men under you who will use it do not know the equipment. Of the following methods, which is the BEST to take in explaining to them how to operate this equipment?

18.___

   A. Ask the men to watch other crews using the equipment.
   B. Show one reliable man how to operate the equipment and ask him to teach the other men.
   C. Ask the men to read the instructions in the manual for the equipment.
   D. Call the men together and show them how to operate the equipment.

19. One supervisor assigns work to his men by calling his crew together each week and describing what has to be done that week. He then tells them to arrange individual assignments among themselves and to work as a team during the week.
This method of scheduling work is a

19.___

   A. *good* idea because this guarantees that the men will work together
   B. *bad* idea because responsibility for doing the job is poorly fixed
   C. *good* idea because the men will finish the job in less time, working together
   D. *bad* idea because the supervisor should always stay with his men

20. Suppose that an employee came to his supervisor with a problem concerning his assignment.
For the supervisor to listen to this problem is a

20.___

   A. *good* idea because a supervisor should always take time off to talk when one of his men wants to talk
   B. *bad* idea because the supervisor should not be bothered during the work day
   C. *good* idea because it is the job of the supervisor to deal with problems of job assignment
   D. *bad* idea because the employee could start annoying the supervisor with all sorts of problems

21. Suppose that on the previous afternoon you were looking for an experienced employee   21._____
in order to give him an emergency job and he was missing from his job location. The next
morning, he tells you that he got sick suddenly and had to go home, but could not tell you
since you were not around. He has never done this before.
What should you do?

    A.   Tell the man he is excused and that in such circumstances he did the wisest thing.
    B.   Bring the man up on charges because whatever he says he could still have notified
         you.
    C.   Have the man examined by a doctor to see if he really was sick the day before.
    D.   Explain to the man that he should make every effort to tell you or to get a message
         to you if he must leave.

22. An employee had a grievance and went to his supervisor about it. The employee was not   22._____
satisfied with the way the supervisor tried to help him and told him so. Yet, the supervisor
had done everything he could under the circumstances.
The PROPER action for the supervisor to take at this time is to

    A.   politely tell the employee that there is nothing more for the supervisor to do about
         the problem
    B.   let the employee know how he can bring his complaint to a higher authority
    C.   tell the employee that he must solve the problem on his own since he did not want
         to follow the supervisor's advice
    D.   suggest to the employee that he ask another supervisor for assistance

23. In which of the following situations is it BEST to give your men spoken rather than written   23._____
orders?

    A.   You want your men to have a record of the instructions.
    B.   Spoken instructions are less likely to be forgotten.
    C.   An emergency situation has arisen in which there is no time to write up instruc-
         tions.
    D.   There are instructions on time and leave regulations which are complicated.

24. One of your employees tells you that a week ago he had a small accident on the job but   24._____
he did not bother telling you because he was able to continue working.
For the employee not to have told his supervisor about the accident was

    A.   *good* because the accident was a small one
    B.   *bad* because all accidents should be reported, no matter how small
    C.   *good* because the supervisor should be bothered only for important matters
    D.   *bad* because having an accident is one way to get excused for the day

25. For a supervisor to deal with each of his subordinates in exactly the same manner is   25._____

    A.   *poor* because each man presents a different problem and there is no one way of
         handling all problems
    B.   *good* because once a problem is handled with one man, he can handle another
         man with the same problem
    C.   *poor* because the men will resent it if they are not handled each in a better way
         than others
    D.   *good* because this assures fair and impartial treatment of each subordinate

KEY (CORRECT ANSWERS)

1.	B		11.	B
2.	D		12.	A
3.	D		13.	C
4.	C		14.	A
5.	C		15.	D
6.	D		16.	B
7.	B		17.	D
8.	B		18.	D
9.	A		19.	B
10.	C		20.	C

21.	D
22.	B
23.	C
24.	B
25.	A

TEST 2

DIRECTIONS: Each question or incomplete statement is followed by several suggested answers or completions. Select the one that BEST answers the question or completes the statement. *PRINT THE LETTER OF THE CORRECT ANSWER IN THE SPACE AT THE RIGHT.*

1. Jim Johnson has been on your staff for over four years. He has always been a conscientious and productive worker. About a month ago, his wife died; and since that time, his work performance has been very poor.
    As his supervisor, which one of the following is the BEST way for you to deal with this situation?

    A.   Allow Jim as much time as he needs to overcome his grief and hope that his work performance improves.
    B.   Meet with Jim to discuss ways to improve his performance.
    C.   Tell Jim directly that you are more concerned with his work performance than with his personal problem.
    D.   Prepare disciplinary action on Jim as soon as possible.

1.____

2. You are responsible for the overall operation of a storehouse which is divided into two sections. Each section has its own supervisor. You have decided to make several complex changes in the storekeeping procedures which will affect both sections.
    Of the following, the BEST way to make sure that these changes are understood by the two supervisors is for you to

    A.   meet with both supervisors to discuss the changes
    B.   issue a memorandum to each supervisor explaining the changes
    C.   post the changes where the supervisors are sure to see them
    D.   instruct one supervisor to explain the changes to the other supervisor

2.____

3. You have called a meeting of all your subordinates to tell them what has to be done on a new project in which they will all be involved. Several times during the meeting, you ask if there are any questions about what you have told them.
    Of the following, to ask the subordinates whether there are any questions during the meeting can BEST be described as

    A.   *inadvisable* because it interferes with their learning about the new project
    B.   *advisable* because you will find out what they don't understand and have a chance to clear up any problems they may have
    C.   *inadvisable* because it makes the meeting too long and causes the subordinates to lose interest in the new project
    D.   *advisable* because it gives you a chance to learn which of your subordinates are paying attention to what you say

3.____

4. As a supervisor, you are responsible for seeing to it that absenteeism does not become a problem among your subordinates.
    Which one of the following is NOT an acceptable way of controlling the problem of excessive absences?

    A.   Distribute a written statement to your staff on the policies regarding absenteeism in your organization.
    B.   Arrange for workers who have the fewest absences to talk to those workers who have the most absences.
    C.   Let your subordinates know that a record is being kept of all absences.
    D.   Arrange for counseling of those employees who are frequently absent.

4.____

5. One of your supervisors has been an excellent worker for the past two years. There are 5.__
no promotion opportunities for this worker in the foreseeable future. Due to the city's
present budget crisis, a salary increase is not possible.
Under the circumstances, which one of the following actions on your part would be
MOST likely to continue to motivate this worker?

    A. Tell the worker that times are bad all over and jobs are hard to find.
    B. Give the worker less work and easier assignments.
    C. Tell the worker to try to look for a better paying job elsewhere.
    D. Seek the worker's advice often and show that the suggestions provided are appreciated.

6. As a supervisor in a warehouse, it is important that you use your available work force to 6.__
its fullest potential. Which one of the following actions on your part is MOST likely to
increase the effectiveness of your work force?

    A. Assigning more workers to a job than the number actually needed.
    B. Eliminating all job training to allow more time for work output.
    C. Using your best workers on jobs that average workers can do.
    D. Making sure that all materials and equipment used are maintained in good working
order.

7. You learn that your storage area will soon be undergoing changes which will affect the 7.__
work of your subordinates. You decide not to tell your subordinates about what is to happen.
Of the following, your action can BEST be described as

    A. wise because your subordinates will learn of the changes for themselves
    B. unwise because your subordinates should be advised about what is to happen
    C. wise because it is better for your subordinates to continue working without being
disturbed by such news
    D. unwise because the work of your subordinates will gradually slow down

8. In making plans for the operation of your unit, you are MOST likely to see these plans 8.__
carried out successfully if you

    A. allow your staff to participate in developing these plans
    B. do not spend any time on the minor details of these plans
    C. base these plans on the past experiences of others
    D. allow these plans to interact with outside activities in other units

9. As a supervisor in charge of the total operation of a food supply warehouse, you find 9.__
vandalism to be a potentially serious problem. On occasion, trespassers have gained
entrance into the facility by climbing over an unprotected 8-foot fence surrounding the
warehouse whose dimensions measure 100 feet by 100 feet.
Assuming that all of the following would be equally effective ways in preventing these
breaches in security in the situation described above, which one would be LEAST
costly?

    A. Using two trained guard dogs to roam freely throughout the facility at night.
    B. Hiring a security guard to patrol the facility after working hours.
    C. Installing tape razor wire on top of the fence surrounding the facility.
    D. Installing an electronic burglar alarm system requiring the installation of a new
fence.

10. The area for which you have program responsibility has undergone recent changes. Your staff is now required to perform many new tasks, and morale is low.
The LEAST effective way for you to improve long-term staff morale would be to

    A. develop support groups to discuss problems
    B. involve staff in job development
    C. maintain a comfortable social environment within the group
    D. adequately plan and give assignments in a timely manner

10.____

11. As a supervisor in a large office, one of your subordinate supervisors stops you in the middle of the office and complains loudly that he is being treated unfairly. The rest of the staff ceases work and listens to the complaint. The MOST appropriate action for you to take in this situation is to

    A. ignore this unprofessional behavior and continue on your way
    B. tell the supervisor that his behavior is unprofessional and he should learn how to conduct himself
    C. explain to the supervisor why you believe he is not being treated unfairly
    D. ask the supervisor to come to your office at a specific time to discuss the matter

11.____

12. You are told that one of your subordinates is distributing literature which attempts to recruit individuals to join a particular organization. Several workers complain that their rights are being violated. Of the following, the BEST action for you to take FIRST is to

    A. ignore the situation because no harm is being done
    B. discuss the matter further with your supervisor
    C. ask the worker to stop distributing the literature
    D. tell the workers that they do not have to read the material

12.____

13. You have been assigned to develop a short training course for a recently issued procedure.
In designing this course, which of the following statements is the LEAST important for you to consider?

    A. The learning experience must be interesting and meaningful in terms of the staff member's job.
    B. The method of teaching must be strictly followed in order to develop successful learning experiences.
    C. The course content should incorporate the rules and regulations of the agency.
    D. The procedure should be consistent with the agency's objectives.

13.____

14. As a supervisor, there are several newly-promoted employees under your supervision. Each of these employees is subject to a probationary period PRIMARILY to

    A. assess the employee's performance to see if the employee should be retained or removed from the position
    B. give the employee the option to return to his former employment if the employee is unhappy in the new position
    C. give the employee an opportunity to learn the duties and responsibilities of the position
    D. judge the employee's potential for upward mobility in the future

14.____

15. An employee under your supervision rushes into your office to tell you he has just   15.__
received a telephone bomb threat.
As the administrative supervisor, the FIRST thing you should do is

    A. evacuate staff from the floor
    B. call the police and building security
    C. advise your administrator
    D. do a preliminary search

16. After reviewing the Absence Control form for a unit under your supervision, you find that   16.__
one of your staff members has a fifth undocumented sick leave within a six-month period.
In this situation, the FIRST action you should take is to

    A. discuss the seriousness of the matter with the staff member when he returns to
work and fully document the details of the discussion
    B. review the case with the location director and warn the staff member that future
use of sick leave will be punished
    C. submit the proper disciplinary forms to ensure that the staff member is penalized
for excessive absences
    D. request that the timekeeper put the staff member on doctor's note restriction

17. A subordinate supervisor recently assigned to your office begins his first conference with   17.__
you by saying that he has learned something that another supervisor is doing that you
should know about.
After hearing this statement, of the following, the BEST approach for you to take is to

    A. explain to the supervisor that the conference is to discuss his work and not that of
his co-workers
    B. tell the supervisor that you do not encourage a spy *system* among the staff you
supervise
    C. tell the supervisor that you will listen to his report only if the other supervisor is
present
    D. allow the supervisor to continue talking until you have enough information to make
a decision on how best to respond

18. Assume that you are a supervisor recently assigned to a new unit. You notice that, for the   18.__
past few days, one of the employees in your unit whose work is about average has been
stopping work at about four o'clock and has been spending the rest of the afternoon
relaxing at his desk.
The BEST of the following actions for you to take in this situation is to

    A. assign more work to this employee since it is apparent that he does not have
enough work to keep him busy
    B. observe the employee's conduct more closely for about ten days before taking any
more positive action
    C. discuss the matter with the employee, pointing out to him how he can use the extra
hour daily to raise the level of his job performance
    D. question the previous supervisor in charge of the unit in order to determine
whether he had sanctioned such conduct when he supervised that unit

19. A new supervisor was assigned to your program four months ago. Although he tries   19.____
hard, he has been unable to meet certain standards because he still has a lot to learn. As
his supervisor, you are required to submit performance evaluations within a few days.
How would you rate this employee on the tasks where he fails to meet standards
because of lack of experience?

    A. Satisfactory   B. Conditional
    C. Unsatisfactory   D. Unratable

20. You find that there is an important procedural error in a memo which you distributed to   20.____
your staff several days ago. The BEST approach for you to take at this time is to

    A. send a corrected memo to the staff, indicating what prior error was made
    B. send a corrected memo to the staff without mentioning the prior error
    C. tell the staff about the error at the next monthly staff meeting
    D. place the corrected memo on the office bulletin board

21. Your superior asks you, a supervisor, about the status of the response to a letter from a   21.____
public official concerning a client's case. When you ask the subordinate who was
assigned to prepare the response to give you the letter, the subordinate denies that it
was given to him. You are certain that the subordinate has the letter, but is withholding it
because the response has not yet been prepared.
Of the following, in order to secure the letter from the subordinate, you should FIRST

    A. accuse the subordinate of lying and demand that the letter be given to you immedi-
ately
    B. say that you would consider it a personal favor if the subordinate would find the let-
ter
    C. continue to question the subordinate until he admits to having been given the letter
    D. offer a face-saving solution, such as asking the subordinate to look again for the
letter

22. As a supervisor, you have been assigned to write a few paragraphs to be included in the   22.____
agency's annual report, describing a public service agency department this year as compared to last year.
Which of the following elements basic to the agency is LEAST likely to have changed
since last year?

    A. Mission   B. Structure
    C. Technology   D. Personnel

23. As a supervisor, you have been informed that a grievance has been filed against you,   23.____
accusing you of assigning a subordinate to out-of-title tasks. Of the following, the BEST
approach for you to take is to

    A. waive the grievance so that it will proceed to a Step II hearing
    B. immediately change the subordinate's assignment to avoid future problems
    C. respond to the grievance, giving appropriate reasons for the assignment
    D. review the job description to ensure that the subordinate's tasks are not out-of-title

24. Which of the following is NOT a correct statement about agency group training programs in a public service agency?

   A. Training sessions continue for an indefinite period of time.
   B. Group training sessions are planned for designated personnel.
   C. Training groups are organized formally through administrative planning.
   D. Group training is task-centered and aimed toward accomplishing specific educational goals.

24.__

25. As a supervisor, you have submitted a memo to your superior requesting a conference to discuss the performance of a manager under your supervision. The memo states that the manager has a good working relationship with her staff; however, she tends to interpret agency policy too liberally and shows poor administrative skills by missing some deadlines and not keeping proper controls.
   Which of the following steps should NOT be taken in order to prepare for this conference with your superior?

   A. Collect and review all your notes regarding the manager's prior performance.
   B. Outline your agenda so that you will have sufficient time to discuss the situation.
   C. Tell the manager that you will be discussing her performance with your superior.
   D. Clearly define objectives which will focus on improving the manager's performance.

25.__

_____

KEY (CORRECT ANSWERS)

1.	B		11.	D
2.	A		12.	C
3.	B		13.	B
4.	B		14.	A
5.	D		15.	B
6.	D		16.	A
7.	B		17.	D
8.	A		18.	C
9.	C		19.	B
10.	C		20.	A

21.	D
22.	A
23.	C
24.	A
25.	C

_____

BASIC FUNDAMENTALS OF
ELECTRICAL MEASUREMENT

CONTENTS

BASIC FUNDAMENTALS OF ELECTRICAL MEASUREMENT

I. INTRODUCTION TO DC PARAMETERS

The use of electrical instruments and equipment to make measurements has become a major source of information and data in the complex manufacturing system as it is known today. Sophisticated techniques for electrical measurement were not introduced until the twentieth century, although the study of electrical phenomena dates back to the time of Benjamin Franklin and the American Revolution.

Measurement for electrical parameters is primarily the measurement of voltage, current, resistance, and frequency. However, most electrical measurements require only the measurement of current and voltage. The symbols for the basic electrical measurement parameters are:

I = Current   where   I =

E = Voltage   E =

R = Resistance   R =

F = Frequency

Diagrammatic symbolization of these basic parameters in direct and alternating current are:

$\textcircled{I}$ and → =   Current

⊪   =   Voltage

〰 =   Resistance

Voltage is the force that makes current move through the wires of a circuit. Current is the actual movement of electrons through a wire. Resistance is the force that controls the amount of current that can pass through a wire. Frequency in alternating current is the number of cycles occurring in each second of time.

Both voltage and current can be measured with a simple electrical meter which uses magnetism and magnetic characteristics to measure the amount of current that flows. When a meter is connected to an electrical circuit, the flow of current through the coils of the meter creates a magnetic force. This magnetic force is used to move a needle. The amount of voltage, current, and resistance is shown by the position of the needle. The greater the current or voltage, the more the needle moves. To make the measurement easier, a scale is placed behind the needle to measure its movement. This scale is marked to show the value of current on voltage or resistance. The element the meter will measure is determined by the way the meter circuit is constructed and the way the meter is connected to the electrical circuit.

Where a meter is used to measure electrical values, a different circuit is required for each type of measurement. To determine the circuits used, a definition of series and parallel circuits must be made. Resistance in a series circuit is depicted as follows:

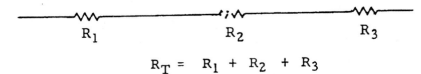

$$R_T = R_1 + R_2 + R_3$$

When two resistors are connected in parallel, they are illustrated as:

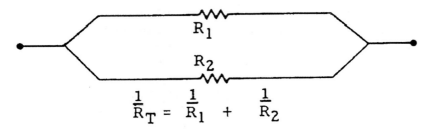

$$\frac{1}{R_T} = \frac{1}{R_1} + \frac{1}{R_2}$$

In a parallel circuit, if either resistor is disconnected, current can still flow through the other resistor. In a series circuit, if either resistor is disconnected, current flow stops because the circuit is broken.

Most circuits have both series and parallel connections and they are called series-parallel circuits. The following figure shows two resistors in series and both in parallel with a third resistor.

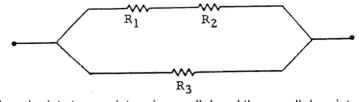

The figure below depicts two resistors in parallel and the parallel resistors in series with a third resistor.

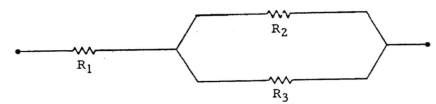

The coil in a meter has some resistance, but more resistance is usually needed. To measure voltage, a large resistance is placed in series with the meter coils as shown below:

For this circuit, the meter is called a voltmeter.

To measure current flow, a small resistance is placed in series with the meter coil and a second small resistor is placed in parallel with the meter and first resistor as shown below:

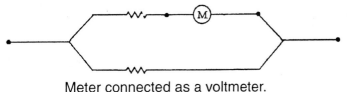

Meter connected as a voltmeter.

A simplified diagram of a D-C moving galvonometer is shown below:

D-C Moving-Coil Galvanometer.

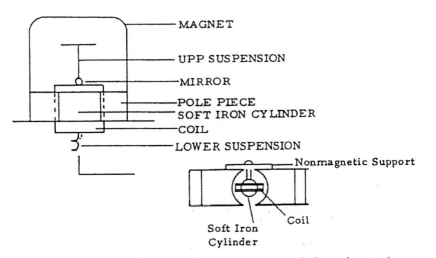

The galvonometer is a basic D'arsonval movement consisting of a stationary permanent magnet and a movable coil with attached mirror and pointer. The use of a pointer permits over-all simplicity in that the use of a light source and a system of mirrors is avoided. However, the use of a pointer introduces the problem of balance, especially if the pointer is long.

II. AMMETERS, VOLTMETERS, WATTMETERS, OHMMETER, AND OSCILLOSCOPE
Ammeter

The basic D'arsonval movement may be used to indicate or measure only very small currents. A simplified diagram of an ammeter is shown below:

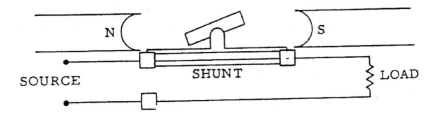

The resistance of the shunt is equal to the voltage drop for full-scale deflection divided by the rated current of the shunt.

Current measuring instruments must always be connected in series with a circuit and never in parallel.

Most ammeters indicate the magnitude of the current by being deflected from left to right. If the meter is connected with reversed polarity, it will be deflected backwards, and this action may damage the movement. The proper polarity should be observed in connecting the meter in the circuit. The meter should always be connected so that the electron flow will be into the negative terminal and out of the positive terminal. Common ammeter shunts are illustrated below:

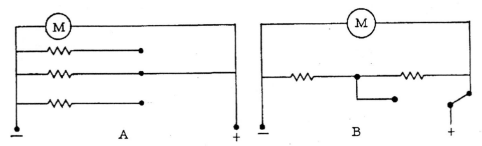

A   B

Voltmeter

The D'arsonval meter used as the basic meter for the ammeter may also be used to measure voltage if a high resistance is placed in series with the moving coil of the meter. A simplified voltmeter circuit is:

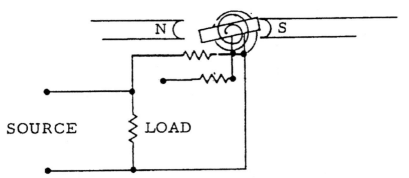

N   S

SOURCE   LOAD

The value of the necessary series resistance is determined by the current required for full-scale deflection of the meter and by the range of voltage to be measured. As an example, assume that the basic meter is to be made into a voltmeter with a full-scale reading of 1 volt. The coil resistance of the basic meter is 100 ohms, and .0001 ampere causes full-scale deflection. The total resistance, R, of the meter coil and the series resistance is:

R = E/I = 1/.0001 = 10,000 Ohms
and the series resistance alone is:
R = 10,000 - 100 = 9,900 Ohms.

Voltage measuring instruments are connected across (in-parallel with) a circuit.

The function of a voltmeter is to indicate the potential difference between two points in a circuit.

Wattmeter

Electric power is measured by means of a wattmeter. Because electric power is the product of current and voltage,

$$P = I E.$$

A wattmeter must have two elements, one for current and the other for voltage. For this reason, wattmeters are usually of the electrodynamometer type which multiplies the instantaneous current through the load by the instantaneous voltage across the load.

Ohmmeter

The series-type ohmmeter consists essentially of a sensitive milliammeter, a voltage source, and a fixed and a variable resistor all connected in series between the two terminals of the instrument, as shown below:

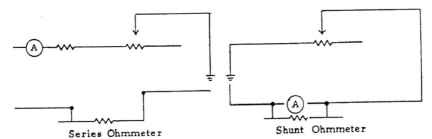

Series Ohmmeter   Shunt Ohmmeter

Before the unknown resistance is measured the test leads are shorted together and the variable resistance is adjusted for full-scale deflection. The point on the meter scale corresponding to full-scale deflection is marked "zero resistance."

The Oscilloscope

Oscilloscopes are used to obtain information about current or voltage in an electrical circuit either to supplement the information given by indicating instruments or to replace the instruments where speed is inadequate. Oscilloscopes permit determination of current and voltage variations that take place very rapidly. These devices are frequently used to obtain qualitative information about a circuit such as current and voltage waves or time relationships between events in a circuit.

This form of measurement also allows determinations of frequency in the form of a graphical illustration. Some examples of the various forms that can be illustrated on an oscilloscope are:

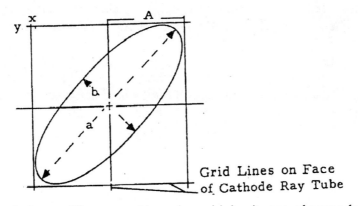

Grid Lines on Face
of Cathode Ray Tube

Determination of phase difference of two sinusoidal voltages of same frequency by the pattern on the face of cathode-ray tube.

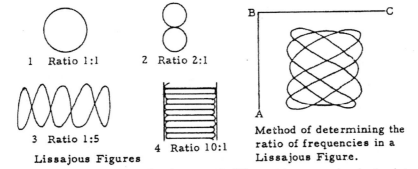

1 Ratio 1:1   2 Ratio 2:1

3 Ratio 1:5

4 Ratio 10:1

Lissajous Figures

Method of determining the ratio of frequencies in a Lissajous Figure.

Lissajous figures are patterns of voltages of different frequencies but related by a simple integral ratio as shown in the preceding figures.

6

III. AC VOLTAGE AND CURRENT

An alternating current (AC) consists of electrons that move first in one direction and then in another. The direction of flow changes periodically. Because most of the theory of electric power and communications deals with currents that surge back and forth in a certain manner known as sine-wave variation, the sine-wave is of considerable importance in alternating current. Symbols are:

I or → = Current   ∿∿ = Resistance   ⊥⊥⊥ = Inductance
⊝ = Voltage   ⊢ = Capacitance   Ⓩ = Impedance

Important characteristics of alternating current are:
1. Cycle - As rotation of a generator continues, the two sides of the loop interchange positions and the generated voltage in each of them is the opposite direction. One complete revolution of the loop results in one cycle of induced AC voltage. This theory is illustrated as shown in the following diagram:

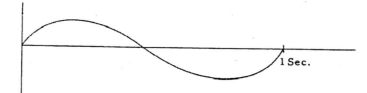

Points 0 to 1 represent one complete cycle of voltage in sine-wave form.
2. Frequency - The number of complete cycles occurring in each second of time. This is symbolized as "F".
3. Period - The time for one complete cycle of the generating force. This is illustrated as 1/f. (For example, the period of a 60-cycle voltage is 1/60 of a second.)
4. Phase Angle - The angle between vectors relative to the positions these vectors represent at any instant of time. This parameter is illustrated as angle 9. One complete cycle of 360 electrical degrees is indicated in the equation:

$e = E\eta \sin \theta$

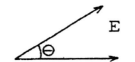

where   e   = instantaneous voltage
          $E\eta$ = maximum voltage
          0   = the angle in electrical degrees representing the instantaneous position of the rotating vector. Therefore, when

6 = 60', $E\eta$ = 100 volts, e = 100 sin 60° = 86.6 volts.

a. Inductance
    Inductance is that property of a circuit that opposes any current change in the circuit. It is also the property whereby energy may be stored in a magnetic field. Therefore, a coil of wire possesses the property of inductance because a magnetic field is established around the coil when current flows in the coil. The relationship of inductance is illustrated by the symbol "L".
    In a simple circuit, the relationship of inductance is shown as follows:

    In a simple circuit, the relationship of capacitance is *shown* as follows:

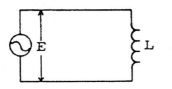

Where E is the applied
voltage and L is the
inductance.

b. Capacitance
Capacitance is that quality of a circuit that enables energy to be stored in the electric
field. In simple form, it has been shown to consist of two parallel metal plates separated by an insulator, called a dielectric.

In a simple circuit, the relationship of capacitance is *shown* as follows:

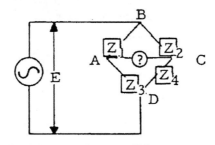

Where E is the applied
.voltage and C is the
capacitance.

IV. MEASUREMENT OF INDUCTANCE AND CAPACITANCE

Measurements of inductance and capacitance may be made conveniently and accurately by A-C bridge circuits. The simple form of the A-C bridge bears a strong resemblance
to the wheatstone bridge. It consists of four arms, a power source furnishes alternating current of the desired frequency and suitable magnitude to the bridge. A four-arm bridge is illustrated in the following diagram:

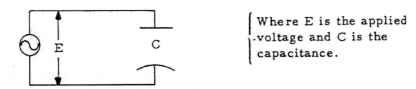

Four arm A-C bridge (using Impedances Z_x).

An inductance comparison bridge is similar to form except that the bridge is made up of
resistance and inductance relationships. An illustration is as follows:

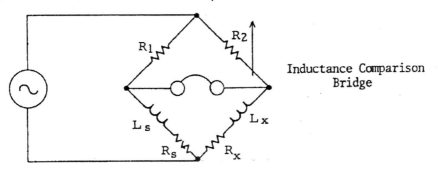

Inductance Comparison
Bridge

In the inductance bridge, the relationship shows that the unknown inductance L_x is derived from the equation--

$$L_x = L_s \frac{R_2}{R_1}$$

A capacitance bridge relationship is used to determine an unknown capacitance by comparison to a known capacitance. The relationship is illustrated in the following diagram:

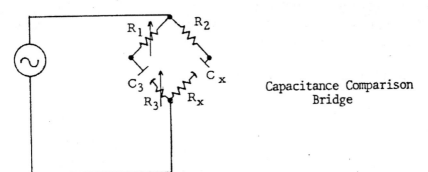

Capacitance Comparison
Bridge

Other measurements of inductance and capacitance can be made by using the following bridges:

1. Maxwell Bridge - Permits measurement of inductance in terms of capacitance.
2. Hay Bridge - Differs from the Maxwell Bridge only in having a resistance in series with the standard capacitor, instead of in parallel with it.
3. Owen Bridge - Another circuit for measurement of inductance in terms of a standard capacitor. One arm consists of the standard capacitor only, and an adjacent arm contains a resistance and capacitance in series.
4. Schering Bridge - One of the most important A-C bridges. It is used to measure capacitance in general and in particular, is used to measure properties of insulators, condenser bushings, insulating oil, and other insulating materials. This bridge is illustrated diagrammatically since it is very important.

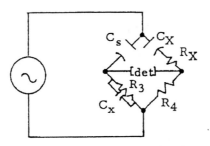

Schering bridge.

R_x = resistance in unknown Capacitor Cx
C_x = adjustable capacitor.
C_s = a high grade mica capacitor.
C_x = air capacitor
The equation is: $C_x = C_s R_3/R_4$

V. MEASUREMENT OF FREQUENCY

Several types of instruments have been devised to determine frequency. Some of them are: (refer to section on oscilloscope operation and use.)

1. Moving Iron Type - Has a moving element consisting of a soft-iron vane and two crossed stationary coils that are connected with some sort of frequency-discriminating network, so that one coil is stronger at low frequencies and the other at high frequencies.
2. Resonant Electrical Type - Two tuned circuits, one tuned to resonance slightly below the low end of the instrument scale, the other slightly above the high end. These two circuits may be combined with a crossed-coil instrument or an electro-dynamometer to make a frequency meter.
3. Mechanical Resonance Type - A series of reeds fastened to a common base that is flexibly mounted and that carries the armature of an electromagnet whose coil is energized from the A-C line whose frequency is to be measured.
4. Transducer Type - The frequency measuring function is entirely separated from the indicating instrument, which in this case is a simple D-C meter. Two parallel off-resonance circuits are used, one resonant below the instrument range and one above.

VI. ACTIVITIES

1. It is possible to make a simple meter to measure electricity. The materials needed to build a meter are as follows:
   a. One frozen concentrate juice container made of cardboard or a cardboard cylinder of about the same diameter.
   b. One 10 D (penny) nail or a piece of soft steel rod about three inches long and one eighth (1/8) inch diameter welding rod obtained from your teacher.
   c. Enameled wire approximately 28 gauge (American Wire Gauge) about 25 feet. Sources: Industrial Arts or Science teacher, the coil on the back of an old TV picture tube or a hobbie store. NOTE: Get the wire from an old TV, unwrap it carefully so that it does not break, kink, or knot up.
   d. One "D" cell battery or any flashlight battery with 1.5 volts (a 9-volt transistor radio battery will not work for this meter).

   e. Two 3x5 note cards.

   f. One small elastic or rubber band.

   g. One flash light bulb.

   h. Masking tape.

   i. Tools: scissors, file, pliers, hacksaw, ruler, and permanent magnet.

   The steps for the construction of the meter are as follows:

   Once the juice container has been washed out, measure two inches along the side of the container, from the open end, and cut this part off to make a cylinder two inches long. This will open the cylinder at both ends. Cut two "V" notches as shown in Figure 4(a), page 16.

Now wrap the wire around the outside of the cylinder. To do this, begin about six inches from the end of the wire and tape the wire to the cylinder 1/8" below one of the "V" notches. Beginning at the notch, wrap the wires neatly around the cylinder each turn next to the other covering approximately one inch of the cylinder. At this point, begin another layer of wire and continue winding on top of the first. Wind this layer in the same direction as the first. Wind layer on layer until sixty-five turns have been made. When it is done, finish at the notch opposite one at which you started and tape the wire in place with a small tab of masking tape. Cut the wire leaving about six inches of lead, save the rest of the wire.

The pointer is made by cutting the head off of the nail. Then mark a point one-third the length from the end of the nail. File both sides of the nail for the two-thirds length until the nail balances at the mark [Figure 4(b), page 16[4]].

Once this is finished, the short round end of the pointer must be magnetized. To do this, rub one pole of a permanent magnet in one direction over the short round end of the pointer until it is magnetized.

Cut a two-inch piece from the end of a note card. Fold this in half, parallel to the long side to make a "V" shape three inches long and one-inch on a side.

Push the pointer through the center of the card and fasten in place with the elastic, Figure 4(c), page 16 . Position the pointer so that when the card is placed in the "V" notches of the cylinder, it balances and stands up straight.

Attach a 3 x 5 note card to the cylinder so that it is vertical and the pointer can move freely in front of the card. This is a place to mark your readings when you experiment with your meter, Figure 4(d), page 18.

Once the meter is made, you can take measurements. This meter will measure low value of DC (Direct Current) only. CAUTION - DO NOT MEASURE ANY ELECTRICITY OTHER THAN BATTERIES LABELED 1. 5 V DC. These batteries are marked "D", "C", "A", "AA", "AM", "AAAA".

Scrape the insulation off the ends of the wires from the meter coil. Connect each of the meter leads to one of the poles of a "D" cell battery. The meter pointer should move. The position in which it stops should indicate 1.5 volts. Note where this position is.

Clean the varnish insulation from the ends of the wire left over after you wound the meter coil. Connect one end of this to one of the meter leads. Now reconnect the battery with the long length of wire in the meter circuit. Does the meter pointer move as far this time?
Connect a flashlight bulb to the battery so that it lights. Touch the two leads of the meter to the contacts of the bulb. The movement of the pointer to a position on the scale shows the amount of voltage used to get the light to light.

Disconnect your meter and reconnect it so that one end of the battery is connected to the meter and the meter to the bulb, and then the other contact of the bulb to the battery (this is a series circuit). See Figure 5, page 17: The deflection of the meter needle is showing the current used by the light bulb.

The meter constructed is a device much the same as meters made and used in industry. Electrical properties measured are basic to the study and use of electricity. If more information is required on the subject, it is available from several sources.

Among the best sources for information is the nearest library, for both basic and advanced manuals and textbooks. Science teachers in high schools or colleges or graduate engineers, electricians, telephone repairmen, can also help. Many hobby shops and electric supply stores have a selection of basic manuals for sale which provide good background material and a number of experiments with electricity.

In order to build the circuits found in most of these books, a meter movement of greater sensitivity is needed. This can also be purchased at low cost from hobby or electrical supply houses. The meter con-structed from this instruction is only a model to demonstrate how simple electricity is to measure.

2. Visit the electrical laboratory in your school and ask the teacher to demonstrate basic electrical measurements on the meter available. Perhaps the teacher will allow you to practice making simple measurements under close supervision.

3. Arrange a plant visitation at a local electronic or electrical assembly plant. Ask the tour guide to demonstrate the different meters and how they are used in basic measurements.

4. Purchase a Heath Kit or similar meter brand name and assemble as directed. A basic ohmmeter or vacuum tube voltmeter would be a good starting point.

STEPS FOR CONSTRUCTION OF A METER

Figure 4

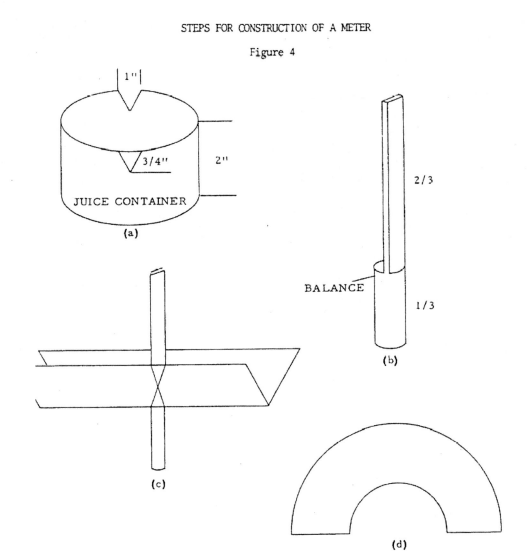

SERIES CIRCUIT
Figure 5

SERIES CIRCUIT

Figure 5

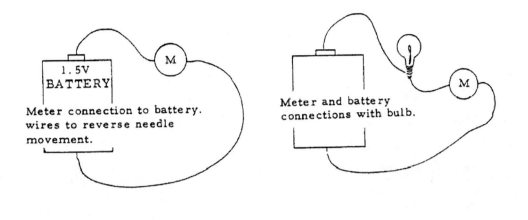

Meter connection to battery. wires to reverse needle movement.

Meter and battery connections with bulb.

BASIC FUNDAMENTALS OF BRIDGES
IN ELECTRICAL MEASUREMENT

CONTENTS

———

BASIC FUNDAMENTALS OF BRIDGES IN ELECTRICAL MEASUREMENT

1. Introduction

A bridge is a sensitive device used to measure resistance, capacitance, or inductance when great accuracy of measurement is desired. The bridges can be used also for measuring reactance, impedance, and frequency. All bridge circuits include a source of a-c or d-c voltage; an indicating device, usually a sensitive galvanometer or headphones; an adjustable standard, usually a resistor or capacitor; the unknown whose value is to be measured; and a method of determining how much the un- known value differs from the standard.

2. Wheatstone Bridge

a. The most common type of bridge used is the *Wheatstone* bridge (fig. 00). The bridge shown is known as the *diamond* arrangement, because the four resistors are shown schematically in the form of a diamond. Resistor R_x is the unknown resistor, R_a and R_b are known as *ratio arms,* and R_s as the *standard arm* of the bridge. R_a and R_b are fixed resistors in the bridge that provide a specific ratio of R_a/R_b, and maximum accuracy and sensitivity result when this ratio is 1/1. With the unknown resistor, R_x, inserted in the bridge, rheostat R_s is adjusted until the galvanometer reads zero.

When this occurs, the voltage drops across R_a and R_b equal the voltage drops across Rs and R_x. In A, where R_a equals R_b, the ohmic value of R_s (450 ohms) must equal that of R_x for this condition to exist.

b. In B, a slightly different condition exists and the ratio of R_a/R_b is made equal to 200/600 or 1/3. To balance the bridge so that the galvanometer reads zero, the ratio of R_s/R_x must also be 1/3. Since R_s equals 150 ohms, then R_x must equal 450 ohms. This line of reasoning, when put in mathematical form, is shown by the formula,

$$\frac{R_a}{R_b} = \frac{R_s}{R_x}$$

Transposing this equation,

$$R_x = \frac{R_s \times R_b}{R_a} = \frac{150 \times 600}{200} = 450 \text{ ohms.}$$

c. Another Wheatstone bridge circuit, known as a slide-wire bridge, is shown in figure 01. A slide wire, made of a material such as man-ganin and consisting of a single wire divided in 100 equal parts, forms the ratio arm of the bridge. A contact point that can be moved manually along the wire is provided; the re-

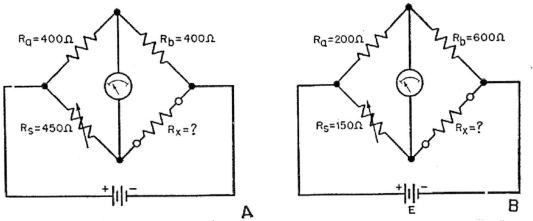

Figure 00. *Determining an unknown resistance using diamond arrangement of Wheatstone bridge.*

2

sistance to the left of the contact point represents R_a and that to the right represents resistor R_b. Moving the manually operated contact point along the slide wire varies the R_a/R_b, ratio. The standard resistor, R_s, has four steps of 1, 10, 100, or 1,000 ohms, making it possible for the bridge to measure different ranges of resistance. An example of the method used to find the value of an unknown resistor can be shown by setting selector switch S to place 10 ohms in the arm. With the contact point in the position shown, scale A gives the value of R_a

as 40 ohms, and scale B gives the value of R_b or 60 ohms. The unknown resistor, R_x, then can be found by the formula

$$R_x = \frac{R_s \times R_b}{R_a} = \frac{10 \times 60}{40} = 15 \, \text{ohms}$$

Nonuniformity of the resistance of the slide wire makes this type of bridge less accurate than the diamond arrangement.

3 . Measuring Capacitance with a Bridge

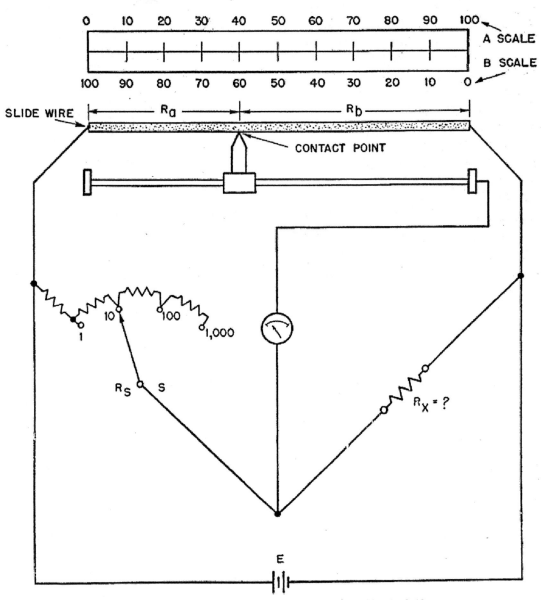

Figure 91. Determining an unknown resistance using slide-wire bridge.

a. When measuring an unknown capacitance on a bridge, an a-c source of voltage must be used. This is necessary because the reactance of the unknown capacitor is used to determine its capacitive value. Some typical methods of determining an unknown capacitance are given in figure 102. In the *series-resistance* capacitive bridge, in A, an a-c generator replaces the battery used in resistance measurements. Headphones are used as null indicators instead of a galvanometer, since their pick-up response is dependent on the reactance presented by the unknown capacitance. The ratio arms consist of R_a and R_b, with R_a adjustable so that the R_a/R_b ratio can be varied. In the standard arm, a calibrated variable capacitor, C_s, is in series with an adjustable resistor R_s. Capacitor C_x is the unknown capacitance, and *Rex* represents the leakage resistance of the capacitor. When the bridge is balanced, the voltage drops across R^a, C_s, and R_s equal those across R_b, C_x, and R_{cx}. R_a is adjusted to give a specific R_a/R_b ratio, R_s is adjusted to compensate for the effects of R_{cx}, and C_s is adjusted to equal C_x. R_s and C_s are varied alternately until a zero beat is obtained in the headphones. The dial setting of C_s represents the unknown capacitance. The unknown capacitance can be computed mathematically by the relationship

$$C_x = C_s \times \frac{R_a}{R_b}.$$

6. Another method of determining the un-

known capacitance, C_x, is illustrated in B. This is known as the *Schering* type of capacitance bridge. The distinguishing feature of this bridge is that the leakage resistance, R_{cx}, of the unknown capacitor is compensated for by the adjustable capacitor, C_a, which is in parallel with R_a. The fixed ratio arm, R_a, and the adjustable ratio arm, R_b, are connected across the headphones. C_a and the standard calibrated capacitor, C_s, are tuned until a zero beat is obtained in the headphones.

c. The capacitance of *electrolytic* capacitors, also, can be determined by using a capacitance bridge. However, a polarizing voltage supplied by a battery must be applied to the electrolytic capacitor, as shown in C. Capacitor C_r must be large enough that its reactance at the frequency of the a-c generator is a minimum so that the a-c voltage will be bypassed around the battery. The operation of this type of bridge arrangement is the same as the operation of other types of capacitance bridges.

d. When an unknown capacitance is small in value and great accuracy is desired, a *substitution* method is used commonly to determine its value. In this method, the resistors comprising the two ratio arms are made equal in value, and a known capacitor is connected across the terminals that are used to measure the unknown capacitor. The bridge then is balanced by adjusting the standard capacitor, and the reading of the dial setting is noted. The unknown capacitor is connected in parallel with the known capacitor, and the bridge is balanced once more by adjusting the standard capacitor. The

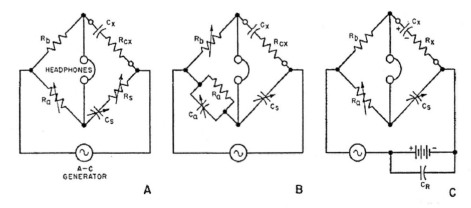

Figure 02. Typical bridge circuits for determining an unknown capacitance.

new reading of the dial setting is noted. The *difference* in the two readings is equal to the capacitance of the unknown.

e. The dissipation factor is the ratio of the resistance of a capacitor to its reactance and is a direct check of the capacitors quality. It is equal to

$$D = \frac{R_{cx}}{X_{cx}}, \text{ or } R_{cx} \times 2\pi f c_x$$

where D is the dissipation factor, R_{cx} is the leakage resistance, and X_{cx} the capacitive reactance of the capacitor. The greater the leakage resistance, the greater the dissipation factor, and when the capacitor has a higher dissipation factor than the value specified by the manufacturer, the capacitor should be discarded. In many capacitance bridges, provisions are made to measure the *dissipation, factor* of a capacitor, and many equipments have dials on which it is indicated directly.

4. Measuring Inductance with a Bridge

a. An unknown inductance can be determined by using the Maxwell bridge shown in A of figure 03. R_a and Rb are the ratio arms, and both are adjustable to obtain various R_a/R_b ratios. I_x represents the unknown inductance and R_x the resistance of the inductor. The standard resistance, R_s, is adjusted to cancel the effects of R_x, the standard inductance, and Ls is adjusted to balance the bridge and obtain zero beat in the headphones. The inductance of L_s as read on a calibrated dial equals that of the unknown inductance. The unknown induc-

tance also can be computed by the relationship

$$L_x = \frac{L_s \times R_b}{R_s}.$$

b. Since it is difficult to calibrate accurately a standard variable inductor, variable capacitors often are used as the standard instead of inductors. One type of bridge using a capacitor as its standard (B, fig. 103) is a variation of the Maxwell bridge. The standard capacitor, C_s, is adjusted to obtain the proper voltage drops around the circuit, and Rs is adjusted to cancel the effects of R_x. The ratio arms, R_a and R_b, are used to help balance the bridge and are connected to opposite sides of L_x. Dials on the equipment are read to determine directly the inductive value of L_x in henrys, millihenrys, or microhenrys. Inductance also can be directly computed from the relationship

$$L_x = C_s \times R_a \times R_b.$$

c. Another bridge used for inductance meas- urements, known as an Owen bridge, is shown in A of figure 04. As in the Maxwell bridge, L_x is located opposite the standard capacitor, C_s, so that a comparison can be made between C_s and L_x. A fixed capacitor or a series of capacitors which are switched into the arm, one at a time, can be used to replace C_s. The variable capacitor, C_a, is used to balance out R_x, and R_a. and Rb balance the bridge. The mathematical relationship used for determining the unknown

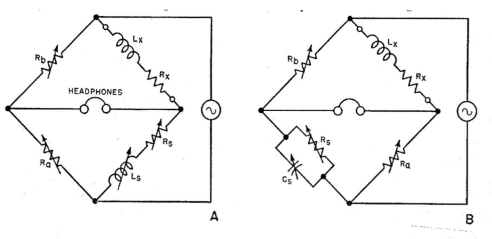

Figure 03. Methods for determining an unknown inductance, using a bridge circuit.

inductance in the Owen bridge is identical to that of the Maxwell bridge. Figure 04 shows the similarity between the Hay bridge and the Owen bridge. The standard capacitor, C_s, located opposite the unknown inductance, L_x, is in series with R_s. Rx is balanced by R_s, L_x is balanced by C_s, and the variable resistors, Ra and R_b, complete the balance of the bridge. This type generally is used for measuring inductances having a $Q(X_L/R)$ greater than 10.

    d. Just as the dissipation factor is used to measure the quality of a capacitor, *storage factor* sometimes is used to measure the quality of an inductor. Storage factor is defined as the reciprocal of the dissipation factor and is equal to

$$S = \frac{X_L}{R_L}$$

where X_L is the inductive reactance of the coil and R_L the resistance of the inductor. This is identical to the Q (figure of merit) of a coil and it is desirable for an inductance to have a , high storage factor.

5 . Practical Impedance Bridge

    a. SCHEMATIC DIAGRAM.

  1. The schematic of a practical impedance bridge used to measure resistance, capacitance, inductance, dissipation factor and storage factor is shown in figure 05. When measuring resistance, the unknown resistor is connected to the RES terminals. When

measuring inductance or capacitance, the unknown reactor is connected to the L-C terminals. Switches S_2 *and* S_3 are ganged and when positioned as shown (R position), resistance can be measured. Switch S_1 determines the amount of resistance in the ratio arms. The resistors of S_1–A represent R_a and those of S_1_B represent R_b as used in previous bridge explanations.

  2. With S_2 and S_3 in the C position, inductance, dissipation factor, and storage factor can be measured. The L-C terminals are connected, and the RES terminal is disconnected from the bridge. The lower sections of S_2 and S_3 connect positions, D, DQ, and Q. When in the D position, the upper sections of S_2 and S_3 are in the C position and the dissipation factor can be measured. The DQ position is used when it is desired to measure storage factor where the Q of the coil is less than 10, and the Q position is used for values of Q greater than 10. When measuring capacitance or dissipation factor, R_{11}, R_{13}, and C_1 are included in the bridge circuit. R_{11} and R_{13} help balance the bridge, and C_1 is a d-c blocking capacitor. When measuring inductance or storage factor, R_{11}, R_{12}, and C_2 are included in the bridge circuit. R_{11} is used to balance the bridge for a storage factor greater than 10,

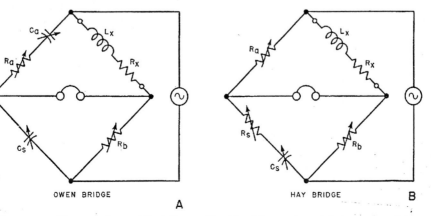

OWEN BRIDGE   A   HAY BRIDGE   B

Figure 04. Owen and Hay bridges used for determining an unknown inductance.

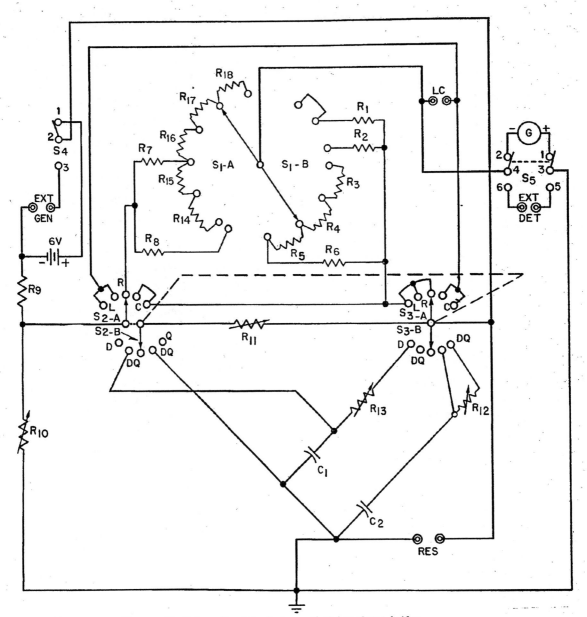

Figure 05. Schematic of typical practical impedance bridge.

and R_{12} for a storage factor less than 10. C_2 is a d-c blocking capacitor.

3. When resistance is being measured, switch S_5 is in the position shown, and the galvanometer is in the bridge circuit. When $S5$ is in positions 5 and 6, headphones can be connected to the EXT DET terminals of the bridge circuit. S_5 remains in this position when measuring inductance or capacitance. When measuring resistance,

with S_4 in the position shown, a 6-volt battery is inserted in the bridge circuit. When S_4 is thrown so that the EXT GEN terminals are connected to the bridge instead of the battery, an external a-c source, usually an audio oscillator, can be connected to the bridge. This is the position in which inductance and capacitance are measured. Resistor $R9$ is a current-limiting resistor for the external a-c generator.

b. CIRCUIT FOR MEASURING RESIS-TANCE. If the circuit of figure 05 is used to measure resistance, the conditions shown in the simplified diagram (fig. .06) exist. With switches S_2 and S_3 in the R positions and S_1–A as shown, the R_a ratio arm consists of R_7, R_{16}, and R_{17}. Switch S_1–B puts R_5 and R_6 in the ratio arm $R_{b'}$. With S_5 in the position shown, the galvanometer also is in the bridge and the 6-volt battery is connected in the circuit. The unknown resistor, R_x, is inserted between the RES terminals, and the calibrated resistor, R_{10} (the standard) is adjusted to balance the bridge. The ohmic value of the unknown resistor is read on the panel of the bridge equipment. Its reading is dependent upon the ohmic values of the two ratio arms and R_{10}.

c. MAXWELL BRIDGE. The Maxwell bridge circuit arrangement of figure 05 can be used also to measure inductance and storage factor (fig. 07). With S_2 and Ss in the L, DQ positions, headphones are connected to the EXT DET terminals, and an audio oscillator is connected to the EXT GEN terminals. The unknown inductor, L_x, then is connected to the L-C terminals and R_{10} and R_{11} are adjusted to balance the bridge (minimum indication in the headphones). Resistor Rx represents the d-c resistance of the unknown inductor. Inductance and storage factor are read directly from dials on the bridge equipment.

d. HAY BRIDGE. The circuit shown in figure 105 can be connected as a Hay bridge to measure inductance and storage factor (fig..08). The Hay bridge is used to measure storage factors greater than 10. The arrangement of all the switches in the Hay bridge is the same as those for the Maxwell bridge with the exception of S_2 and S_3. These switches are arranged so that their lower sections are connected to the Q position, their upper sections remaining in the L position. Resistor R_{12} in series with capacitor C_1 is the standard arm of the bridge. The remainder of the Hay bridge is identical to the Maxwell bridge arrangement.

e. CIRCUIT FOR MEASURING CAPACITANCE. The-circuit of figure 05 also can be arranged (fig. 09) to measure an unknown capacitor and dissipation factor. Switches S_2 and S_3 are arranged so that their upper sections are in the C position and their lower sections are in the D position. This causes C_1 to be in series with R_{13} *in* the standard arm. R_5 and R_6 become the R_b ratio arm. C_x represents the capacitance to be measured, and R_x the d-c resistance of the capacitor. The bridge is balanced by adjusting R_{10} and R_{13}. A minimum indication is heard in the headphones, and capacitance, or dissipation factor, is read directly on the panel of the bridge.

6. Summary

a. A bridge is a sensitive device which is used to measure an unknown resistance, capacitance, inductance, or reactance.

b. The most common bridge used to measure an unknown resistance is the Wheatstone bridge.

c. The mathematical relationship for determining an unknown resistance in a bridge circuit is

$$R_x = \frac{R_s \times R_b}{R_a}.$$

d. A slide-wire Wheatstone bridge uses a single piece of high-resistance wire as the R_a and R_b ratio arms.

e. When measuring an unknown capacitance, an a-c generator and headphones are used instead of a battery and galvanometer as in a Wheatstone bridge.

f. The mathematical relationship for determining an unknown capacitor in a bridge circuit is

$$C_x = C_s \times \frac{R_a}{R_b}.$$

g. Dissipation factor determines the leakage resistance of a capacitor and is equal to the leakage resistance divided by the reactance of the capacitor, or $R_{cx} \times 2\pi fc_x$

h. Inductance bridges often use variable capacitors instead of variable inductors as the standard because they are easier to calibrate.

i. The mathematical relationship for determining an unknown inductor in a bridge circuit is

$$L_x = C_s \times R_a \times R_b.$$

j. Storage factor determines the worth of an inductor and is equal to its reactance divided by its d-c resistance.

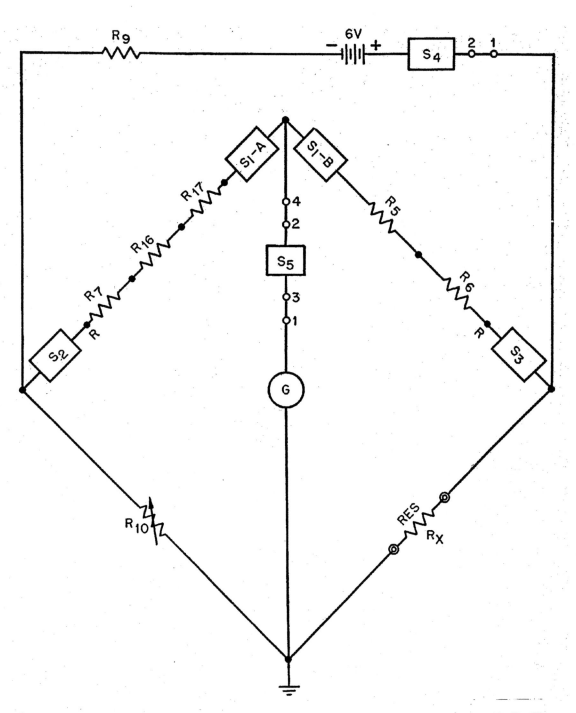

Figure 06. *Circuit for measuring resistance.*

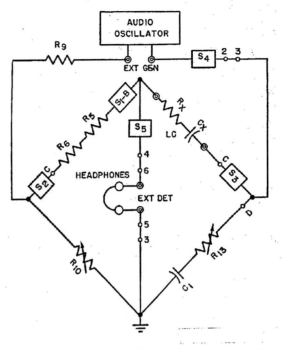

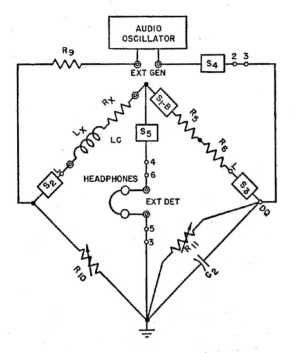

Figure 07. Maxwell bridge circuit for measuring inductance and storage factor.

Figure 09. Circuit for measuring capacitance and dissipation factor.

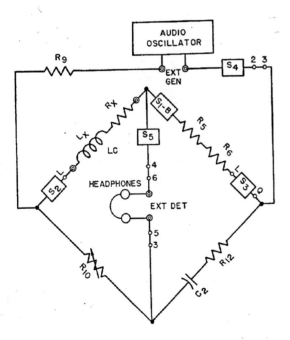

Figure 08. Hay bridge circuit for measuring inductance and storage factor.

7. Review Questions

a. Define a bridge circuit.

b. Can a Wheatstone bridge be used to measure an unknown reactance?

c. Why is it desirable to have the R_b/R_a ratio in a Wheatstone bridge equal to 1 ?

d. What is the distinguishing characteristic of a slide-wire type Wheatstone bridge?

e. Why are a-c generators and headphones used in reactive bridge circuits instead of batteries and galvanometers ?

f. What changes must be made in a capacitive bridge circuit when measuring an electrolytic capacitor?

g. Explain the difference between dissipation factor and storage factor.

h. If capacitive bridges use capacitors as the standard, then why do not inductive bridges use inductors as the standard?

i. What are the mathematical relationships for determining an unknown resistor, capacitor, and inductor in a bridge circuit?

j. What is a storage factor?

BASIC FUNDAMENTALS OF ELECTRICAL WIRING

TABLE OF CONTENTS

Basic Fundamentals Of Electrical Wiring

SECTION I. INTRODUCTION

1-1. PURPOSE AND SCOPE

These notes provide practical information in the basics and procedures of electrical wiring, a full exposition of the electrician's tools and equipment, and a description of the common components or general-use materials of the many different wiring systems currently in use which vary from the simple to the complex.

1-2. COMMENTARY

The student is encouraged to proceed on from this basic plateau to a study of specialized areas of the subject of interior wiring, such as design and layout, open wiring, cable wiring, and maintenance.

Section II. FUNDAMENTALS AND PROCEDURES OF ELECTRICAL WIRING

1-3. Fundamentals of Electricity

a. Throughout this part, emphasis is placed on the constructional aspects of electric wiring. Detailed coverage of electrical fundamentals may be found in standard text books .The term "phase" is used when refer ring to the angular displacement between two or more like quantities, either alternating electromotive force (EMF) or alternating currents. It is likewise used in distinguishing the different types of alternating current generators. For example, a machine designed to generate a single EMF wave is called a single-phase alternator, and one designed to generate two or more EMF waves is called a polyphase alternator.

b. Power generators will produce single or three-phase voltages that may be used for electrical power systems at generated voltages or through transformer systems.

(1) Single-phase generators are normally used only for small lighting and single-phase motor loads. If the generated voltage is 120 volts then a two-wire system is used, see table C-1(A). One of the conductors is grounded and the other is ungrounded or hot. The generated single-phase voltage may be 240 volts. This voltage is normally used for larger single-phase motors. In order to provide power for lighting loads, the 240-volt phase is center-tapped to provide a three-wire single-phase system, see table C-1(B). The center tap is the grounded neutral conductor. The voltage from this grounded conductor to either of the two ungrounded

ITEM	SYMBOL
WIRING CONCEALED IN CEILING OR WALL	————————
WIRING CONCEALED IN FLOOR	— — —
EXPOSED BRANCH CIRCUIT	- - - - -
BRANCH CIRCUIT HOME RUN TO PANEL BOARD (NO. OF ARROWS EQUALS NO. OF CIRCUITS, DESIGNATION IDENTIFIES DESIGNATION AT PANEL;	A1 A3
THREE OR MORE WIRES (NO. OF CROSS LINES EQUALS NO. OF CONDUCTORS TWO CONDUCTORS INDICATED IF NOT OTHERWISE NOTED)	///
INCOMING SERVICE LINES	
CROSSED CONDUCTORS, NOT CONNECTED	—⊢ OR ⊥—
SPLICE OR SOLDERED CONNECTION	—•— OR ⊥
CABLED CONNECTOR (SOLDERLESS)	—■—
WIRE TURNED UP	———○
WIRE TURNED DOWN	———●

 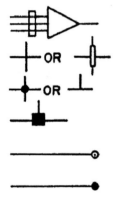

Figure 1-1. Standard electrical symbols (sheet 1).

(hot) conductors is 120 volts. This is one half of the total phase value. The voltage between the two ungrounded conductors is 240 volts. This system provides power for both lighting and single-phase 240-volt motors.

(2) The most common electrical system is the three-phas'e system. The generated EMF's are 120 degrees apart in phase. As shown in table C-1 (C, D, E), three-phase systems may be carried by three or four wires. If connected in a delta (A), the common phase voltage is 240 volts. Some systems generate 480 or 600 volts. If the delta has a grounded center tap neutral, then a voltage equal to one half the phase voltage is available. If the phases are wye (y) con-

nected then the phase voltage is equal to $\sqrt{3}$ (1.73) times the phase-to-neutral voltage. The most common electrical system found in the military is the three-phase four-wire 208/120 volt system.

c. Single-phase three-wire and three-phase four-wire systems provide voltages for both lighting and power loads. If the load between each of the three phases or between the two ungrounded conductors and their grounded center tapped neutral are equal, a balanced circuit exists. When this occurs there is no current flowing in the neutral conductor. Because of this, two ungrounded conductors and one grounded neutral may be used to feed two circuits.

COMMON SYMBOLS AND LINE CONVENTIONS USED IN WIRING PLANS

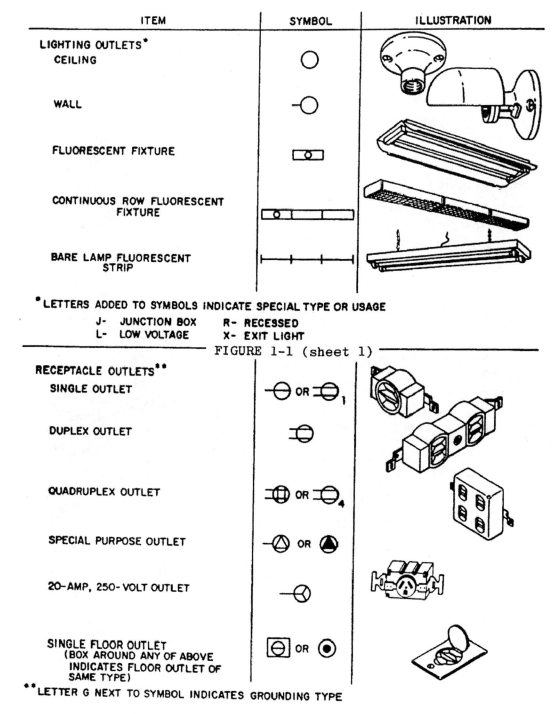

ITEM	SYMBOL	ILLUSTRATION
LIGHTING OUTLETS* CEILING		
WALL		
FLUORESCENT FIXTURE		
CONTINUOUS ROW FLUORESCENT FIXTURE		
BARE LAMP FLUORESCENT STRIP		

*LETTERS ADDED TO SYMBOLS INDICATE SPECIAL TYPE OR USAGE

J- JUNCTION BOX   R- RECESSED
L- LOW VOLTAGE   X- EXIT LIGHT

FIGURE 1-1 (sheet 1)

RECEPTACLE OUTLETS** SINGLE OUTLET		
DUPLEX OUTLET		
QUADRUPLEX OUTLET		
SPECIAL PURPOSE OUTLET		
20-AMP, 250-VOLT OUTLET		
SINGLE FLOOR OUTLET (BOX AROUND ANY OF ABOVE INDICATES FLOOR OUTLET OF SAME TYPE)		

**LETTER G NEXT TO SYMBOL INDICATES GROUNDING TYPE

Figure 1-1—Continued (sheet 2)

Thus, three conductors may be used where otherwise four are normally required.

d. The preceding discussion leads logically into one-, two-, and three-phase electric light circuits. Electric lamps for indoor lighting in the United States are generally operated at 110 to 120 volts from constant-potential circuits. Two- and three-wire distri-

4

ITEM	SYMBOL	ILLUSTRATION
SWITCHES		
SINGLE POLE SWITCH	S	
DOUBLE POLE SWITCH	S_2	
THREE WAY SWITCH	S_3	
SWITCH AND PILOT LAMP	S_P	
CEILING PULL SWITCH	Ⓢ	
PANEL BOARDS AND RELATED EQUIPMENT PANEL BOARD AND CABINET		
SWITCHBOARD, CONTROL STATION OR SUBSTATION		
SERVICE SWITCH OR CIRCUIT BREAKER	▬ OR ▬ OR ⊗	
EXTERNALLY OPERATED DISCONNECT SWITCH	⬭	
MOTOR CONTROLLER	⧓ OR MC	
MISCELLANEOUS TELEPHONE	▶	
THERMOSTAT	—Ⓣ	
MOTOR	Ⓜ	

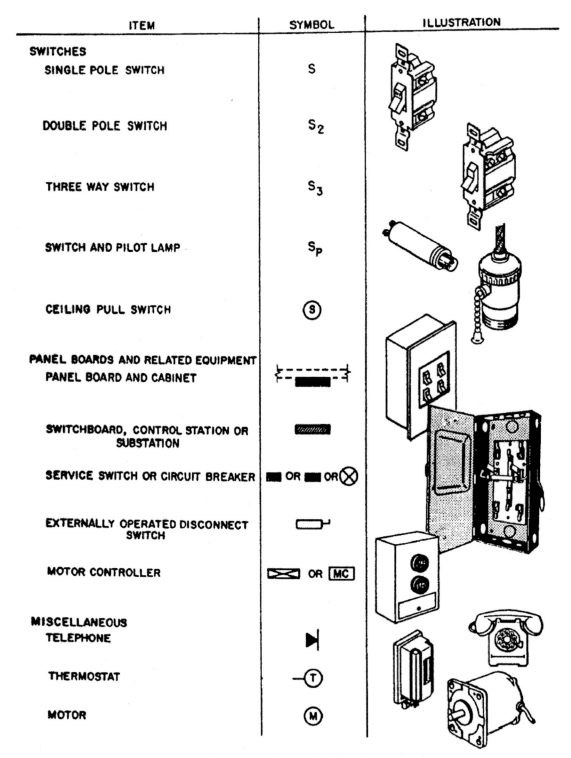

Figure 1-1—Continued (sheet 3)

bution systems, either direct current or single-phase alternating current, are widely used for lighting installations.

e. These systems of distribution are capable of handling both lamp and motor loads connected in parallel between the constant-potential lines. The three-wire system provides twice the potential difference between the outside wires than it does between either of the outside wires and the central or neutral wire. This system makes it possible to operate the larger motors at 240 volts while the lamps and smaller motors operate at 120 volts. When the load is unbalanced, a current in the neutral wire will correspond to the difference in current taken by the two sides. A balance of load is sought in laying out the wiring for lighting installations.

1-4. Drawing Symbols and Blueprint Reading

The electrician must be able to interpret simple blueprints since his construction orders will ordinarily be in that form. He needs the ability to make simple engineering sketches to describe work for which he receives only verbal orders.

a. Symbols. The more common symbols and line conventions used in wiring plans are shown in figure 1-1. These symbols enable precise location of any electrical equipment in a building from the study of a drawing.

b. Schematic Wiring Diagrams. Electrical plans show what items are to be installed, their approximate location, and the circuits to which they are to be connected. A typical electrical plan for a post exchange is shown in figure 1-2. The plan shows that the incoming service consists of three No. 8 wires and that two circuit-breaker panels are to be installed. Starting at the upper left, the plan shows that nine ceiling lighting outlets and two duplex wall outlets are to be installed in the bulk storage area. The arrow designated "B2" indicates that these outlets are to be connected to circuit 2 of circuit-breaker panel B. Note that three wires are indicated from this point to the double home-

run arrows designated "B1, B2." These are, the hot wire from the bulk storage area to circuit 2 of panel B, the hot wire from the administration area to circuit 1 of panel B, and a common neutral. The two hot conductors must be connected to different phases at the panel. This allows a cancellation of current in the neutral when both circuits are fully loaded (para 1-3c). From the double arrowhead, these wires are run to the circuit breaker panel without additional connections.

b. Schematic Wiring Diagrams. This is the form of wiring plans used most frequently for construction drawings (fig. 1-2). Single lines indicate the location of wires connecting the fixtures and equipment. Two conductors are indicated in a schematic diagram by a single line. If there are more than two wires together, short parallel lines through the line symbols indicate the number of wires represented by the line. Connecting wires are indicated by placing a dot at the point of intersection. No dot is used where wires cross without connecting. The electrician may encounter drawings in which the lines indicating the wiring have been omitted. In this type of drawing only the fixture and equipment symbols are shown; the location of the actual wiring is to be determined by the electrician. No actual dimensions or dimension lines are shown in electrical drawings. Location dimensions and spacing requirements are given in the form of notes or follow the standard installation principles shown in figure 1-1.

c. Drawing Notes. A list of drawing notes is ordinarily provided on a schematic wiring diagram to specify special wiring requirements and indicate building conditions which alter standard installation methods.

1-5. Color Coding
The National Electrical Code requires that a grounded or neutral conductor be identified by an outer color of white or natural gray for Number 6 wire or smaller. For larger conductors the outer identification of white or natural gray may be used, or they should be identified

by white markings at the terminals. The ungrounded conductors of a circuit should be identified with insulation colored black, red, and blue, used in that order, in two-, three-, or four-wire circuits, respectively. All circuit conductors of the same color shall be connected to the same ungrounded (hot) feeder conductor throughout the installation. A grounding conductor, used solely for grounding purposes, should be bare or have a green covering.

1-6. Splices

A spliced wire must be as good a conductor as a continuous conductor. Figure 1-3 shows many of the variations of splicing used to obtain an electrically secure joint. Though

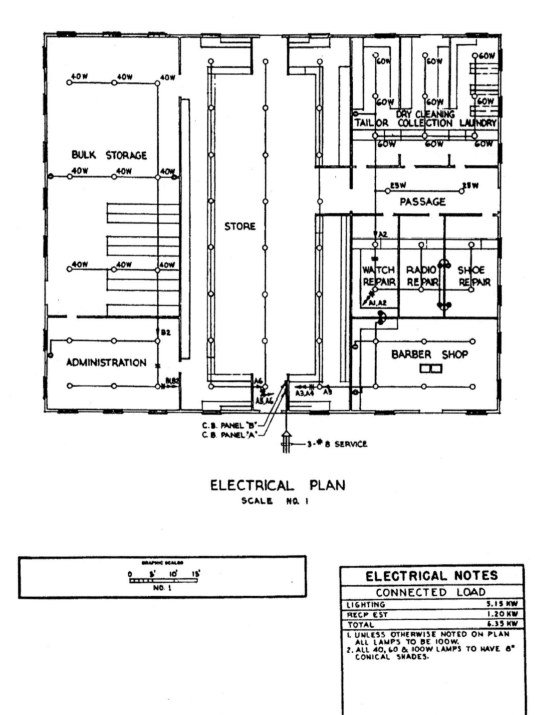

ELECTRICAL PLAN
SCALE NO. 1

ELECTRICAL NOTES	
CONNECTED LOAD	
LIGHTING	5.15 KW
RECP EST	1.20 KW
TOTAL	6.35 KW
1. UNLESS OTHERWISE NOTED ON PLAN ALL LAMPS TO BE 100W. 2. ALL 40, 60 & 100W LAMPS TO HAVE 6" CONICAL SHADES.	

Figure 1-2. Typical wiring diagram.

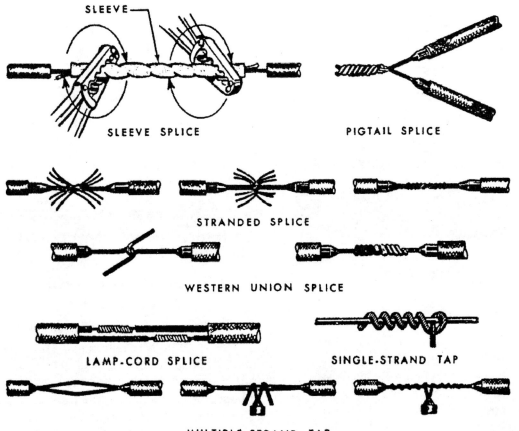

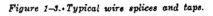

Figure 1–3. Typical wire splices and taps.

splices are permitted wherever accessible in wiring systems, they should be avoided whenever possible. The best wiring practice (including open wiring systems) is to run continuous wires from the service box to the outlets. UNDER NO CONDITIONS SHOULD SPLICES BE PULLED THROUGH CONDUIT. SPLICES MUST BE PLACED IN APPROPRIATE ELECTRICAL BOXES.

1-7. Solderless Connectors

Figure 1-4 illustrates connectors used in place of splices because of their ease of installation. Since heavy wires are difficult to splice and solder properly, split-bolt connectors (1, fig. 1-4) are commonly used for wire joining. Solderless connectors, popularly called wire nuts, which are used for connecting small-gage and fixture wires, are illustrated in 2, figure 1-4. One design shown consists of a funnel-shaped metal-

spring insert molded into a plastic shell, into which the wires to be joined are screwed. The other type shown has a removable insert which contains a setscrew to clamp the wires. The plastic shell is screwed onto the insert to cover the joint.

1-8. Soldering

a. When a solderless connector is not used, the splice must be soldered before it is considered to be as good as the original conductor. The primary requirements for obtaining a good solder joint are a clean soldering iron, a clean joint, and a nonacid flux. These requirements can be satisfied by using pure rosin on the joint or by using a rosin core solder.

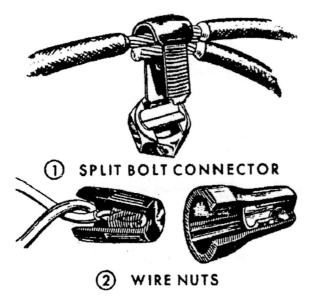

① SPLIT BOLT CONNECTOR

② WIRE NUTS

Figure 1-4. Solderless connectors.

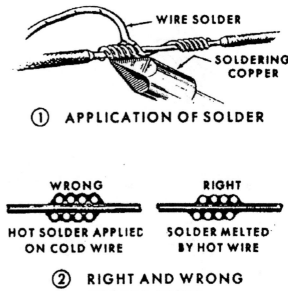

① APPLICATION OF SOLDER

WRONG / **RIGHT**

HOT SOLDER APPLIED ON COLD WIRE / SOLDER MELTED BY HOT WIRE

② RIGHT AND WRONG SOLDER JOINT

Figure 1-5. Soldering and solder joints.

b. To insure a good solder joint, the electric heated or copper soldering iron should be applied to the joint (1, fig. 1-5) until the joint melts the solder by its own heat. Two, figure 1-5 shows the difference between a good and bad solder joint. The bad joint has a weak crystalline structure.

c. Figure 1-6 illustrates dip soldering. This method of soldering is frequently used by experienced electricians because of its convenience and relative speed for soldering pigtail splices.

1-9. Taping Joints

a. Every soldered joint must be covered with a coating of rubber, or varnished cambric, and friction tape to replace the wire insulation of the conductor. In taping a spliced solder joint (fig. 1-7), the rubber or cambric tape is started on the tapered end of the wire insulation and advances toward the other end, with each succeeding wrap, by overlapping the windings. This procedure is repeated from one end of the splice to the other until the original thickness has been restored. The joint is then covered with several layers of friction tape.

b. Though the method in a above for taping joints is still considered to be standard, the plastic electrical tape, which serves as an insulation and a protective covering, should be used whenever available. This tape materially reduces the time required to tape a joint and reduces the space needed by the joint because a satisfactory protective and insulation covering can be achieved with three-layer taping.

1-10. Insulation and Making Wire Con-nections

a. When attaching a wire to a switch or an electrical device or when splicing it to another wire, the wire insulation must be removed to bare the copper conductor. One, figure 1-8 shows the right and wrong way to remove insulation. When the wire-stripping tool is applied at right angles to the wire, there is danger that the wire may be nicked and thus weakened. Therefore extreme caution must be used to make sure the wire is not nicked. To avoid nicks, the cut is made at an angle to the conductor. After the protective insulation is removed, the conductor is scraped or sanded thoroughly to remove all traces of insulation and oxide on the wire.

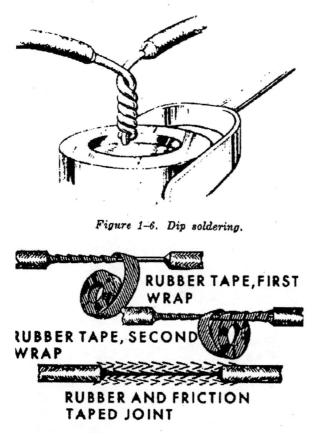

Figure 1-6. Dip soldering.

RUBBER TAPE, FIRST WRAP

RUBBER TAPE, SECOND WRAP

RUBBER AND FRICTION TAPED JOINT

Figure 1-7. Rubber- and friction-tape insulating.

b. Two and three, figure 1-8 show the correct method of attaching the trimmed wire to terminals. The wire loop is always inserted under the terminal screw, as shown, so that tightening the screw tends to close the loop. The loop is made so that the wire insulation ends close to the terminal.

1-11. Job Sequence

a. *Scope.* The installation of interior wiring is generally divided into two major divisions called roughing-in and finishing. Roughing-in is the installation of the outlet boxes, cable, wire, and conduit. Finishing is the installation of the switches, receptacles, covers, fixtures, and the completion of the service. The interval between these two work periods is used by other trades for plastering, enclosing walls, finishing floors, and trimming.

b. *Roughing-in.*

(1) The first step in the roughing-in phase of a wiring job is the mounting of out-let boxes. The mounting can be expedited if the locations of all boxes are first marked on the studs and joists of the building.

(2) All the boxes are mounted on the building members on their own or by special brackets. For concealed installation, all boxes must be installed with the forward edge or plaster ring of the boxes flush with the finished walls.

(3) The circuiting and installation of wire for open wiring, cable, or conduit should be the next step. This involves the drilling and cutting-out of the building members to allow for the passage of the conductor or its protective covering. The production-line method of drilling the holes for all runs (as the installations between boxes are called) at one time, and then installing all of the wire, cable, or conduit, will expedite the job.

(4) The final roughing-in step in the installation of conduit systems is the pulling-in of wires between boxes. This can also be included as the first step in the finishing phase and requires care in the handling of the wires to prevent the marring of finished wall or floor surfaces.

c. Finishing.

(1) The splicing of joints in the outlei and junction boxes and the connection of the bonding circuit is the initial step in the completion phase of a wiring job.

(2) Upon completion of the first finishing step, the proper leads to the terminals of switches, ceiling and wall outlets, and fixtures are then installed.

(3) The devices and their cover plates are then attached to the boxes. The fixtures are generally supported by the use of special mounting brackets called fixture studs or hick-eys.

(4) The service-entrance cable and fusing or circuit breaker panels are then connected and the circuits fused.

(5) The final step in the wiring of any building requires the testing of all outlets by the insertion of a test prod or test lamp, the operation of all switches in the building, and the loading of all circuits to insure proper circuiting has been installed.

SECTION III. ELECTRICIAN'S TOOLS AND EQUIPMENT

1-12. Purpose

The electrical apparatus and materials that an electrician is required to install and maintain are different from other building materials. Their installation and maintenance require the use of special handtools. This section describes and illustrates the tools normally used by an Army electrician in interior wiring. For additional information on proper tool usage, refer to standard textbooks.

1-13. Pliers

Pliers are furnished with either uninsulated or insulated handles. Although the insulated handle pliers are always used when working on or near "hot" wires, they must not be considered sufficient protection alone and other precautions must be taken. Long-nose pliers are used for close work in panels or boxes. Wire clippers are used to cut wire to size. One type of wire clippers shown in figure 1-9 has a plastic cushion in the cutting head which grips the clipped

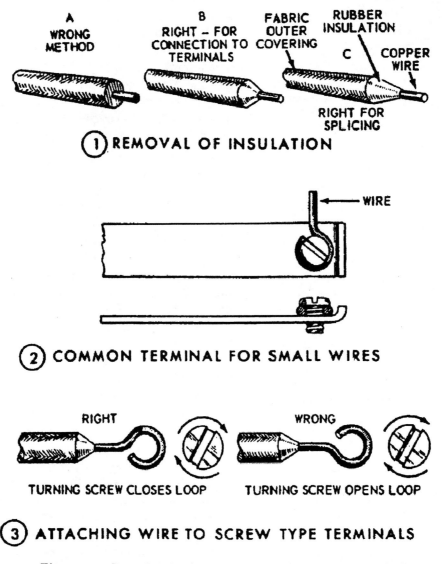

Figure 1-8. Removing insulation and attaching wire to terminals.

wire end and prevents the clipped piece from flying about and injuring personnel. The slip-joint pliers are used to tighten locknuts or small nuts on devices.

1-14. Fuse Puller

The fuse puller shown in figure 1-10 is designed to eliminate the danger of pulling and replacing cartridge fuses by hand. It is also used for bending fuse clips, adjusting loose cutout clips, and handling live electrical parts.

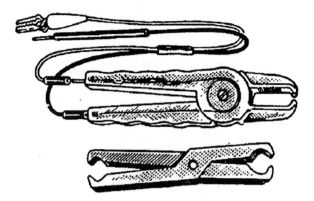
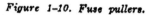

Figure 1-10. Fuse pullers.

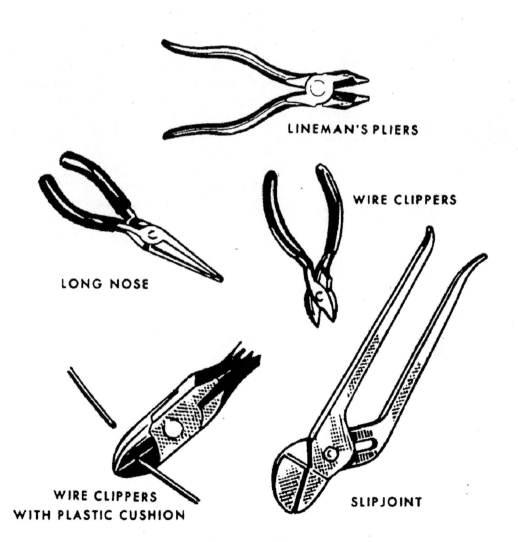

Figure 1-9. Pliers.

The second type of fuse puller, although having the same general configuration, is made of molded plastic. Encased in the handle is an electrical circuit similar to a voltmeter except that the indicating device is a neon glow tube. Test probes are attached to the handle of this fuse puller and may be used to determine if voltage is present in a circuit.

1-15. Screwdrivers

Screwdrivers *(fig. 1-11)* are made in many sizes and tip shapes. Those used by electricians should have insulated handles. Generally the electrician uses screwdrivers in attaching electrical devices to boxes and attaching wires to terminals. One variation of the screwdriver is the screwdriver bit which is held in a brace and used for heavy-duty work. For safe and efficient application, screwdriver tips should be kept square and properly tapered and should be selected to match the screw slot.

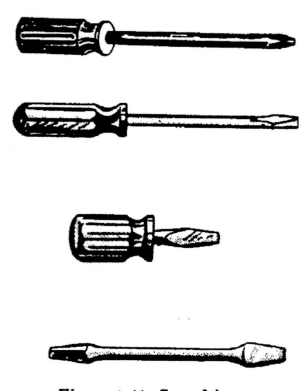

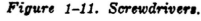

Figure 1-11. Screwdrivers.

1-16. Wrenches

Figure 1-12 shows four types of wrenches used by electricians. Adjustable open-end wrenches, commonly called crescent wrenches, open end, closed end, and socket wrenches are used on hexagonal and square fittings such as machine bolts, hexagon nuts, or conduit unions. Pipe wrenches are used for pipe and conduit work and should not be used where crescent, open end, closed end, or socket wrenches can be used. Their construction will not permit the application of heavy pressure on square **or** hexagonal material, and the continued misuse of the tool in this manner will deform the teeth on the jaw faces and mar the surfaces of the material being worked.

1-17. Soldering Equipment
A standard soldering kit (fig. 1-13) used by electricians consists of nonelectric or electric soldering irons or both, a blowtorch (for heating a nonelectric soldering iron and pipe or wire joints), a spool of solid tin-lead wire solder or flux core solder, and soldering paste. An alcohol or propane torch may also be used in place of the blowtorch. Acid core solder should never be used in electrical wiring.

1-1-8. Drilling Equipment
Drilling equipment (fig. 1-14) consists of a brace, a joist-drilling fixture, an extension bit to allow for drilling into and through deep cavities, an adjustable bit, and a standard wood bit. These are required in electrical work to drill holes in building structures for the passage of conduit or wire in new or modified construction. Similar equipment is required for drilling holes in sheet-metal cabinets and boxes. In this case high speed drills should be used. Carbide drills are used for tile or concrete work. Electric power drills aid in this phase of an electrician's work.

1-19. Woodworking Tools
The crosscut and keyhole saws and wood chisels shown in figure 1-15 are used by electri- cians to remove wooden structural members obstructing a wire or conduit run and to notch studs and joists to take conduit, cable, or box-mounting brackets. They are also used in

the construction of wood-panel mounting
brackets. The keyhole saw may again be used
to cut openings in walls of existing buildings
where boxes are to be added.

1-20. Metalworking Tools
The cold chisels and center punches shown in
figure 1-16, besides several other types of metalworking tools employed by the electrical
trade, are used when working on steel panels.
The knockout punch is used either in making
or enlarging a hole in a steel cabinet or outlet
box. The hacksaw is usually used by an electri-

cian to cut conduit, cable, or wire too large for
wire cutters. A light steady stroke of about 40
to 50 times a minute is best. A new blade
should always be inserted with the teeth point-
ing away from the handle. The tension wing-
nut is tightened until the blade is rigid. Care
must be taken because insufficient tension will
cause the blade to twist and jam whereas too
much tension will caus[c] the blade to break.
Blades have 14, 18, 24, and 32 teeth per inch.
The best blade for general use is one having
18 teeth per inch. A blade with 32 teeth per
inch is best for cutting thin material. The mill

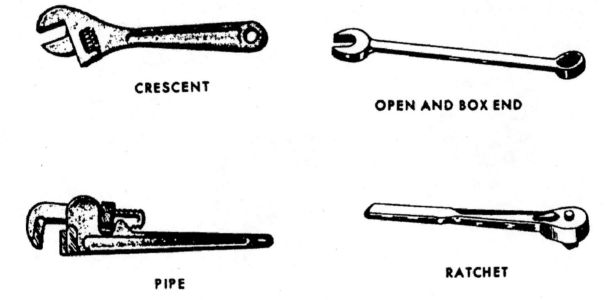

CRESCENT

OPEN AND BOX END

PIPE

RATCHET

Figure 1-12. Wrenches.

file shown in the figure is used in filing the
sharp ends of cutoffs as a precaution against
short circuits.
1-21. Masonry-Working Tools
An electrician should have several sizes of
masonry drills in his tool kit. These normally
are carbide-tipped and are used to drill holes in

brick or concrete walls either for anchoring
apparatus with expansion screws or for the
passage of conduit or cable. Figure 1-17
shows the carbide-tipped bit used with a power
drill and a hand-operated masonry drill.
1-22. Conduit Threaders and Dies
Rigid conduit is normally threaded for installation. Figure 1-18 illustrates one type of con-

duit threader and dies used in cutting pipe
threads on conduit. The tapered pipe reamer is
used to ream the inside edge of the conduit as
a precaution against wire damage. The conduit
cutter is used when cutting thin-wall conduit
and has a tapered blade attachment for reaming the conduit ends.

1-22. Conduit Threaders and Dies
Rigid conduit is normally threaded for installation. Figure 1-18 illustrates one type of conduit threader and dies used in cutting pipe
threads on conduit. The tapered pipe reamer is
used to ream the inside edge of the conduit as
a precaution against wire damage. The conduit
cutter is used when cutting thin-wall conduit

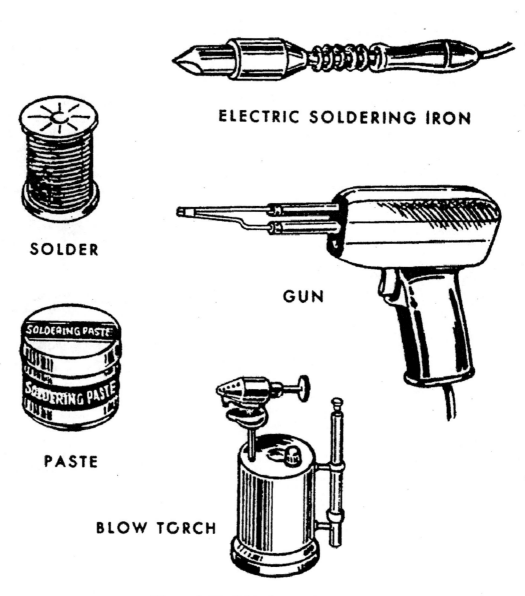

Figure 1-13. Soldering equipment.

and has a tapered blade attachment for reaming the conduit ends.

1-23. Knives and Other Insulation-Stripping Tools

Wire and cable insulation is stripped or removed with the tools shown in figure 1-19. The knives and patented wire strippers are used to bare the wire of insulation before making connections. The scissors shown are used to cut insulation and tape. A multipurpose tool designed to cut and skin wires, attach termi-

nals, gage wire, and cut small bolts may also be

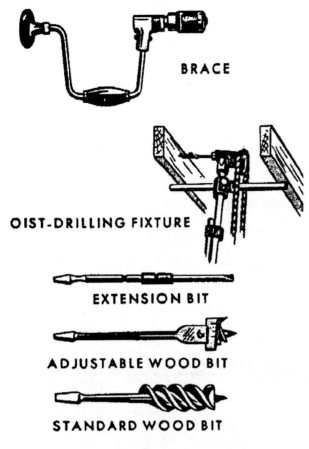

BRACE

OIST-DRILLING FIXTURE

EXTENSION BIT

ADJUSTABLE WOOD BIT

STANDARD WOOD BIT

Figure 1-14. Drilling equipment.

1-24. Hammers
Hammers are used either in combination with other tools such as chisels or in nailing equipment to building supports. Figure 1-20 shows

a carpenter's clawhammer and a machinist's ball peen hammer, both of which can be

advantageously used by electricians in their work.

1-25. Tape
Various types of tapes are used to replace insulation and wire coverings. Friction tape is a cotton tape impregnated with an insulating adhesive compound. It provides weather resistance and limited mechanical protection to a splice already insulated. Rubber or varnished cambric tape may be used as an insulator when replacing wire covering. Plastic electrical tape is made of a plastic material with adhesive on one face. It has replaced friction and rubber tape in the field for 120- and 208-volt circuits, and as it serves a dual purpose in taping joints, it is preferred over the former methods. This is discussed in paragraph 1-9.

1-26. Fish Wire and Drop Chain
a. *Fish Wire.* Fish wires are used primarily to pull wires through conduits. Many pulls are

16

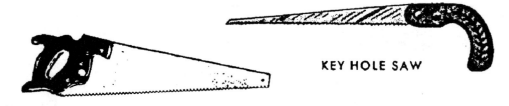

KEY HOLE SAW

CROSSCUT SAW

CHISEL

Figure 1-15. Woodworking tools.

HACKSAW AND BLADE

KNOCKOUT PUNCH

MILL FILE

COLD CHISELS AND PUNCHES

Figure 1-16. Metalworking tools.

quite difficult and require a fish-wire "grip" or "pull" to obtain adequate force on the wire in pulling. The fish wire is made of tempered spring steel about 1/4-inch wide and is available in lengths to suit requirements. It is stiff enough to preclude bending under normal operation but can be pushed or pulled easily around the bends or conduit elbows.

b. Drop Chain. When pulling wires and cables in existing buildings, the electrician will normally employ a fish wire or drop chain between studs. A drop chain consists of small chain links attached to a lead or iron weight. It is used only to feed through wall openings in a vertical plane.

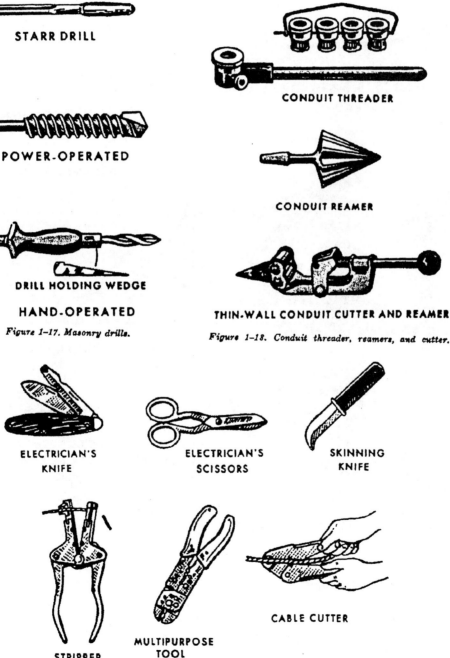

STARR DRILL

POWER-OPERATED

DRILL HOLDING WEDGE

HAND-OPERATED

Figure 1-17. Masonry drills.

CONDUIT THREADER

CONDUIT REAMER

THIN-WALL CONDUIT CUTTER AND REAMER

Figure 1-18. Conduit threader, reamers, and cutter.

ELECTRICIAN'S KNIFE

ELECTRICIAN'S SCISSORS

SKINNING KNIFE

STRIPPER

MULTIPURPOSE TOOL

CABLE CUTTER

Figure 1-19. Insulation-stripping tools.

CARPENTER'S CLAW HAMMER

MACHINIST'S BALL-PEEN HAMMER

Figure 1-20. Hammers.

WIRE GRIP   **SPLICING CLAMP**

Figure 1-21. Wire grip and splicing clamp.

RUBBER-HANDLE GUARDS

Figure 1-22. Extension light (without bulb).

1-27. Ruler and Measuring Tape
As an aid in cutting conduit to exact size as well as in determining the approximate material quantities required for each job, the electrician should be equipped with a folding rule and a steel tape.

1-28. Wire Clamps and Grips
To pull wire through conduit and to pull open-wire installations tight, the wire grip shown in

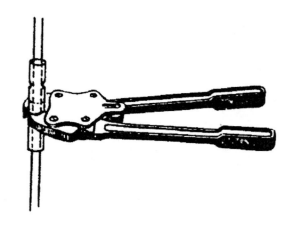

Figure 1-23. Thin-wall conduit impinger.

120 VOLTS (LAMPS DIM)

208 VOLTS (LAMPS BRIGHT)

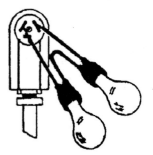 

120 OR 208 VOLTS TEST LAMP   **FOR 120 VOLT ONLY**

Figure 1-24. Test lamps.

figure 1-21 is an invaluable aid. As seen in the figure, the wire grip has been designed so that the harder the pull on the wire, the tighter the wire will be gripped. Also shown in the figure is the splicing clamp used to twist the wire pairs into a uniform and tight joint when making splices.

1-29. Extension Cord and Light
The extension light shown in figure 1-22 normally is supplied with a long extension cord and is used by the electrician when normal building lighting has not been installed or is not functioning.

1-30. Thin-Wall Conduit Impinger

When the electrician uses indenter type couplings and connectors with thin-wall conduit, an indenter tool (a thin-wall conduit impinger shown in fig. 1-23) must be used to attach these fittings permanently to the conduit. This

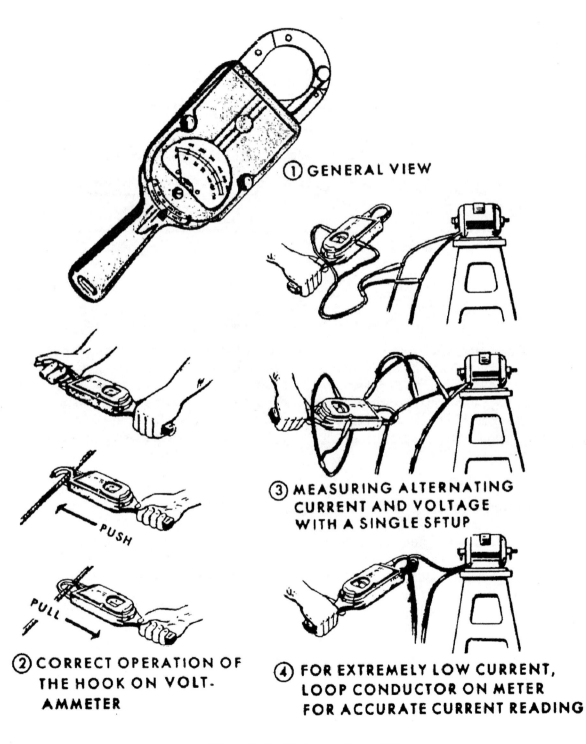

① GENERAL VIEW

③ MEASURING ALTERNATING CURRENT AND VOLTAGE WITH A SINGLE SETUP

PUSH

PULL

② CORRECT OPERATION OF THE HOOK ON VOLT-AMMETER

④ FOR EXTREMELY LOW CURRENT, LOOP CONDUCTOR ON METER FOR ACCURATE CURRENT READING

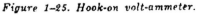

Figure 1-25. Hook-on volt-ammeter.

tool has points which, when pressed against the fittings, form indentations in the fitting and are pressed into the wall of the tubing to hold it on the conduit. The use of these slip-on fittings and the impinger materially reduces the installation time required in electrical installations and thus reduces the cost of thin-wall conduit installations considerably.

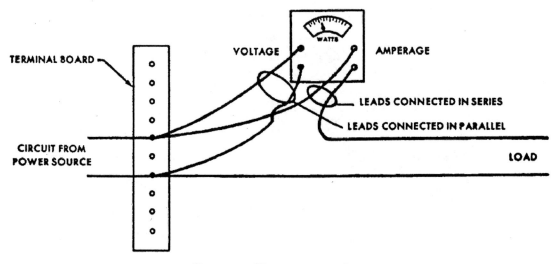

Figure 1-26. Wattmeter connection.

1-31. Wire Code Markers
Tapes with identifying numbers or nomenclature are available for the purpose of permanently identifying wires and equipment. These are particularly valuable to identify wires in complicated wiring circuits, in fuse circuit breaker panels, or in junction boxes.

1-32. Meters and Test Lamps
    a. Test Lamps. An indicating voltmeter or test lamp is useful when determining the system voltage or locating the ground lead, and for testing circuit continuity through the power source. They both have a light which glows in the presence of voltage. Figure 1-24 shows a test lamp used as a voltage indicator.
    b. Hook-On Volt-Ammeter. A modern method of measuring current flow in a circuit uses the hook-on volt-ammeter (1, fig. 1-25) which does not need to be hooked into the circuit. Two, figure 1-25 shows its ease of operation. To make a measurement, the hook-on section is opened by hand and the meter is placed against the conductor. A slight push on the handle snaps the section shut; a pull springs the hook on the C-shaped current transformer open and releases the conductor. Applications of this meter are shown in 3, figure 1-25 where voltage is being measured using the meter leads. Current is measured using the hook-on section. With three coils around the meter (4, fig. 1-25) the current reading will be three times the actual current flowing through the wire. To obtain the true current, therefore, this reading is divided by 3. The hook-on volt-ammeter can be used only on alternating current circuits and can measure current only in a single conductor.
    c. Wattmeter. The basic unit of measurement for electric power is the watt. In the power ratings of electric devices used by domestic consumers of electricity, the term watts signifies that, when energized at the normal line voltage, the apparatus will use electricity at the specified rate. In alternating-current circuits, power is the product of three quantities: the potential (volt), the current (amperes), and the power factor (percent). Power is measured by a wattmeter

(fig. 1-26). This instrument is connected (fig. 1-26) so that the current in the measured circuit flows through the stationary field coils in the wattmeter and the voltage across the measured circuit is impressed upon the watt-meter-armature circuit, which includes movable coils and a fixed resistor. The power factor is automatically included in the measurement because the torque developed in the wattmeter is always proportional to the product of the instantaneous values of current and voltage. Consequently, the instrument gives a true indication of the power, or rate at which energy is being utilized.

SECTION IV. WIRING MATERIALS

1-33. Introduction

There are many different wiring systems currently in use which vary in complexity from the simple-to-install open wiring to the more complex conduit systems. These various systems contain common components. This section describes these common or general use materials.

1-34. Electrical Conductors

a. *Single Conductors.* Electrical conductors that provide the paths for the flow of electric current generally consist of copper or aluminum wire or cable over which an insulating material is formed. The insulating material insures that the path of current flow is through the conductor rather than through extraneous paths, such as conduits, water pipes, and so on. The wires or conductors are initially classified by type of insulation applied and wire gage. The various types of insulation are in turn subdivided according to their maximum operating

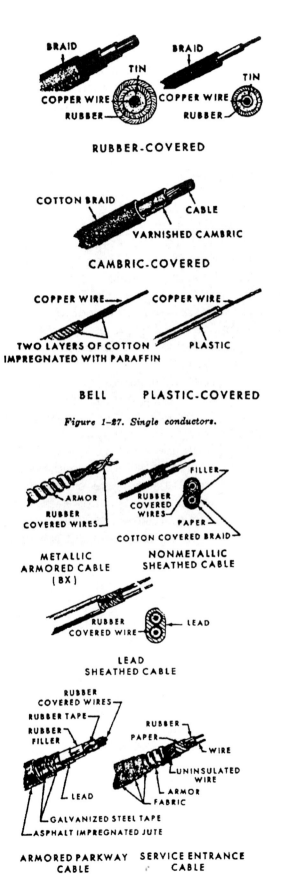

Figure 1-27. Single conductors.

Figure 1-28. Multiconductor cables.

temperatures and nature of use. Figure 1-27 illustrates the more common single conductors used in interior wiring systems. Table C-2 lists the common trade classification of wires and compares them as to type, temperature rating, and recommended use.

b. Wire Sizes. The wire sizes are denoted by the use of the American Wire Gage (AWG) standards. The largest gage size is No. 0000. Wires larger than this are classified in size by their circular mil cross-sectional area. One circular mil is the area of a circle with a diameter of 1/1,000 of an inch. Thus, if a wire has a diameter of 0.10 inch or 100 mil, the cross sectional area is 100 X 100 or 10,000 circular mils. The most common wire sizes used in interior wiring are 14, 12, and 10 and they are usually of solid construction. Some characteristics of the numbering system are

(1) As the numbers become larger, the size of the wire decreases.

(2) The sizes normally used have even numbers, e.g., 14, 12, and 10.

(3) Numbers 8 and 6 wires, which are furnished either solid or stranded, are normally used for heavy-power circuits or as service-entrance leads to buildings. Wire sizes larger than these are used for extremely heavy loads and for poleline distributions.

c. Multiconductor Cables. There are many types of installations of electrical wiring where the use of individual conductors spaced and supported side by side becomes an inefficient as well as hazardous practice. For these installations, multiconductor cables have been designed and manufactured. Multiconductor cables consist of the individual conductors as outlined in *b* above, arranged in groups of two or more. An additional insulating or protective shield is formed or wound around the group of conductors. The individual conductors are color coded for proper identification. Figure 1-28 illustrates some of the types of multiconductors. The description and use of each type are given in (1) through (5) below.

(1) Armored cable, commonly referred to as BX, can be supplied either in two- or three-wire types and with or without a lead sheath. The wires in BX, matched with a bare equipment ground wire, are initially twisted together. This grouping, totaling three or four wires with the ground, is then wrapped in coated paper and a formed self-locking steel armor. The cable without a lead sheath is widely used for interior wiring under dry conditions. The lead sheath is required for installation in wet locations and through masonry or concrete building partitions where added protection for the copper conductor wires is required.

(2) Nonmetallic sheathed cable consists of two or three rubber- or thermoplastic-insulated wires, each covered with a jute type of filler material which acts as a protective insulation against mishandling. This in turn is covered with an impregnated cotton braid. The cable is light in weight, simple to install, and comparatively low priced. It is used quite extensively in interior wiring, but is not approved for use in wet locations. A dual-purpose plastic sheathed cable with solid copper conductors can be used underground outdoors or indoors. It needs no conduit, and its flat shape and gray or ivory color make it ideal for surface wiring. It resists moisture, acid, and corrosion and can be run through masonry or between studding.

(3) Lead-covered cable consists of two or more rubber-covered conductors surrounded by a lead sheathing which has been extruded around it to permit its installation in wet and underground locations. Lead-covered cable can also be immersed in water or installed in areas where the presence of liquid or gaseous vapors would attack the insulation on other types.

(4) Parkway cable provides its own protection from mechanical injury and therefore can be used for underground services by burying it in the ground without any protecting conduit. It normally consists of rub-

ber-insulated conductors enclosed in a lead sheath and covered with a double spiral of galvanized steel tape which acts as a mechanical protection for the lead. On top of the tape, a heavy braid of jute saturated with a waterproofing compound is applied for additional weather protection.

(5) Service-entrance cable normally has three wires with two insulated and braided conductors laid parallel and wound with a bare conductor. Protection against damage for this assembly is obtained by encasing the wires in heavy tape or armor, which serves as an inner cushion, and covering the whole assembly with braid. Though the cable normally serves as a power carrier from the exterior service drop to the service equipment of a building, it may also be used in interior-wiring circuits to supply power to electric ranges and water heaters at voltages not exceeding 150 volts to ground pro

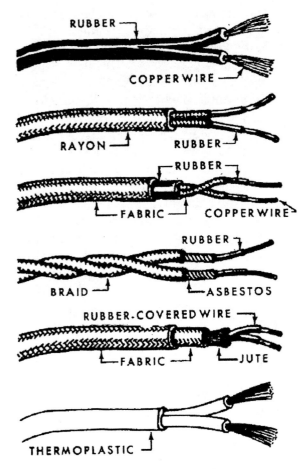

Figure 1-29. Types of flexible cords.

vided the outer covering is armor. It may also be used as a feeder to other buildings on the same premises under the same conditions, if the bare conductor is used as an equipment grounding conductor from a main distribution center located near the main service switch.

d. Cords. Many items using electrical power are either of the pendant, portable, or vibration type. In these cases the use of cords as shown in figure 1-29 is authorized for delivery of power. These can be grouped and designated as either lamp, heater, or heavy-duty power cords. Lamp cords are supplied in many forms. The most common types are the single-paired rubber-insulated and twisted-paired cords. The twisted-paired cords consist of two cotton-wound conductors which have been covered with rubber and rewound with cotton braid. Heater cords are similar to this latter type except that the first winding is replaced by heat-resistant asbestos. Heavy-duty or hard-service cords are normally supplied with two or more conductors surrounded by cotton and rubber insulation. In manufacture, these are first twisted or stranded. The voids created in the twisting process are then filled with jute and the whole assembly covered with rubber. All cords, whether of this type or of the heater or lamp variety, have the conductors color coded for ease of identification. Table C-8 groups by common trade terms the cords found in general use and illustrates some of their characteristics.

1-35. Electrical Boxes

a. Design. Outlet boxes bind together the elements of a conduit or armored cable system in a continuous grounded system. They provide a means of holding the conduit in position, a space for mounting such devices as switches and receptacles, protection for the device, and space for making splices and connections. Outlet boxes are manufactured in either sheet steel, porcelain, bakelite, or cast iron and are either round, square, octagonal, or rectangular. The fabricated steel box is available in a number of different designs. For example, some boxes are of the sectional or "gang" variety, while others have integral brackets for mounting on studs and joists. Moreover, some boxes have been designed to receive special cover plates so that switches, receptacles, or lighting fixtures may be more easily installed. Other designs facilitate installation in plastered surfaces. Regardless of the design or material, they all should have sufficient interior volume to allow for the splicing of conductors or the making of connections. For this reason the allowable minimum depth of outlet boxes is limited to 11/2 inches in all cases except where building-supporting members would have to be cut. In this case the minimum depth can be reduced to 1/2 inch.

b. Selection. The selection of boxes in an electrical system should be made in accordance with tables C-9 and C-10 which list the maximum allowable conductor capacity for each type of box. In these tables a conductor running through the box

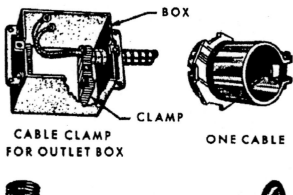

CABLE CLAMP
FOR OUTLET BOX

ONE CABLE

TWO CABLE

ARP.CORNER
NE CABLE

ANTISHORT
BUSHING

Figure 1–30. Armored-cable fittings.

is counted along with each conductor terminating in the box. For example, one conductor running through a box and two terminating in the box would equal three conductors in the

box. Consequently, any of the boxes listed would be satisfactory. The tables apply for boxes that do not contain receptacles, switches, or similar devices. Each of these items mounted in a box will reduce by one the maximum number of conductors allowable as shown in the tables.

c. Outlet Boxes for Rigid and Thin-Watt Circuit and Armored Cable. Steel or cast iron outlet boxes are generally used with rigid and thin-wall conduit or armored cable. The steel boxes are either zinc- or enamel-coated, the zinc coating being preferred when installing conduit in wet locations. All steel boxes have "knockouts." These knockouts are indentations in the side, top, or back of an outlet box, sized to fit the standard diameters of conduit fittings or cable connectors. They usually can be removed with a small cold chisel or punch to facilitate entry into the box of the conduit or cable. Boxes designed specifically for armored-cable use also have integral screw clamps located in the space immediately inside the knockouts and thus eliminate the need for cable connectors. This reduces the cost and labor of installation. Box covers are normally required when it is necessary to reduce the box openings, provide mounting lugs for electrical devices, or to cover the box when it is to be used as a junction. Figure 1-30 illustrates several types of cable connectors and also a cable clamp for use in clamping armored cable in an outlet box. The antishort bushing shown in the figure is inserted between the wires and the armor to protect the wire from the sharp edges of the cut armor when it is cut with a hacksaw or cable cutter.

d. Outlet Boxes for Nonmetallic Sheathed Cable and Open Wiring.

(1) *Steel.* Steel boxes are also used for nonmetallic cable and open wiring. However, the methods of box entry are different from those for conduit and armored-cable wiring because the electrical conductor wires are not protected by a hard surface. The connectors and interior box clamps used in nonmetallic and open wiring are formed to provide a smooth surface for securing the

cable rather than being the sharp-edged type of closure normally used.

(2) *Nonmetallic.* Nonmetallic outlet boxes made of either porcelain or bakelite may also be used with open or nonmetallic sheathed wiring. Cable or wire entry is generally made by removing the knockouts of preformed weakened blanks in the boxes.

(3) *Special.* In open wiring, conductors should normally be installed in a loom from the last support to the outlet box. Although all of the boxes described in (1) and (2) above are permissible for open wiring, a special loom box is available which has its back corners "sliced off" and allows for loom and wire entry at this sliced-off position.

e. Attachment Devices for Outlet Boxes. Outlet boxes which do not have brackets are supported by wooden cleats or bar hangers as illustrated in figure 1-31.

(1) *Wooden cleats.* Wooden cleats are first cut to size and nailed between two wooden members. The boxes are then either nailed or screwed to these cleats through holes provided in their back plates.

(2) *Strap hangers.* If the outlet box is to be mounted between studs, mounting straps are necessary. The readymade straps are handy and accommodate not only a single box, but a 2, 3, 4, or 5 gang box.

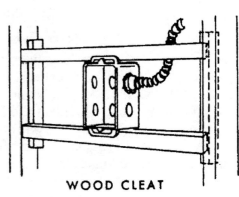

WOOD CLEAT

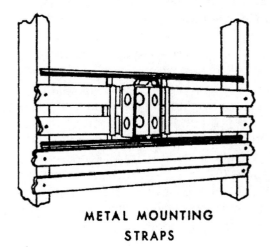

METAL MOUNTING STRAPS

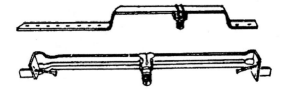

BAR HANGERS

Figure 1-31. Typical box mountings.

(3) *Bar hangers.* Bar hangers are prefabricated to span the normal 16-inch and 24-inch joist and stud spacings and are obtainable for surface or recessed box installation. They are nailed to the joist or stud exposed faces. The supports for recessed boxes normally are called offset bar hangers.

(4) *Patented supports.* When boxes have to be installed in walls that are already plastered, several patented supports can be used for mounting. These obviate the need for installing the boxes on wooden members and thus eliminate extensive chipping and replas-tering.

1-36. Knobs, Tubes, Cleats, Loom, and Special Connectors

Open wiring requires the use of special insulating supports and tubing to insure a safe installation. These supports, called knobs and cleats, are smooth-surfaced and made of porcelain. Knobs and cleats support the wires which are run singly or in pairs on the surface of the joists or studs in the buildings. Tubing or tubes, as they are called, protect the wires froir abrasion when passing through wooden members. Insulation of loom of the "slip-on" type is used to cover the wires on box entry and at wire-crossover points. The term "loom" is applied to a continuous flexible tube woven of cambric material impregnated with varnish.

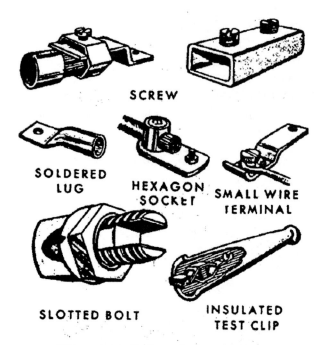

SCREW

SOLDERED LUG　**HEXAGON SOCKET**　**SMALL WIRE TERMINAL**

SLOTTED BOLT　**INSULATED TEST CLIP**

Figure 1–32. Cable and wire connectors.

At points where the type of wiring may change and where boxes are not specifically required, special open wiring to cable or conduit wiring connectors should be used. These connectors are threaded on one side to facilitate connection to a conduit and have holes on the other side to accommodate wire splices but are designed only to carry the wire to the next junction box. The specific methods of installation and use of these items are covered in standard textbooks.

1-37. Cable and Wire Connectors

Code requirements state that "Conductors shall be spliced or joined with splicing devices approved for the use or by brazing, welding, or soldering with a fusible metal or alloy. Soldered splices shall first be so spliced as to be mechanically and electrically secure without solder and then soldered." Soldering or splicing devices are used as added protection because of the ease of wiring and the high quality of connection of these devices. Assurance of high quality is the responsibility of the electrician who selects the proper size of connector relative to the number and size of wires.

27

Figure 1-32 shows some of the many types of cable and wire connectors in common use.

1-38. Straps and Staples

a. *Policy.* All conduits and cables must be attached to the structural members of a building in a manner that will preclude sagging. The cables must be supported at least every 4 1/2 feet for either a vertical or horizontal run and must have a support in the

form of a strap or staple within 12 inches of every outlet box. Conduit-support spacings vary with the size and rigidity of the conduit. See table C-11 for support of rigid nonmetallic conduit and paragraph 6-2 for rigid metal conduit.

b. *Cable Staples.* A very simple and effective method of supporting BX cables on wooden members is by the use of cable staples as shown in 1, figure 1-33.

c. *Insulating Staples.* Bell or signal wires

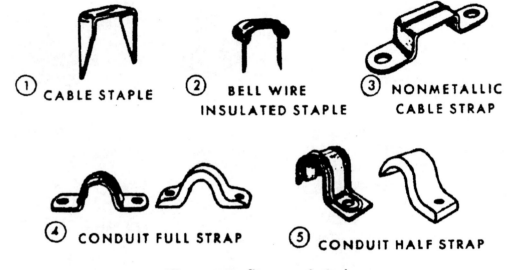

Figure 1-33. Straps and staples.

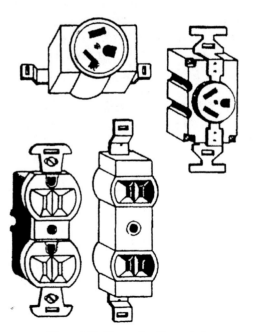

Figure 1-34. Types of wall receptacles.

are normally installed in pairs in signal systems. The operating voltage and energy potential is so low in these installations (12 to 24 volts) that protective coverings such as conduit or loom are not required. To avoid any possibility of shorting in the circuit, they are normally supported on wood joists or studs by insulated staples of the type shown in 1, figure 1-33.

d. *Straps.* Conduit and cable straps (3, 4, and 5, fig. 1-33) are supplied as either one-hole or two-hole supports and are formed to fit the contour of the specific material for which they are designed. The conduit and cable straps are attached to building materials by "anchors" designed to suit each type of supporting material. For example, a strap is attached to a wood stud or joist by nails or screws. Expanding anchors are used for box or strap attachment to cement or brick structures and also to plaster or plaster-substitute surfaces. Toggle and "molly" bolts are used where the surface wall is thin and has a concealed air space which will allow for the release of the toggle or expanding sleeve.

1-39. Receptacles, Fixtures, and Receptacle Covers

a. *Applicability.* Portable appliances and devices are readily connected to an electrical supply circuit by means of an outlet called a receptacle. For interior wiring these outlets are installed either as single or duplex receptacles. Receptacles previously installed, and their replacements in the same box, may be two-wire receptacles. All others must be the three-wire type. The third wire on the three-wire receptacle is used to provide a ground lead to the equipment which receives power from the receptacle. This guards against dangers from current leakage due to faulty insulation or exposed wiring and helps prevent accidental shock. The receptacles are constructed to receive plug prongs either by a straight push action or by a twist-and-turn push action. Fixtures are similar to receptacles but are used to connect the electrical supply circuit directly to lamps inserted in their sockets.

b. *Knob-and-Tube- Wiring.* Receptacles with their entire enclosures made of some insulating material, such as bakelite, may be used without metal outlet boxes for exposed, open wiring or nonmetalli sheathed cable.

c. *Conduit and Cable.* The receptacles (fig. 1-34) commonly used with conduit and cable installations are constructed with yokes to facilitate their installation in outlet boxes. In this case they are attached to the boxes by metal screws through the yokes, threaded into the box. Wire connections are made at the receptacle terminals by screws which are an integral part of the outlet. Receptacle covers made of either brass, steel, or nonmetallic materials are then attached to box and receptacle installations to afford complete closure at the out-lets.quick inexpensive electrical wiring installation method since they aie installed on the

wall surface instead of inside the wall (fig. 1-35).

(1) Surface metal raceway is basically of two types: one-piece construction or two-piece construction. When working with the one-piece construction type, the metal raceway is installed like conduit, then the wires are "pulled" to make the necessary electrical connections. If working with the two-piece construction type, the base piece is installed along

ADAPTER

2 — POLE
RUBBER MOLDED
WITH FINGER GRIP

3 — POLE
TWIST - LOCK

GROUNDED PLUG

Figure 1-86. Attachment plugs.

a. *Surface Metal Raceways.* These provide a quick inexpensive electrical wiring installation method since they aie installed on the wall surface instead of inside the wall (fig. 1-35).

1-40. Plugs and Cord Connectors

a. *Plugs.* Portable appliances and devices that are to be connected to receptacles have their electrical cords equipped with plugs (fig. 1-86) that have prongs which mate with the slots in the outlet receptacles. A three-prong

(1) Surface metal raceway is basically of two types: one-piece construction or two-piece construction. When working with the one-piece construction type, the metal raceway is installed like conduit, then the wires are "pulled" to make the necessary electrical

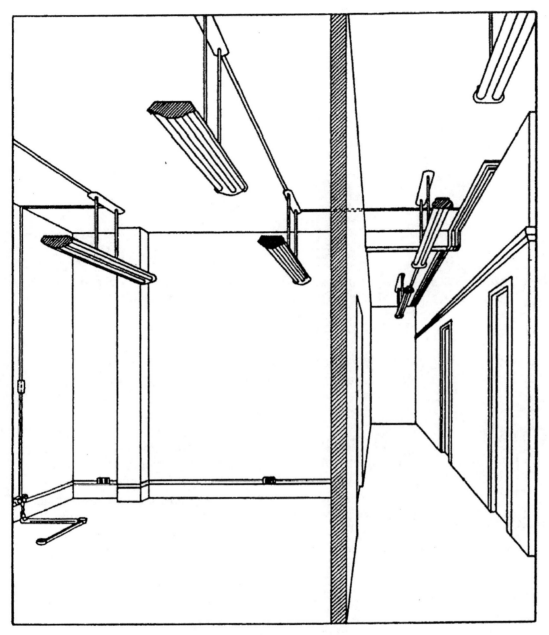

Figure 1–35. Surface metal raceways.

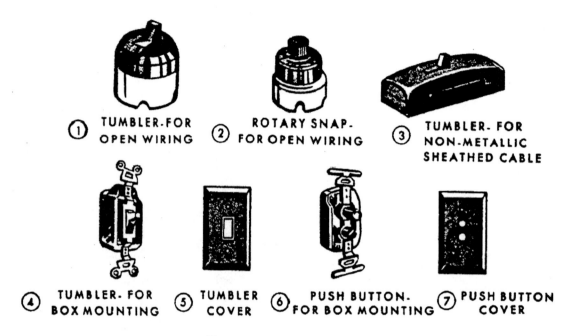

① TUMBLER-FOR OPEN WIRING   ② ROTARY SNAP- FOR OPEN WIRING   ③ TUMBLER- FOR NON-METALLIC SHEATHED CABLE

④ TUMBLER- FOR BOX MOUNTING   ⑤ TUMBLER COVER   ⑥ PUSH BUTTON- FOR BOX MOUNTING   ⑦ PUSH BUTTON COVER

Figure 1-38. Switches and covers.

connections. If working with the two-piece construction type, the base piece is installed along

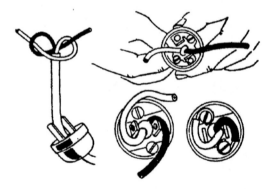

Figure 1-37. The Underwriters knot.

plug can fit into a two-prong receptacle by using an adapter. If the electrical conductors connected to the outlet have a ground system, the lug on the lead wire of the adapter is connected to the center screw holding the receptacle cover to the box. Many of these plugs are permanently molded to the attached cords. There are other types of cord-grips that hold the cord firmly to the plug. Twist-lock plugs have patented prongs that catch and are firmly held to a mating receptacle when the plugs are inserted into the receptacle slots and twisted. Where the plugs do not have cord-grips, the cords should be tied with an Underwriters knot (fig. 1-37) at plug entry to eliminate tension on

the terminal connections when the cord is connected and disconnected from the outlet receptacle. Figure 1-37 shows the steps to be used in tying this type of knot.

   b. Cord Connectors. There are some operating conditions where a cord must be connected to a portable receptacle. This type of receptacle, called a cord connector body or a female plug, is attached to the cord in a manner similar to the attachment of the male plug outlined in *a* above.

1-41. Switches and Covers
   a. *Definition. A* switch is a device used to connect and disconnect an electrical circuit from the source of power. Switches may be either one-pole or two-pole for ordinary lighting or receptacle circuits. If they are of the one-pole type, they must be connected to break the hot or ungrounded conductor of the circuit. If of the two-pole type, the hot and ground connection can be connected to either pole on the line side of the switch. Switches are also available that can be operated in combinations of two, three, or more in one circuit. These are called three-way and four-way switches and are discussed fully in paragraph 3-15.

b. Open and Nonmetallic Sheathed Wiring. Switches used for exposed open wiring and nonmetallic sheathed cable wiring are usually of the tumbler type with the switch and cover in one piece. Other less common ones are the rotary-snap and push-button types. These switches are generally nonmetallic in composition (1, 2, and 3, fig. 1-38).

c. Conduit and Cable Installations. The tumbler switch and cover plates (4 and 5, fig. 1-38) normally used for outlet-box installation are mounted in a manner similar to that for box type receptacles and covers and are in two pieces. Foreign installations may still use pushbutton switches as shown in 6 and 7, figure 1-38.

d. Entrance Installations. At every power-line entry to a building a switch and fuse combination or circuit breaker switch of a type similar to that shown in figure 1-39 must be installed at the service entrance. This switch must be rated to disconnect the building load while in use at the system voltage. Entrance or service switches, as they are commonly called,consist of one "knife" switch blade for every hot wire of the power supplied. The switch is generally enclosed and sealed in a sheet-steel cabinet. When connecting or disconnecting the building circuit, the blades are operated simultaneously through an exterior handle by the rotation of a common shaft holding the blades. The neutral or grounded conductor is not switched but is connected at a neutral terminal within the box. Many entrance switches are equipped with integral fuse blocks or circuit breakers which protect the building load. The circuit breaker type of entrance switch is preferred, particularly in field installations, because of its ease of resetting after the overload condition in the circuit has been cleared.

Figure 1-39. Service switch box.

1-42. Fuses and Fuse Boxes

a. Fuses. The device for automatically opening a circuit when the current rises beyond the safety limit is technically called a cutout, but more commonly is called a fuse. All circuits and electrical apparatus must be protected from short circuits or dangerous overcurrent conditions through correctly rated fuses.

(1) *Standard.* The cartridge type fuse is used for current rating above 30 amperes in interior wiring systems. The ordinary plug or screw type fuse is satisfactory for incandescent lighting or heating appliance circuits.

(2) *Special.* On branch circuits, wherever motors are connected, time-lag fuses should be used instead of the standard plug or cartridge type fuse. These fuses have self-compensating elements which maintain and hold the circuit in line during a momentary heavy ampere drain, yet cut out the circuit under normal short-circuit conditions. The heavy ampere demand normally occurs in motor circuits when the motor is started.

Examples of such circuits are the ones used to power oil burners or air conditioners.

b. *Fuse Boxes.* As a general rule the fusing of circuits is concentrated at centrally located fusing or distribution panels. These panels are normally located at the service-entrance switch in small buildings or installed in several power centers in large buildings. The number of service centers or fuse boxes in the latter case would be determined by the connected power load. Fuses and a fuse box are shown in figure 1-40.

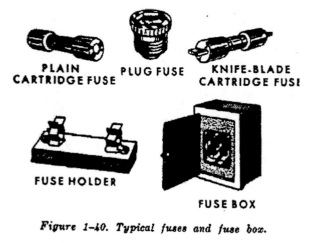

PLAIN CARTRIDGE FUSE   PLUG FUSE   KNIFE-BLADE CARTRIDGE FUSE

FUSE HOLDER   FUSE BOX

Figure 1-40. Typical fuses and fuse box.

1-43. Circuit Breaker Panels

Circuit breakers are devices resembling switches that trip or cut out the circuit in case of overamperage. They perform the same

function as fuses and can be obtained with time-lag opening features similar to the special fuses outlined in paragraph 1-42. Based on their operation, they may be classified as a thermal, magnetic, or combination thermal-magnetic reaction type. A thermal type circuit breaker has a bimetallic element integrally built within the breaker that responds only to fluctuations in temperature within the circuit. The element is made by bonding together two strips of dissimilar metal, each of which has a different coefficient of expansion. When a current is flowing in the circuit, the heat created by the resistance of the bimetallic element will expand each metal at a different rate causing the strip to bend. The element acts as a latch in the circuit as the breaker mechanism is adjusted so that the element bends just far enough under a specified current to trip the breaker and open the circuit. A magnetic circuit breaker responds to changes in the magnitude of current flow. In operation an increased current flow will create enough magnetic force to "pull up" an armature, opening the circuit. The motor circuits for closer adjustment to motor rating while the circuit conductors are protected, as usual, by another circuit breaker. The thermal-magnetic breaker, as the name implies, combines the features of the thermal and magnetic types. Practically all of the

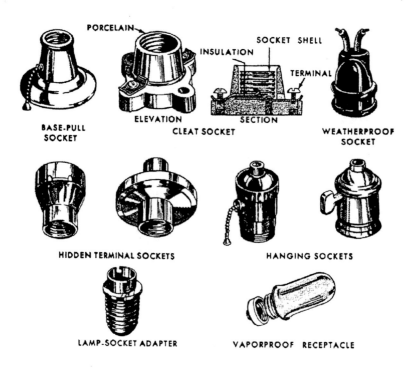

PORCELAIN   SOCKET SHELL
INSULATION   TERMINAL

BASE-PULL SOCKET   ELEVATION   SECTION   WEATHERPROOF SOCKET
CLEAT SOCKET

HIDDEN TERMINAL SOCKETS   HANGING SOCKETS

LAMP-SOCKET ADAPTER   VAPORPROOF RECEPTACLE

molded case magnetic circuit breaker is usually used in

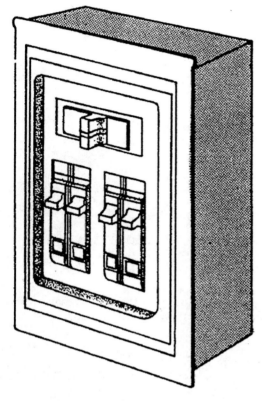

Figure 1-41. Typical circuit breaker box.

circuit breakers used in lighting panelboards are of this type. The thermal element protects against overcurrents in the lower range and the magnetic element prof- .ts against the higher range usually occurri.ig from short circuits. During the last decade, circuit breakers have been used to a greater extent than fuses because they can be manually reset after tripping, whereas fuses require replacement. Fuses may easily be replaced with higher capacity ones that do not protect the circuit. This is difficult to do with circuit breakers. In addition they combine the functions of fuse and switch, and when tripped by overloads or short circuits, all of the ungrounded conductors of a circuit are opened simultaneously. Each branch circuit must have a fuse or circuit breaker protecting each ungrounded conductor. Some installations may or may not have amain breaker that disconnects everything. As a guide during installation, if it does not require more than six movements of the hand to open

all the branch circuit breakers, a main breaker or switch is not required ahead of the branch-circuit breaker. However, if more than six movements of the hand are required, a separate disconnecting main circuit breaker is required ahead of the branch-circuit breaker. Each 120-volt circuit requires a single-pole (one-pole) breaker which has its own handle. Each 208-volt circuit requires a double-pole (two-pole) breaker to protect both ungrounded conductors. You can, however, place two single-pole breakers side by side, and tie the two handles together mechanically to give double-pole protection. Both handles can then be moved by a single movement of the hand. A two-pole breaker may have one handle or two handles which are mechanically tied together, but either one requires only one movement of the hand to break the circuit. Figure 1-41 illustrates a typical circuit breaker panel.

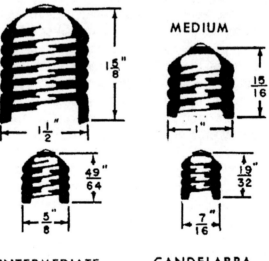

Figure 1-43. General lamp-socket sizes.

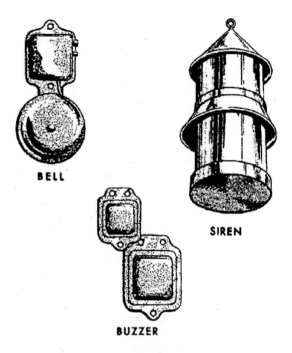

BELL

SIREN

BUZZER

Figure 1-44. Types of signal equipment.

① CONE   ② DOME

③ FLOODLIGHT

Figure 1-45. Types of reflectors.

1-44. Lampholders and Sockets

Lamp sockets as shown in figure 1-42 are generally screw-base units placed in circuits as holders for incandescent lamps. A special type of lampholder has contacts, rather than a screw base, which engage and hold the prongs of fluorescent lamps when they are rotated in the holder. The sockets can generally be attached to a hanging cord or mounted directly on a wall or ceiling in open wiring installations by using screws or nails in the mounting holes provided in the nonconducting material which is molded or formed around the lamp socket. The two mounting holes in a procelain lamp socket are spaced so the sockets may also be attached to outlet box "ears" or a plaster ring with machine screws. The screw threads molded or rolled in the ends of the lampholder sockets also facilitate their ready integration in other types of lighting fixtures such as table lamps, floor lamps, or hanging fixtures which have reflectors or decorative shades. In an emergency, a socket may also be used as a receptacle. The socket is converted to a receptacle by screwing in a female plug. One type of ceiling lampholder has a grounded outlet located on the side. Lamp sockets are produced in many different sizes and shapes. A few of the most common sizes are shown in figure 1-43.

1-45. Signal Equipment

Figure 1-44 illustrates the most common components in interior wiring signal systems. Their normal operating voltages are 6, 12, 18, or 24 volts, ac or dc. As a general rule they are connected by open-wiring methods and are used as interoffice or building-to-building signal systems.

1-46. Reflectors and Shades

Figure 1-45 shows several types of reflectors and shades which are used to focus the lighting effect of bulbs. Of these, some are used to flood an area with high intensity light and are called floodlights. Others, called spotlights, concentrate the useful light on a small area. Both floodlights and spotlights can come in two- or three-light clusters with swivel holders. They can be mounted on walls or posts or on spikes pushed into the ground. One and two, figure 1-45 illustrate reflectors that deliver normal building light of average intensity in a pattern similar to the floodlight shown in 3, figure 1-45.

1-45. Signal Equipment
Figure 1-44 illustrates the most common components in interior wiring signal systems.

1-47. Incandescent Lamps

The most common light source for general use is the incandescent lamp. Though it is the least efficient type of light, its use is preferred over the fluorescent type because of its low initial cost, ease of maintenance, convenience, and flexibility. Its flexibility and convenience is readily seen by the wide selection of wattage ratings that can be inserted in one type socket. Further, since its emitted candlepower is directly proportional to the voltage, a lower voltage application will dim the light. A high rated voltage application from a power source will increase its intensity. Although an incandescent light is economical, it is also inefficient because a large amount of the energy supplied to it is converted to heat rather than light. Moreover, it does not give a true light because the tungsten filament emits a great deal more red and yellow light than does the light of the sun. Incandescent lamps are shown in figure 1-46. Incandescent lights are normally built to last 1,000 hours when operating at their rated voltage.

1-48. Fluorescent Lamps

Fluorescent lamps (fig. 1-47) are either of the conventional "hot cathode" or "cold cathode" type. The "hot cathode" lamp has a coiled wire type of electrode, which when heated gives off electrons. These electrons collide with mercury

Figure 1-46. Incandescent lamps.

atoms, provided by mercury vapor in the tubes, which produces ultraviolet radiation. Fluorescent powder coatings on the inner walls of the tubes absorb this radiation and transform the energy into visible light. The "cold cathode" lamp operates in a similar manner except that its electrode consists of a cylindrical tube. It receives its name because the heat is generated over a larger area and, therefore, the cathode does not reach as high a temperature as in the "hot cathode" tube. The "cold cathode" is less efficient but has a longer operating life than the "hot cathode" unit. It is used most frequently on flashing circuits. Because of the higher light output per watt input, more illumination and less heat is obtained per watt from fluorescent lamps than from incandescent ones. Light diffusion is also better, and surface brightness is lower. The life of fluorescent lamps is also longer compared to filament types. However, the fluorescent lamp, because of its design, cannot control its beam of light as well as the incandescent type and has a tendency to produce stroboscopic effects which are counteracted by phasing arrangements. Moreover, when voltage fluctuations are severe, the lamps may go out prematurely or start slowly. Finally, the higher initial cost in fluorescent lighting, which requires auxiliary equipment such as starters, ballasts, special landholders, and fixtures (fig. 1-47), is also a disadvantage compared with other types of illumination.

a. *Construction.* The fluorescent lamp is an electric discharge lamp that consists of an elongated tubular bulb with an oxide-coated filament sealed in each end to comprise two electrodes (fig. 1-48). The bulb contains a drop of mercury and a small amount of argon gas. The inside surface of the bulb is coated with a fluorescent phosphor. The lamp produces invisible, short wave (ultraviolet) radiation by the discharge through the mercury vapor in the bulb. The phosphor absorbs the invisible radiant energy and reradiates it over a band of wavelengths that are sensitive to the eye.

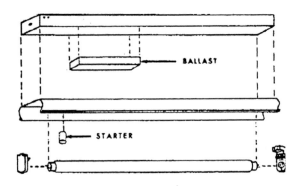

Figure 1-47. Fluorescent light accessories.

(1) Detail illumination is required where the intensity of general illumination is not sufficient, and in engineering spaces for examination of gages. The fixtures for detail illumination commonly use single fluorescent lamps. One and two, figure 1-48, illustrates the wiring arrangement for these single units, and three, figure 1-48, shows a multiple unit.

(2) Because of greater cost and shorter life of 8-watt fluorescent lamps, as compared to 15-watt and 20-watt lamps, fixtures with 8-watt lamps are used only for detail illumination and general illumination within locations where space is restricted.

(3) Although the fluorescent lamp is basically an ac lamp, it can be operated on dc with the proper auxiliary equipment. The current is controlled by an external resistance in series with the lamp (4, fig. 1-48). Since there is no voltage peak, starting is

more difficult and thermal switch starters are required. The lamp tends to deteriorate at one end due to the uniform direction of the current. This may he par-tially overcome by reversing the lamp position or the direction of current periodically.

(4) Because of the power lost in the resistance ballast box in the dc system, the overall lumens per watt efficiency of the dc system is about 60 percent of the ac system. Also, lamps operated on dc may provide as little as 80 percent of rated life.

(5) The fluorescent lamp, like all discharge light sources, requires special auxiliary control equipment for starting and stabilizing the lamp. This equipment consists of an iron-core choke coil, or ballast, and an automatic starting switch connected in series with the lamp filaments. The starter (starting switch) can be either a glow switch or a thermal switch. A resistor must be connected in series with the ballast in dc circuits because the ballast alone does not offer sufficient resistance to maintain the arc current steady.

(6) Each lamp must be provided with an individual ballast and starting switch, but the auxiliaries for two lamps are usually enclosed in a single container.. The auxiliaries for fluorescent lighting fixtures are mounted inside the fixture above the reflector. The starting switches (starters) project through the reflector so that they can be replaced readily. The circuit diagram for the fixture appears on the ballast container.

b. *Operation.* A fluorescent lamp equipped with a glow-switch starter is illustrated in 1, figure 1-48. The glow-switch starter is essentially a glow lamp containing neon or argon gas and two metallic electrodes. One electrode has a fixed contact, and the other electrode is a U-shaped, bimetal strip having a movable contact. These contacts are normally open.

(1) When the circuit switch is closed, there is practically no voltage drop across the ballast, and the voltage across the starter, S, is sufficient to produce a plow around the bimetallic strip in the glow lamp.

37

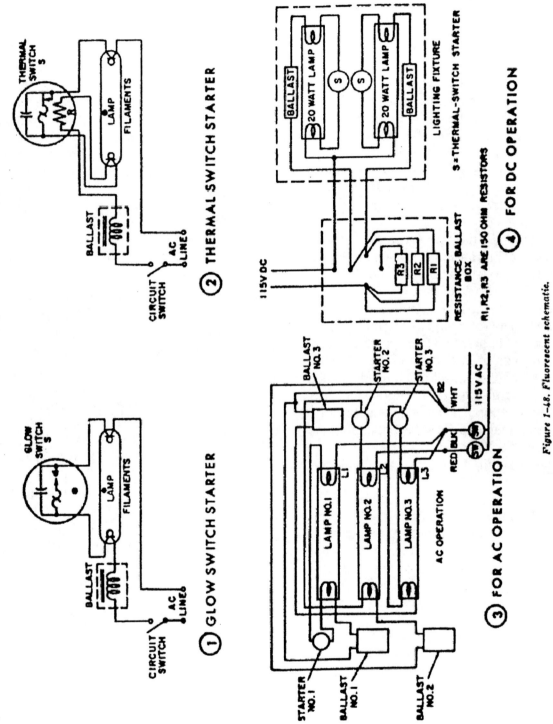

Figure 1–48. Fluorescent schematic.

The heat from the glow causes the bimetal   strip to distort and touch the fixed electrode.

This action shorts out the glow discharge and the bimetal strip starts to cool as the starting circuit of the fluorescent lamp is completed. The starting current flows through the lamp filament in each end of the fluorescent tube, causing the mercury to vaporize. Current does not flow across the lamp between the electrodes at this time because the path is short circuited by the starter and because the gas in the bulb is nonconducting when the electrodes are cold. The preheating of the fluorescent tube continues until the bimetal strip in the starter cools sufficiently to open the starting circuit.

(2) When the starting circuit opens, the decrease of current in the ballast produces an induced voltage across the lamp electrodes. The magnitude of this voltage is sufficient to ionize the mercury vapor and start the lamp. The resulting glow discharge (arc) through the fluorescent lamp produces a large amount of ultraviolet radiation that impinges on the phosphor, causing it to fluoresce and emit a relatively bright light. During normal operation the voltage across the fluorescent lamp is not sufficient to produce a glow in the starter. Hence, the contacts remain open and the starter consumes no energy.

(3) A fluorescent lamp equipped with a thermal-switch starter is illustrated in 1, figure 1-48. The thermal-switch starter consists of two normally closed metallic contacts and a series resistance contained in a cylindrical enclosure. One contact is fixed, and the movable contact is mounted on a bimetal strip.

(4) When the circuit switch is closed, the starting circuit of the fluorescent lamp is completed (through the series resistance, R) to allow the preheating current to flow through the electrodes. The current through the series resistance produces heat that causes the bimetal strip to bend and open the starting circuit. The accompanying induced voltage produced by the ballast starts the lamp. The normal operating current holds the thermal switch open.

(5) The majority of thermal-switch starters use some energy during normal operation of the lamp. However, this switch insures more positive starting by providing an adequate preheating period and a higher induced starting voltage.

c. Characteristics. The failure of a hot-cathode fluorescent lamp usually results from loss of electron-emissive material from the electrodes. This loss proceeds gradually throughout the life of the lamp and is accelerated by frequent starting. The rated average life of the lamp is based on normal burning periods of 3 to 4 hours. Blackening of the ends of the bulb progresses gradually throughout the life of the lamp.

(1) The efficiency of the energy conversion of a fluorescent lamp is very sensitive to changes in temperature of the bulb. The maximum efficiency occurs in the range of 100° F. to 120° F., which is the operating temperature that corresponds to an ambient room temperature range of 65° to 85° F. The efficiency decreases slowly as the temperature is increased above normal, but also decreases very rapidly as the temperature is decreased below normal. Hence, the fluorescent lamp is not satisfactory for locations in which it will be subjected to wide variations in temperature. The reduction in efficiency with low ambient room temperature can be minimized by operating the fluorescent lamp in a tubular glass enclosure so that the lamp will operate at more nearly the desired temperature.

(2) Fluorescent lamps are relatively efficient compared with incandescent lamps. For example, a 40-watt fluorescent lamp produces approximately 2800 lumens, or 70 lumens per watt. A 40-watt fluorescent lamp produces six times as much light per watt as does the comparable incandescent lamp.

(3) Fluorescent lamps should be operated at voltage within 8 percent of their rated voltage. If the lamps are operated at lower voltages, uncertain starting may result, and if operated at higher voltages, the ballast may overheat. Operation of the lamps at either lower or higher voltages results in decreased lamp life. The characteristic

curves for hot-cathode fluorescent lamps show the effect of variations from rated voltage on the condition of lamp operation. Also, the performance of fluorescent lamps depends to a great extent on the characteristics of the ballast, which determines the power delivered to the lamp for a given line voltage.

(4) When lamps are operated on ac circuits, the light output executes cyclic pulsations as the current passes through zero. This reduction in light output produces a flicker that is more noticeable in fluorescent lamps than in incandescent lamps at frequencies of 50 and 60 cycles and may cause unpleasant stro-boscopic effects when moving objects are viewed. The cyclic flicker can be minimized by combining two or three lamps in a fixture and operating the lamps on different phases of a three-phase system. Where only single-phase circuits are available, leading current may be supplied to one lamp and lagging current to another through a lead-lag ballast circuit so that the light pulsations compensate each other.

(5) The fluorescent lamp is inherently a high power-factor device, but the ballast required to stabilize the arc is a low power-factor device. The voltage drop across the ballast is usually equal to the drop across the arc, and the resulting power factor for a single-lamp circuit with ballast is about 50 percent. The low power factor can be corrected in a single-lamp ballast circuit by a capacitor shunted across the line. This correction is accomplished in a two-lamp circuit by means of a "tulamp" auxiliary that connects a capacitor in series with one of the lamps to displace the lamp currents, and, at the same time, to remove the unpleasant stroboscopic effects when moving objects come into view.

d. Glow Lamps. Glow lamps are electric discharge light sources, which are used as indicator or pilot lights for various instruments and on control panels. These lamps have relatively low light output, and thus are used to indicate when circuits are energized or to indicate the operation of electrical equipment installed in remote locations.

(1) The glow lamp consists of two closely spaced metallic electrodes sealed in a glass bulb that contains an inert gas. The color of the light emitted by the lamp depends on the gas. Neon gas produces a blue light. The lamp must be operated in series with a current-limiting device to stabilize the discharge. This current-limiting device consists of a high resistance that is usually contained in the lamp base.

(2) The glow lamp produces light only when the voltage exceeds a certain striking voltage. As the voltage is decreased somewhat below this value, the glow suddenly vanishes. When the lamp is operated on alternating current, light is produced only during a portion of each half cycle, and both electrodes are alternately surrounded with a glow. When the lamp is operated on direct current, light is produced continuously, and only the negative electrode is surrounded with a glow. This characteristic makes it possible to use the glow lamp as an

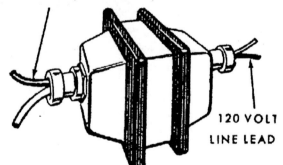

Figure 1-49. Transformer.

indicator of alternating current and direct current. It has the advantages of small size, ruggedness, long life, and negligible current consumption, and can be operated on standard lighting circuits.

1-49. Transformers
The transformer is a device for changing alternating current voltages into either high voltages for efficient powerline transmission or low voltages for consumption in lamps, electrical

devices, and machines. Transformers vary in size according to their power handling rating. Their selection is determined by input and output voltage and load current requirements. For example, the transformer used to furnish power for a doorbell reduces 115-volt alternating current to about 6 to 10 volts. This is accomplished by two primary wire leads which are permanently connected to the 115-volt circuit and two secondary screw terminals from the low voltage side of the transformer. Figure 1-49 shows a common type of signal system transformer. It is used to lower the building voltage of 120 volts or 240 volts ac to the 6, 12,

18, or 24 volts ac. The wires shown are input and output leads. In figure 1-49 the input leads are smaller than the output leads because the current in the output circuit is greater than in the input circuit.

1-50. Rotating Equipment

Generally, lighting circuits outnumber motor or power circuits in every installation.

However, the energy consumption of motors and power loads is probably greater than the lighting-circuit consumption. The electrician should study in order to further his knowledge of motors, motor controls, their maintenance and repair.

APPENDIX
ELECTRIC DATA

Table C-1. Characteristics of Electrical Systems

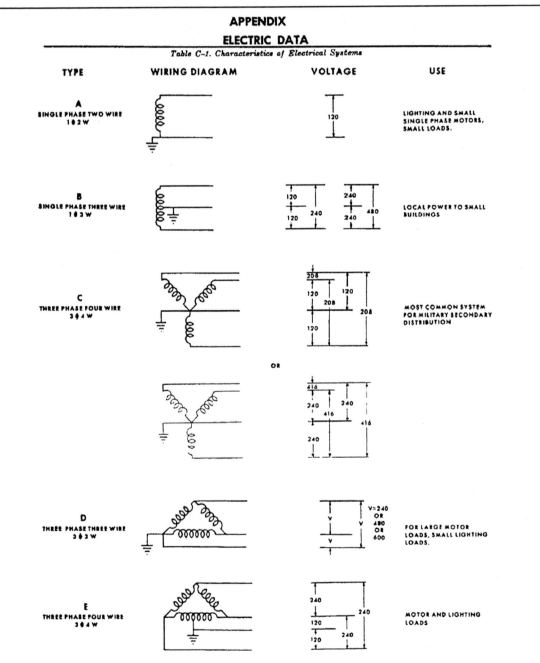

Table C-2. Conductor Insulation

Trade Name	Type Letter	Temp. rating	Application Provisions
Rubber-Covered Fixture Wire	*RF-1	60°C 140°F	Fixture wiring. Limited to 300 V.
Solid or 7-Strand	*RF-2	60°C 140°F	Fixture wiring.
Rubber-Covered Fixture Wire	*FF-1	60°C 140°F	Fixture wiring. Limited to 300 V.
Flexible Stranding	*FF-2	60°C 140°F	Fixture wiring.
Heat-Resistant Rubber-Covered Fixture Wire	*RFH-1	75°C 167°F	Fixture wiring. Limited to 300 V.
Solid or 7-Strand	*RFH-2	75°C 167°F	Fixture wiring.
Heat-Resistant Rubber-Covered Fixture Wire	*FFH-1	75°C 167°F	Fixture wiring. Limited to 300 V.
Flexible Stranding	*FFH-2	75°C 167°F	Fixture wiring.
Thermoplastic-Covered Fixture Wire—Solid or Stranded	*TF	60°C 140°F	Fixture wiring.
Thermoplastic-Covered Fixture Wire—Flexible Stranding	*TFF	60°C 140°F	Fixture wiring.
Cotton-Covered, Heat-Resistant, Fixture Wire	*CF	90°C 194°F	Fixture wiring. Limited to 300 V.
Asbestos-Covered Heat-Resistant, Fixture Wire	*AF	150°C 302°F	Fixture wiring. Limited to 300 V. and Indoor Dry Location.
Silicone Rubber Insulated Fixture Wire	*SF-1	200°C 392°F	Fixture wiring. Limited to 300 V.
Solid or 7 Strand	*SF-2	200°C 392°F	Fixture wiring
Silicone Rubber Insulated Fixture Wire	*SFF-1	150°C 302°F	Fixture wiring. Limited to 300 V.
Flexible Stranding	*SFF-2	150°C 302°F	Fixture wiring.
Code Rubber	R	60°C 140°F	Dry locations.
Heat-Resistant Rubber	RH	75°C 167°F	Dry locations.
Heat Resistant Rubber	RHH	90°C 194°F	Dry locations.
Moisture-Resistant Rubber	RW	60°C 140°F	Dry and wet locations. For over 2000 volts, insulation shall be ozone-resistant.
Moisture and Heat Resistant Rubber	RH-RW	60°C 140°F	Dry and wet locations. For over 2000 volts, insulation shall be ozone-resistant.

*Fixture wires are not intended for installation as branch circuit conductors nor for the connection of portable or stationary appliances.

ELECTRICAL TERMS AND FORMULAS

CONTENTS

ELECTRICAL TERMS AND FORMULAS

Terms

AGONIC.—An imaginary line of the earth's surface passing through points where the magnetic declination is 0°; that is, points where the compass points to true north.

AMMETER.—An instrument for measuring the amount of electron flow in amperes.

AMPERE.—The basic unit of electrical current.

AMPERE-TURN.—The magnetizing force produced by a current of one ampere flowing through a coil of one turn.

AMPLIDYNE.—A rotary magnetic or dynamo-electric amplifier used in servomechanism and control applications.

AMPLIFICATION.—The process of increasing the strength (current, power, or voltage) of a signal.

AMPLIFIER.—A device used to increase the signal voltage, current, or power, generally composed of a vacuum tube and associated circuit called a stage. It may contain several stages in order to obtain a desired gain.

AMPLITUDE.—The maximum instantaneous value of an alternating voltage or current, measured in either the positive or negative direction.

ARC.—A flash caused by an electric current ionizing a gas or vapor.

ARMATURE.—The rotating part of an electric motor or generator. The moving part of a relay or vibrator.

ATTENUATOR.—A network of resistors used to reduce voltage, current, or power delivered to a load.

AUTOTRANSFORMER.—A transformer in which the primary and secondary are connected together in one winding.

BATTERY.—Two or more primary or secondary cells connected together electrically. The term does not apply to a single cell.

BREAKER POINTS.—Metal contacts that open and close a circuit at timed intervals.

BRIDGE CIRCUIT.—The electrical bridge circuit is a term referring to any one of a variety of electric circuit networks, one branch of which, the "bridge" proper, connects two points of equal potential and hence carries no current when the circuit is properly adjusted or balanced.

BRUSH.—The conducting material, usually a block of carbon, bearing against the commutator or sliprings through which the current flows in or out.

BUS BAR.—A primary power distribution point connected to the main power source.

CAPACITOR.—Two electrodes or sets of electrodes in the form of plates, separated from each other by an insulating material called the dielectric.

CHOKE COIL.—A coil of low ohmic resistance and high impedance to alternating current.

CIRCUIT.—The complete path of an electric current.

CIRCUIT BREAKER.—An electromagnetic or thermal device that opens a circuit when the current in the circuit exceeds a predetermined amount. Circuit breakers can be reset.

CIRCULAR MIL.—An area equal to that of a circle with a diameter of 0.001 inch. It is used for measuring the cross section of wires.

COAXIAL CABLE.—A transmission line consisting of two conductors concentric with and insulated from each other.

COMMUTATOR.—The copper segments on the armature of a motor or generator. It is cylindrical in shape and is used to pass power into or from the brushes. It is a switching device.

CONDUCTANCE.—The ability of a material to conduct or carry an electric current. It is the reciprocal of the resistance of the material, and is expressed in mhos.

CONDUCTIVITY.—The ease with which a substance transmits electricity.

CONDUCTOR.—Any material suitable for carrying electric current.

CORE.—A magnetic material that affords an easy path for magnetic flux lines in a coil.

COUNTER E.M.F.—Counter electromotive force; an e.m.f. induced in a coil or armature that opposes the applied voltage.

CURRENT LIMITER.—A protective device similar to a fuse, usually used in high amperage circuits.

CYCLE.—One complete positive and one complete negative alternation of a current or voltage.

DIELECTRIC.—An insulator; a term that refers to the insulating material between the plates of a capacitor.

DIODE.—Vacuum tube—a two element tube that contains a cathode and plate; semiconductor—a material of either germanium or silicon that is manufactured to allow current to flow in only one direction. Diodes are used as rectifiers and detectors.

DIRECT CURRENT.—An electric current that flows in one direction only.

EDDY CURRENT.—Induced circulating currents in a conducting material that are caused by a varying magnetic field.

EFFICIENCY.—The ratio of output power to input power, generally expressed as a percentage.

ELECTROLYTE.—A solution of a substance which is capable of conducting electricity. An electrolyte may be in the form of either a liquid or a paste.

ELECTROMAGNET.—A magnet made by passing current through a coil of wire wound on a soft iron core.

ELECTROMOTIVE FORCE (e.m.f.).—The force that produces an electric current in a circuit.

ELECTRON.—A negatively charged particle of matter.

ENERGY.—The ability or capacity to do work.

FARAD.—The unit of capacitance.

FEEDBACK.—A transfer of energy from the output circuit of a device back to its input.

FIELD.—The space containing electric or magnetic lines of force.

FIELD WINDING.—The coil used to provide the magnetizing force in motors and generators.

FLUX FIELD.—All electric or magnetic lines of force in a given region.

FREE ELECTRONS.—Electrons which are loosely held and consequently tend to move at random among the atoms of the material.

FREQUENCY.—The number of complete cycles per second existing in any form of wave motion; such as the number of cycles per second of an alternating current.

FULL-WAVE RECTIFIER CIRCUIT.—A circuit which utilizes both the positive and the negative alternations of an alternating current to produce a direct current.

FUSE.—A protective device inserted in series with a circuit. It contains a metal that will melt or break when current is increased beyond a specific value for a definite period of time.

GAIN.—The ratio of the output power, voltage, or current to the input power, voltage, or current, respectively.

GALVANOMETER.—An instrument used to measure small d-c currents.

GENERATOR.—A machine that converts mechanical energy into electrical energy.

GROUND.—A metallic connection with the earth to establish ground potential. Also, a common return to a point of zero potential. The chassis of a receiver or a transmitter is sometimes the common return, and therefore the ground of the unit.

HENRY.—The basic unit of inductance.

HORSEPOWER.—The English unit of power, equal to work done at the rate of 550 foot-pounds per second. Equal to 746 watts of electrical power.

HYSTERESIS.—A lagging of the magnetic flux in a magnetic material behind the magnetizing force which is producing it.

IMPEDANCE.—The total opposition offered to the flow of an alternating current. It may consist of any combination of resistance, inductive reactance, and capacitive reactance.

INDUCTANCE.—The property of a circuit which tends to oppose a change in the existing current.

INDUCTION.—The act or process of producing voltage by the relative motion of a magnetic field across a conductor.

INDUCTIVE REACTANCE.—The opposition to the flow of alternating or pulsating current caused by the inductance of a circuit. It is measured in ohms.

INPHASE.—Applied to the condition that exists when two waves of the same frequency pass through their maximum and minimum values of like polarity at the same instant.

INVERSELY.—Inverted or reversed in position or relationship.

ISOGONIC LINE.—An imaginary line drawn through points on the earth's surface where the magnetic deviation is equal.

JOULE.—A unit of energy or work. A joule of energy is liberated by one ampere flowing for one second through a resistance of one ohm.

KILO.—A prefix meaning 1,000.

LAG.—The amount one wave is behind another in time; expressed in electrical degrees.

LAMINATED CORE.—A core built up from thin sheets of metal and used in transformers and relays.

LEAD.—The opposite of LAG. Also, a wire or connection.

2

LINE OF FORCE.—A line in an electric or magnetic field that shows the direction of the force.

LOAD.—The power that is being delivered by any power producing device. The equipment that uses the power from the power producing device.

MAGNETIC AMPLIFIER.—A saturable reactor type device that is used in a circuit to amplify or control.

MAGNETIC CIRCUIT.—The complete path of magnetic lines of force.

MAGNETIC FIELD.—The space in which a magnetic force exists.

MAGNETIC FLUX.—The total number of lines of force issuing from a pole of a magnet.

MAGNETIZE.—To convert a material into a magnet by causing the molecules to rearrange.

MAGNETO.—A generator which produces alternating current and has a permanent magnet as its field.

MEGGER.—A test instrument used to measure insulation resistance and other high resistances. It is a portable hand operated d-c generator used as an ohmmeter.

MEGOHM.—A million ohms.

MICRO.—A prefix meaning one-millionth.

MILLI.—A prefix meaning one-thousandth.

MILLIAMMETER.—An ammeter that measures current in thousandths of an ampere.

MOTOR-GENERATOR.—A motor and a generator with a common shaft used to convert line voltages to other voltages or frequencies.

MUTUAL INDUCTANCE.—A circuit property existing when the relative position of two inductors causes the magnetic lines of force from one to link with the turns of the other.

NEGATIVE CHARGE.—The electrical charge carried by a body which has an excess of electrons.

NEUTRON.—A particle having the weight of a proton but carrying no electric charge. It is located in the nucleus of an atom.

NUCLEUS.—The central part of an atom that is mainly comprised of protons and neutrons. It is the part of the atom that has the most mass.

NULL.—Zero.

OHM.—The unit of electrical resistance.

OHMMETER.—An instrument for directly measuring resistance in ohms.

OVERLOAD.—A load greater than the rated load of an electrical device.

PERMALLOY.—An alloy of nickel and iron having an abnormally high magnetic permeability.

PERMEABILITY.—A measure of the ease with which magnetic lines of force can flow through a material as compared to air.

PHASE DIFFERENCE.—The time in electrical degrees by which one wave leads or lags another.

POLARITY.—The character of having magnetic poles, or electric charges.

POLE.—The section of a magnet where the flux lines are concentrated; also where they enter and leave the magnet. An electrode of a battery.

POLYPHASE.—A circuit that utilizes more than one phase of alternating current.

POSITIVE CHARGE.—The electrical charge carried by a body which has become deficient in electrons.

POTENTIAL.—The amount of charge held by a body as compared to another point or body. Usually measured in volts.

POTENTIOMETER.—A variable voltage divider; a resistor which has a variable contact arm so that any portion of the potential applied between its ends may be selected.

POWER.—The rate of doing work or the rate of expending energy. The unit of electrical power is the watt.

POWER FACTOR.—The ratio of the actual power of an alternating or pulsating current, as measured by a wattmeter, to the apparent power, as indicated by ammeter and voltmeter readings. The power factor of an inductor, capacitor, or insulator is an expression of their losses.

PRIME MOVER.—The source of mechanical power used to drive the rotor of a generator.

PROTON.—A positively charged particle in the nucleus of an atom.

RATIO.—The value obtained by dividing one number by another, indicating their relative proportions.

REACTANCE.—The opposition offered to the flow of an alternating current by the inductance, capacitance, or both, in any circuit.

RECTIFIERS.—Devices used to change alternating current to unidirectional current. These may be vacuum tubes, semiconductors such as germanium and silicon, and dry-disk rectifiers such as selenium and copper-oxide.

RELAY.—An electromechanical switching device that can be used as a remote control.

RELUCTANCE.—A measure of the opposition that a material offers to magnetic lines of force.

RESISTANCE.—The opposition to the flow of current caused by the nature and physical dimensions of a conductor.

RESISTOR.—A circuit element whose chief characteristic is resistance; used to oppose the flow of current.

ELECTRICAL TERMS AND FORMULAS

RETENTIVITY.—The measure of the ability of a material to hold its magnetism.

RHEOSTAT.—A variable resistor.

SATURABLE REACTOR.—A control device that uses a small d-c current to control a large a-c current by controlling core flux density.

SATURATION.—The condition existing in any circuit when an increase in the driving signal produces no further change in the resultant effect.

SELF-INDUCTION.—The process by which a circuit induces an e.m.f. into itself by its own magnetic field.

SERIES-WOUND.—A motor or generator in which the armature is wired in series with the field winding.

SERVO.—A device used to convert a small movement into one of greater movement or force.

SERVOMECHANISM.—A closed-loop system that produces a force to position an object in accordance with the information that originates at the input.

SOLENOID.—An electromagnetic coil that contains a movable plunger.

SPACE CHARGE.—The cloud of electrons existing in the space between the cathode and plate in a vacuum tube, formed by the electrons emitted from the cathode in excess of those immediately attracted to the plate.

SPECIFIC GRAVITY—The ratio between the density of a substance and that of pure water, at a given temperature.

SYNCHROSCOPE—An instrument used to indicate a difference in frequency between two a-c sources.

SYNCHRO SYSTEM.—An electrical system that gives remote indications or control by means of self-synchronizing motors.

TACHOMETER.—An instrument for indicating revolutions per minute.

TERTIARY WINDING.—A third winding on a transformer or magnetic amplifier that is used as a second control winding.

THERMISTOR.—A resistor that is used to compensate for temperature variations in a circuit.

THERMOCOUPLE.—A junction of two dissimilar metals that produces a voltage when heated.

TORQUE.—The turning effort or twist which a shaft sustains when transmitting power.

TRANSFORMER.—A device composed of two or more coils, linked by magnetic lines of force, used to transfer energy from one circuit to another.

TRANSMISSION LINES.—Any conductor or system of conductors used to carry electrical energy from its source to a load.

VARS.—Abbreviation for volt-ampere, reactive.

VECTOR.—A line used to represent both direction and magnitude.

VOLT.—The unit of electrical potential.

VOLTMETER.—An instrument designed to measure a difference in electrical potential, in volts.

WATT.—The unit of electrical power.

WATTMETER.—An instrument for measuring electrical power in watts.

Formulas

Ohm's Law for d-c Circuits

$$I = \frac{E}{R} = \frac{P}{E} = \sqrt{\frac{P}{R}}$$

$$R = \frac{E}{I} = \frac{P}{I^2} = \frac{E^2}{P}$$

$$E = IR = \frac{P}{I} = \sqrt{PR}$$

$$P = EI = \frac{E^2}{R} = I^2R$$

Resistors in Series

$$R_T = R_1 + R_2 \cdots$$

Resistors in Parallel
Two resistors

$$R_T = \frac{R_1 R_2}{R_1 + R_2}$$

More than two

$$\frac{1}{R_T} = \frac{1}{R_1} + \frac{1}{R_2} + \frac{1}{R_3}$$

4

R-L Circuit Time Constant equals

$$\frac{L \text{ (in henrys)}}{R \text{ (in ohms)}} = t \text{ (in seconds)}, \text{ or}$$

$$\frac{L \text{ (in microhenrys)}}{R \text{ (in ohms)}} = t \text{ (in microseconds)}$$

R-C Circuit Time Constant equals

R (ohms) X C (farads) = t (seconds)

R (megohms) x C (microfarads) = t (seconds)

R (ohms) x C (microfarads) = t (microseconds)

R (megohms) x C (micromicrofrads = t (microseconds)

Comparison of Units in Electric and Magnetic Circuits.

	Electric circuit	Magnetic circuit
Force	Volt, E or e.m.f.	Gilberts, F, or m.m.f.
Flow	Ampere, I	Flux, Φ, in maxwells
Opposition	Ohms, R	Reluctance, R
Law	Ohm's law, $I = \frac{E}{R}$	Rowland's law $\Phi = \frac{F}{R}$
Intensity of force	Volts per cm. of length	$H = \frac{1.257IN}{L}$, gilberts per centimeter of length
Density	Current density— for example, amperes per cm^2.	Flux density—for example, lines per cm^2., or gausses

Capacitors in Series
Two capacitors

$$C_T = \frac{C_1 C_2}{C_1 + C_2}$$

More than two

$$\frac{1}{C_T} = \frac{1}{C_1} + \frac{1}{C_2} + \frac{1}{C_3}\ldots$$

Capacitors in Parallel

$$C_T = C_1 + C_2\ldots$$

Capacitive Reactance

$$X_c = \frac{1}{2\pi f C}$$

Impedance in an R-C Circuit (Series)

$$Z = \sqrt{R^2 + X_c^{\,2}}$$

Inductors in Series

$$L_T = L_1 + L_2 \ldots \text{(No coupling between coils)}$$

Inductors in Parallel
Two inductors

$$L_T = \frac{L_1 L_2}{L_1 + L_2} \text{(No coupling between coils)}$$

More than two

$$\frac{1}{L_T} = \frac{1}{L_1} + \frac{1}{L_2} + \frac{1}{L_3} \ldots \text{(No coupling between coils)}$$

Inductive Reactance

$$X_L = 2\pi f L$$

Q of a Coil

$$Q = \frac{X_L}{R}$$

Impedance of an R-L Circuit (series)

$$Z = \sqrt{R^2 + X_L^2}$$

Impedance with R, C, and L in Series

$$Z = \sqrt{R^2 + (X_L - X_C)^2}$$

Parallel Circuit Impedance

$$Z = \frac{Z_1 Z_2}{Z_1 + Z_2}$$

Sine-Wave Voltage Relationships
Average value

$$E_{ave} = \frac{2}{\pi} \times E_{max} = 0.637 E_{max}$$

Effective or r.m.s. value

$$E_{eff} = \frac{E_{max}}{\sqrt{2}} = \frac{E_{max}}{1.414} = 0.707 E_{max} = 1.11 E_{ave}$$

Maximum value

$$E_{max} = \sqrt{2} E_{eff} = 1.414 E_{eff} = 1.57 E_{ave}$$

Voltage in an a-c circuit

$$E = IZ = \frac{P}{I \times P.F.}$$

Current in an a-c circuit

$$I = \frac{E}{Z} = \frac{P}{E \times P.F.}$$

Power in A-C Circuit
Apparent power $= EI$
True power

$$P = EI \cos \theta = EI \times P.F.$$

Power factor

$$P.F. = \frac{P}{EI} = \cos \theta$$

$$\cos \theta = \frac{\text{true power}}{\text{apparent power}}$$

Transformers
Voltage relationship

$$\frac{E}{E} = \frac{N}{N} \text{ or } E = E \times \frac{N}{N}$$

Current relationship

$$\frac{I_p}{I_s} = \frac{N_s}{N_p}$$

Induced voltage

$$E_{eff} = 4.44 \, BAfN \, 10^{-8}$$

Turns ratio equals

$$\frac{N_p}{N_s} = \sqrt{\frac{Z_p}{Z_s}}$$

Secondary current

$$I_s = I_p \frac{N_p}{N_s}$$

Secondary voltage

$$E_s = E_p \frac{N_s}{N_p}$$

Three Phase Voltage and Current Relationships
With wye connected windings

$$E_{line} = 1.732 E_{coil} = \sqrt{3} E_{coil}$$

$$I_{line} = I_{coil}$$

With delta connected windings

$$E_{line} = E_{coil}$$

$$I_{line} = 1.732 I_{coil}$$

With wye or delta connected winding

$$P_{coil} = E_{coil} I_{coil}$$

$$P_t = 3 P_{coil}$$

$$P_t = 1.732 E_{line} I_{line}$$

(To convert to true power multiply by $\cos \theta$)

Synchronous Speed of Motor

$$\text{r.p.m.} = \frac{120 \times \text{frequency}}{\text{number of poles}}$$

GREEK ALPHABET

Name	Capital	Lower Case	Designates
Alpha	A	α	Angles.
Beta	B	β	Angles, flux density.
Gamma . . .	Γ	γ	Conductivity.
Delta	Δ	δ	Variation of a quantity, increment.
Epsilon . . .	E	ϵ	Base of natural logarithms (2.71828).
Zeta	Z	ζ	Impedance, coefficients, coordinates.
Eta	H	η	Hysteresis coefficient, efficiency, magnetizing force.
Theta	Θ	θ	Phase angle.
Iota	I	ι	
Kappa	K	κ	Dielectric constant, coupling coefficient, susceptibility.
Lambda . . .	Λ	λ	Wavelength.
Mu	M	μ	Permeability, micro, amplification factor.
Nu	N	ν	Reluctivity.
Xi	Ξ	ξ	
Omicron . . .	O	o	
Pi	Π	π	3.1416
Rho	P	ρ	Resistivity.
Sigma	Σ	σ	
Tau	T	τ	Time constant, time-phase displacement.
Upsilon . . .	Υ	υ	
Phi	Φ	φ	Angles, magnetic flux.
Chi	X	χ	
Psi	Ψ	ψ	Dielectric flux, phase difference.
Omega	Ω	ω	Ohms (capital), angular velocity ($2\pi f$).

COMMON ABBREVIATIONS AND LETTER SYMBOLS

Term	Abbreviation or Symbol
alternating current (noun)	a,c.
alternating-current (adj.)	a-c
ampere	a.
area	A
audiofrequency (noun)	AF
audiofrequency (adj.)	A-F
capacitance	C
capacitive reactance	X_c
centimeter	cm.
conductance	G
coulomb	Q
counterelectromotive force	c.e.m.f.
current (d-c or r.m.s. value)	I
current (instantaneous value)	i
cycles per second	c.p.s.
dielectric constant	K,k
difference in potential (d-c or r.m.s. value)	E
difference in potential (instantaneous value)	e
direct current (noun)	d.c.
direct-current (adj.)	d-c
electromotive force	e.m.f.
frequency	f
henry	h.
horsepower	hp.
impedance	Z
inductance	L
inductive reactance	X_L
kilovolt	kv.
kilovolt-ampere	kv.-a.
kilowatt	kw.
kilowatt-hour	kw.-hr.
magnetic field intensity	H
magnetomotive force	m.m.f.
megohm	M
microampere	μ a.
microfarad	μ f.
microhenry	μ h.
micromicrofarad	$\mu\mu$ f.
microvolt	μ v.
milliampere	ma.
millihenry	mh.
milliwatt	mw.
mutual inductance	M
power	P
resistance	R
revolutions per minute	r.p.m.
root mean square	r.m.s.
time	t
torque	T
volt	v.
watt	w.

8

ANSWER SHEET

USE THE SPECIAL PENCIL.   MAKE GLOSSY BLACK MARKS.

	A	B	C	D	E			A	B	C	D	E			A	B	C	D	E			A	B	C	D	E			A	B	C	D	E
1							26							51							76							101					
2							27							52							77							102					
3							28							53							78							103					
4							29							54							79							104					
5							30							55							80							105					
6							31							56							81							106					
7							32							57							82							107					
8							33							58							83							108					
9							34							59							84							109					
10							35							60							85							110					

Make only ONE mark for each answer.   Additional and stray marks may be
counted as mistakes.   In making corrections, erase errors COMPLETELY.

	A	B	C	D	E			A	B	C	D	E			A	B	C	D	E			A	B	C	D	E			A	B	C	D	E
11							36							61							86							111					
12							37							62							87							112					
13							38							63							88							113					
14							39							64							89							114					
15							40							65							90							115					
16							41							66							91							116					
17							42							67							92							117					
18							43							68							93							118					
19							44							69							94							119					
20							45							70							95							120					
21							46							71							96							121					
22							47							72							97							122					
23							48							73							98							123					
24							49							74							99							124					
25							50							75							100							125					

ANSWER SHEET

TEST NO. _____ PART _____ TITLE OF POSITION _____

PLACE OF EXAMINATION _____ DATE _____

(CITY OR TOWN)   (STATE)

RATING

USE THE SPECIAL PENCIL.   MAKE GLOSSY BLACK MARKS.

	A	B	C	D	E		A	B	C	D	E		A	B	C	D	E		A	B	C	D	E		A	B	C	D	E
1						26						51						76						101					
2						27						52						77						102					
3						28						53						78						103					
4						29						54						79						104					
5						30						55						80						105					
6						31						56						81						106					
7						32						57						82						107					
8						33						58						83						108					
9						34						59						84						109					
10						35						60						85						110					

Make only ONE mark for each answer.   Additional and stray marks may be counted as mistakes.   In making corrections, erase errors COMPLETELY.

	A	B	C	D	E		A	B	C	D	E		A	B	C	D	E		A	B	C	D	E		A	B	C	D	E
11						36						61						86						111					
12						37						62						87						112					
13						38						63						88						113					
14						39						64						89						114					
15						40						65						90						115					
16						41						66						91						116					
17						42						67						92						117					
18						43						68						93						118					
19						44						69						94						119					
20						45						70						95						120					
21						46						71						96						121					
22						47						72						97						122					
23						48						73						98						123					
24						49						74						99						124					
25						50						75						100						125					